The
Whole
Truth

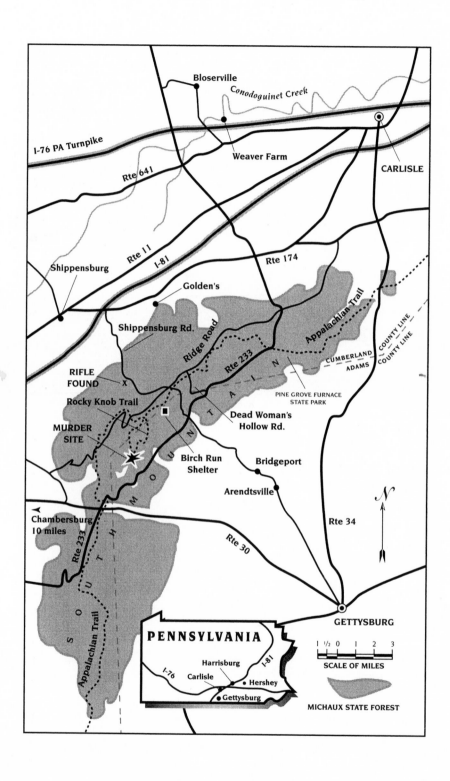

Bloserville

Conodoguinet Creek

I-76 PA Turnpike

Weaver Farm

Rte 641

CARLISLE

Rte 11

I-81

Rte 174

Shippensburg

Golden's

Shippensburg Rd.

Ridge Road

Appalachian Trail

Rte 233

CUMBERLAND
ADAMS

COUNTY LINE
COUNTY LINE

RIFLE
FOUND   X

M
O
U
N
T
A
I
N

PINE GROVE FURNACE
STATE PARK

Rocky Knob Trail

MURDER
SITE

Dead Woman's
Hollow Rd.

Birch Run
Shelter

Bridgeport

Arendtsville

◄ Chambersburg
10 miles

Rte 233

Rte 34

Rte 30

S
O
U
T
H

Appalachian Trail

GETTYSBURG

PENNSYLVANIA

1 ½ 0   1   2   3

SCALE OF MILES

Harrisburg

I-81

I-76

Carlisle

Hershey

Gettysburg

MICHAUX STATE FOREST

N

The Whole Truth

A Case of Murder on the Appalachian Trail

H. L. Pohlman

University of Massachusetts Press   Amherst

Library of Congress Cataloging-in-Publication Data
Pohlman, H. L., 1952–
The whole truth? : a case of murder on the Appalachian Trail /
H. L. Pohlman.
p.   cm.
Includes index.
ISBN 1-55849-165-1 (cloth : alk. paper). — ISBN 1-55849-166-X
(pbk. : alk. paper)
1. Carr, Stephen Roy—Trials, litigation, etc. 2. Trials
(Murder)—Pennsylvania—Gettysburg. 3. Murder—Pennsylvania—Adams
County. 4. Lesbians—Crimes against—Pennsylvania—Adams County.
I. Title.
KF224.C368P64   1999
345.748′4202523—dc21   98-28300
CIP

British Library Cataloguing in Publication data are available.

To
Leon Wight,
his family,
and the memory of
Rebecca

Contents

Prologue

"I was lying on my side and Rebecca was slightly lower down than me, and all of a sudden the world exploded and I grabbed for my right arm."

"You felt something?"

"Yeah."

"Pain?"

"Yes."

"You heard something?"

"Yes."

"Did you know at that point it was a gunshot?"

"No, I didn't know that it was a gunshot. . . . Rebecca said, 'Where did you get shot, Claudia?' I sat up to a sitting position, and I never answered Rebecca, because there were more shots."

"Did you see blood?"

"Yes. . . . [A]fter the first shot in my arm I got hit twice more, three times more and I started to scream after the first shot. . . . I screamed 'Stop!' as loud as I could. 'Enough!' 'Stop!' At the top of my lungs. I thought I was going to die."

"You did not see who was firing the shots; is that correct?"

"That's correct. I knew the direction they came from and I said to Rebecca, 'He came back.'"

The
Whole
Truth

Introduction

I didn't find out about what had happened until Monday. It was late afternoon and I had just returned home from work. I picked up the local *Sentinel* from the stoop, and a headline on the right side of the front page caught my eye: "Hikers Shot On Trail." It wasn't the day's top story. That honor went to a report of a local man suing a credit union because he had been denied a loan after he refused, on biblical grounds, to provide his Social Security number. Below the "Hikers" headline, a six-inch single column sketchily described what had occurred on Friday, May 13, 1988, approximately thirty miles south of my home in Carlisle, Pennsylvania.

Someone had shot two white females camping near the Appalachian Trail, killing one and seriously wounding the other. The incident had taken place in Michaux State Forest, a large wooded area straddling South Mountain in southcentral Pennsylvania, west of Gettysburg. The survivor, Claudia Brenner, had somehow managed to leave the scene of the shootings and make her way ten miles to Shippensburg. She was now recovering in a local hospital that the police would not identify for security reasons. The dead woman's name was Rebecca Wight. She had died "instantly," the paper reported. The assailant was believed to be a man wearing gray sweatpants with a maroon stripe down the side.

In a follow-up story the next day, the *Sentinel* identified the victims as graduate students who had come to the South Mountain area to enjoy a weekend of hiking and camping. Friends were planning a memorial service for Wight later in the week, and her funeral was scheduled for Sunday. An autopsy had recovered the bullet that had killed the twenty-eight-year-old woman, but the police refused to disclose the type or caliber of the murder weapon. Some physical evidence had been found at the crime scene, but the police weren't talking about that, either. Brenner, thirty-one years of age, remained hospitalized. The *Gettysburg Times* reported that a man had been seen flirting with Brenner and Wight prior to the shootings and suggested that the killer had left an unconscious Brenner for dead.

With the identity and whereabouts of the killer unknown, inhabitants of the South Mountain area became increasingly apprehensive. In the May 21st weekend edition of the *Gettysburg Times*, Dr. Mike Silverman, a local psychiatrist, advised people not to "overreact" by carrying guns. Random acts of violence were rare. "The public often [mistakenly] sees violence as being inflicted by a bad person," the doctor explained. "They need [instead] to view it as a public health problem." It arises from familial, social, environmental, and physiological problems. If people followed his advice, Dr. Silverman concluded, they would be able to take commonsense steps to ensure their safety without endangering themselves or others.

On May 23rd, ten days after the shootings, a large-scale police manhunt of South Mountain turned up nothing, adding to the growing impression that Wight's killer would not be caught. The *Sentinel* reported that the Appalachian Trail Conference (ATC) had offered a $1,000 reward for any information leading to an arrest. In the article, David Starzell, executive director of the ATC, pronounced the trail safe but urged hikers to take the sort of precautions appropriate for a journey through "relatively isolated areas." Brian King, director of public affairs, denied that the murder had caused any "real alarm" among ATC members. It put "an element of fear in their minds, especially the long-distance hikers," he added, "but that's natural."

The next day, the state police surprised everyone by naming a suspect—twenty-eight-year-old Stephen Roy Carr, who lived on South Mountain near Cleversburg at the northwestern edge of Michaux State Forest. "Police Searching for a Mountain Man," announced the *Sentinel's* May 24 banner headline. The accompanying story quoted Sergeant John Straka of the Pennsylvania State Police as saying, "We just want to talk to Mr. Carr. He is considered a suspect and may be armed and dangerous. We know that he has no fixed place of abode and that he does wander the mountain area."

On Wednesday, May 25th, the *Sentinel* reported Carr's arrest at a farm ten miles west of Carlisle. His thin, hollow face with its deep-set eyes appeared in a photo in the upper right-hand corner of a front page devoted entirely to the murder case, except for one piece on President Ronald Reagan's departure for his fourth Moscow summit meeting with Mikhail Gorbachev. The arrest took place without incident after an un-known "tipster" had informed the police that Carr was staying with a family of Mennonites. Carr was charged wtih first-degree murder, third-degree murder, attempted murder, and two counts of aggravated assault. Although unable to point to a motive for the shootings, an unidentified state trooper predicted that Carr would face the death penalty. A few weeks later, a story in the *Gettysburg Times* described Carr's attack as "apparently motiveless," yet indicated that the Adams County prosecu-tor, Roy Keefer, would in all likelihood seek the ultimate sanction.

A preliminary hearing to review whether there was sufficient evi-dence to hand Carr over for trial was held on June 24. In her testimony, Claudia Brenner confirmed local rumors that she and Wight had been lovers. The possibility that Carr shot the women because they were lesbians complicated the case, because the jury would be drawn from Adams County, Pennsylvania, a rural, conservative, and religious area. Many of the local residents believed that homosexuality violated God's law and that homosexuals themselves were wicked and sinful.

Carr's attorney, Michael George, compounded the potential jury problem by asking Brenner if the women had "teased" Carr or "put on a show for him." Though the surviving victim vehemently denied they had done anything of the sort, this exchange encouraged gossip and specula-tion. Some local residents were quick to conclude that Brenner and Wight were the type of women who probably had done something "to set Carr off." In the upcoming trial, Brenner's credibility would be pitted against Carr's. Who would the jury believe, an out-of-state lesbian or a local mountain man? Credibility would be crucial. If an Adams County jury concluded that the women had done things to Carr that arguably would have provoked a reasonable person to violence, it could reduce Carr's culpability from capital murder to voluntary manslaughter—a crime that usually receives a five- to ten-year sentence, with the possibility of time off for good behavior.

The *Sentinel* reported that Carr sat quietly throughout the preliminary hearing, holding his head in his palms, a tattoo of a knife with "Roy" underneath it visible on his left hand. Only once did he become visibly upset: when John Holtz, a Pennsylvania state trooper, testified that Carr had neither asked to see an attorney nor refused to answer questions during his interrogation, Carr whispered loudly, "Liar." The implications of Carr's comment were potentially quite important. If his request for an attorney or his refusal to answer questions had been ignored or denied, his confession might be ruled inadmissible on constitutional grounds.

In a press conference immediately after the hearing, Defense Attorney George said he would not "rule out" an insanity or diminished-capacity defense for his client. If a jury decided that Carr was insane, he would be acquitted of the criminal charges against him and civilly committed to a mental institution until he could satisfy state psychiatrists that he was no longer a danger to himself or others. Diminished capacity, in contrast, was a partial defense. If a jury could be persuaded that at the time of the shootings, Carr, though sane, was suffering from a diminished capacity, the jury could reduce his culpability to third-degree murder, a crime carrying a ten- to twenty-year sentence with the possibility of parole. Carr's mental condition thus became the fourth major issue of the case, alongside provocation, the admissibility of Carr's confession, and the legitimacy of the death penalty itself.

As a professor of political science who teaches law-related courses at Dickinson College, I followed with great interest the developments in the Carr case throughout the summer of 1988. The few sensational details of the crime notwithstanding, it was a typical homicide case, tossed into a system that processed it in the same way it processed thousands of others. Since there seemed little doubt that Stephen Carr had shot the two hikers, the case centered on two questions: the level of Carr's culpability—was he guilty of capital murder, first-degree murder, third-degree murder, or voluntary manslaughter?—and the appropriate severity of his punishment (on a scale ranging from five years' imprisonment to the electric chair).

Carr's motive for attacking the women had considerable bearing on these two issues. Was the murder a hate crime? A sex crime? A class crime? If the evidence showed that Carr's actions were premeditated and motivated by homophobia, he would be a strong candidate for the death penalty. If, on the other hand, the shootings were unintentional or if the women had provoked Carr, a less harsh penalty would be in order.

Carr's fate, in other words, depended on the "facts" of what happened on South Mountain on May 13, 1988. The American criminal justice system that would determine what the facts were was adversarial rather than inquisitorial. Intent on magnifying Carr's culpability and maximizing his punishment, the prosecution would paint the darkest possible picture of his crime and motive. The defense would highlight those features of the case that lowered Carr's culpability. Each side would formulate its interpretation of what happened, focusing on the facts that fit its theory and ignoring, or perhaps even hiding, those that didn't. The two versions of the "truth" would presumably clash at Carr's trial, where a jury would decide which one, or whether some combination of the two, made the most sense and would render its verdict accordingly.

By late summer of 1988, the Carr case had faded from the headlines. The fall semester began, and, busy with my courses, I all but forgot about the Appalachian Trail murder and Carr's prosecution. It was not until five years later, amid the public furor of the O. J. Simpson murder trial, that I thought about the case again. From conversations with students, friends, and colleagues, it was clear to me that many people were disgusted not only with the Simpson verdict, but also with the legal system that produced it. Expressions of outrage were often accompanied by calls for reform to prevent similar miscarriages of justice in the future.

Although to some extent I shared those sentiments, I recognized how atypical the Simpson case was. Unlike the Los Angeles district attorney's office in the Simpson case, most prosecutors do not forego seeking the death penalty in a multiple homicide case. Unlike Simpson, most homicide defendants are not wealthy celebrities with the resources to retain a team of high-priced lawyers. Rather, they are poor, psychologically flawed, relatively anonymous individuals represented by public defenders or court-appointed lawyers. Usually there's little doubt that the defendant committed the crime, and often there's a confession, perhaps one gained by police officers not terribly scrupulous about the defendant's constitutional rights. As in the Carr case, the issue is not whether the defendant is guilty and deserves punishment, but rather how guilty the defendant is and how severe the punishment should be.

Members of the public all too readily assume that what goes on in a highly visible homicide case is typical of what happens generally in the criminal justice system. In large part because they are misleading in this way, such cases can inspire reforms of the system that are at worst counterproductive, or at best inconsequential because they have little or no impact on the average homicide case. Assuming that an informed public is perhaps the best way to prevent such flawed reforms, I began my research on the Carr case in the fall of 1994. My goal was to write a narrative of a typical murder case that would be both interesting and informative for the general public.

Most, though not all, of the people involved in the Carr case agreed to talk with me. I sent a letter to Claudia Brenner requesting an interview, but she never responded. John Holtz, one of the four Pennsylvania state troopers who played important parts in the Carr investigation, refused to talk to me, as did a sister of Rebecca Wight. Everyone else cooperated, at least to the point of talking to me on the phone. A few deserve particular mention. Don Blevins and Denny Beaver gave me fascinating insights into a police investigation. After Carr released them from their duty of confidentiality, Michael George, Carr's attorney, and Skip Gochenour, his defense investigator, provided me with information that I could not have found elsewhere. In several interviews, Roy Keefer talked at length about his understanding of the role of the prosecutor. Once he became convinced that my purpose in writing a book on the Carr case was a serious one, Judge Oscar Spicer put aside his reservations about talking to me.

I am very grateful to these six individuals and the others who spoke to me. Their sometimes conflicting recollections of what took place during the prosecution of Stephen Carr in 1988 make up a large part of what follows. Though I have on occasion reordered what these individuals told me, I have accurately quoted and summarized the substance of their opinions. In addition to the participants' recollections, I have interspersed in the narrative my own views on a number of issues. If the text does not attribute an opinion to anyone, the reader may assume it is the author's.

In this book, I extensively used the formal transcripts of the preliminary hearing, the suppression hearing, the pretrial conference, and the trial, in addition to other documents, some of which are on file in the Adams County Clerk's Office. In the first chapter, I quote from the transcript of the preliminary hearing without attribution because the focus of the chapter is on the shootings, not the hearing. In later chapters, when the focus is on the criminal process itself, I identify the speakers by name.

In this book, I have protected the reputations of persons who were only tangentially involved with the Carr case by changing their names.

At the core of our adversarial system of criminal justice is the notion that the truth most readily comes to light when opposing parties place alternative theories and "facts" before an impartial arbiter. This book tests this assumption, challenging readers to sort out the conflicting statements and weigh the significance of each piece of evidence. Fulfilling in this way the role that the jury often plays in our criminal justice system, the reader will have to consider two fundamental questions. Did the system find out the "whole truth" of what happened on South Mountain? Was justice served in this case: did Carr receive the proper punishment? The first question addresses the fact-finding capacity of today's adversarial system of criminal justice; the second considers what factors transform a homicide into a death penalty case. The two questions are related, because no one can assess Carr's culpability without implicitly evaluating whether the system uncovered all the relevant facts. The way we answer these questions has implications not only for our criminal justice system, but for the future of our society.

The Hikers

Several weeks after she and Rebecca Wight were shot, Claudia Brenner told her story of what happened the day her world exploded. Sitting on the witness stand, she answered Prosecutor Roy Keefer's questions in a calm voice that only underscored the horror of what she described. The shootings occurred about 5:00 P.M. She and Wight were lying beside a stream near the Appalachian Trail (A.T.) when she felt a sharp pain in her right arm. She heard something, but she didn't know what it was. A horrible nightmare began to envelope her. Someone was shooting her. Someone was trying to kill her.

"How many times were you struck, could you tell?"

"I was struck first in my arm and then twice in my neck; . . . and [then] once in my face, and then Rebecca said, 'Get down!' because I was sitting up. So I got down and put my hands over my head and got as close to the ground as I could, and I got struck again."

"Where were you struck that last time?"

Some of the information contained in this chapter is drawn from Claudia Brenner and Hannah Ashley, *Eight Bullets: One Woman's Story of Surviving Anti-Gay Violence* (Ithaca, N.Y.: Firebrand Books, 1995). However, all of the quotations attributed to Brenner are taken from the testimony she provided on direct examination at the preliminary hearing.

Birch Run Shelter where Claudia Brenner and Rebecca Wight first encountered a strange mountain man on May 13, 1988. Courtesy Gary Zimmerman.

"The top of my head."

A desperate Brenner pressed herself against the earth as flat as she could, but she couldn't get low enough and the bullets kept coming, five of them. She couldn't see the gunman, but she knew the direction the bullets were coming from. She said to Rebecca, "He came back!"

Brenner was referring to the man they had seen that morning at Birch Run Shelter, a designated camping area on the A.T. about two miles north of the shooting scene. The two women had slept the night before in a tent they had pitched near the camping area's two wooden lean-tos. They had woken up around 9:00 in the morning.

"Rebecca went up to the outhouse and, believing that we were completely alone at the campsite, she wasn't wearing any clothing. When she came back to the tent, she told me that she had met somebody who was in the lean-to area of the campsite."

"Did she indicate whether that person was a male or female?"

"Male."

Rebecca Wight's nudity was not all that exceptional on the A.T., which stretches from Springer Mountain in Georgia to the summit of Mount Katahdin in Maine. Many of those who follow the familiar white blazes that mark the Trail, as it winds its way for 2,144 miles through some of the most scenic areas in the eastern United States, are looking for some relief from the conventions and concerns that burden everyday life. Working and living in densely populated cities and suburbs, they are able to find temporary peace and solace in the natural world of the Trail. And so, when Rebecca Wight walked to the outhouse that morning, she was only doing what came naturally to her. It was perhaps no different from going skinny-dipping after a hot day of hiking.

"Did she [Wight] indicate whether she had had any conversation with that person?"

"Yes, she had had a conversation with him."

"Did she describe that conversation to you?"

"Yes. She had gone over to the lean-to in order to see if there was a logbook at the lean-to."

"What's a logbook?"

"I've never seen one, but Rebecca described them as a book that's kept at a campsite, . . . and campers come and they write notes. Anyone can read them. It's kind of like, you know, at a tourist place there will be a book where you can write your name and address so everyone can see that a boy scout troop came and somebody from England came to the Appalachian Trail, and people write different comments and they are generally stored in these lean-tos out of the rain. She had been interested in me seeing a logbook, so apparently after she went to the outhouse she walked over in that direction and came upon this male individual."

Logbooks enable hikers to share experiences, reflections, and in-sights with each other. They are popular because hikers are rarely solitary creatures. They regularly share food, campsites, and shelters. On the Trail, a love of nature and a sense of community often go hand in hand.

"She [Wight] said something to him like, 'I didn't know you were here.' She repeated to me [that] he said something like, 'I didn't know you were here.' She told me that he asked for cigarettes and she said that she didn't have any."

"Neither of you smoked?"

"Correct. Then she came back to the tent. She told me that there was another individual at the campsite and therefore we should put on some clothes, because neither one of us would ever have been naked or without any kind of appropriate clothing at the campsite if anyone else was around. So I put on some clothes and she put on some clothes, and we went on with the morning."

The presence of the man in the lean-to was disquieting, however. The two friends had come to the woods for a relaxing weekend together, and this would be difficult with him nearby. Wanting the kind of privacy that now didn't seem possible at Birch Run Shelter, they considered whether they should move to another campsite. They checked their map and confirmed that about two miles south of Birch Run Shelter, Rocky Knob Trail branched off the A.T. in a southeastern direction. They decided to try to find a new campsite somewhere along this local loop trail and left the shelter around noon.

"As we packed up and started to leave the campsite, we both noticed he was still there . . . sitting in the lean-to."

"How far were you from this person?"

"Perhaps twenty to thirty feet, although I am not certain of those distances."

"The person that you saw, was that person sitting up, standing up, or lying down?"

"He was leaning against the side of the lean-to with his legs stretched out wearing sweatpants, and that's all I remember, sweatpants."

"Did you have any observations regarding the physical shape of the person at that point?"

"I noticed that he was skinny, that his legs were long and that his hair was unkempt."

"Bushy or wild?"

"No, just not well taken care of. Kind of rough looking."

"Did you see the person's face at that point?"

"Yes."

"Did you see that person's face to a point where you would recognize that face if you saw it again?"

"Yes."

"Did you or Rebecca have any conversation with this man as you walked past him at that point?"

"As we walked past him, we said, 'See you later.' "

"Kind of like, 'Have a nice day.' "

"See ya, yeah."

"Did you really expect to see him again?"

"Never."

But the women did see the skinny, rough-looking man again. After thirty minutes of hiking south on the A.T., they came to an intersection. They stopped to look at their map to see if the trail running perpendicular to the A.T. was the one they wanted. As they checked the distances, the man with the unkempt hair came up behind them.

"He was coming from the same direction you had come?"

"Correct, and he had a rifle that was across his shoulders, which I had not seen before, and his arms were hanging over the rifle and he was very casually walking up the trail."

"You had not seen the rifle at the lean-to?"

"No. He said, 'Are you lost already?'"

"Did you or Rebecca respond to that?"

"At that point, we knew where we were going and I needed no assistance and directions, and I said, 'No, are you?' And then I walked in the direction I intended to walk on the trail."

"Then you and Rebecca went down Rocky Knob Trail?"

"Correct, and the three of us were never in the same place at that junction at the same time."

"How far apart were you when the statements were made, 'Are you lost already' and 'No, are you'?"

"Thirty feet, thirty-five feet. Maybe a little closer."

"Had you seen anyone else on the trail?"

"No one."

"Did you see where the man went at that point?"

"I took a look and I saw him continue south on the Appalachian Trail."

"So he passed that turn-off?"

"To the best of my knowledge."

Brenner looked back several times as the two women left the intersection and proceeded down the left fork of the loop trail. She saw no one, but she remained concerned, especially about the rifle. But as the hours slipped by, her anxieties eased and the two women enjoyed their afternoon. They hiked up a ridge that dropped off steeply, giving them a pretty view of the hills to the east. The going was a bit rough at times. To reach the top of Rocky Knob, they had to engage in some hardy rock climbing, but it was worth it. At the summit, they could see Long Pine

Run Reservoir off to the south nestled in the surrounding hills shimmering in the bright sunshine.

The two women talked incessantly as they enjoyed the sights and sounds of the beautiful spring day. They talked about everything under the sun: moss; gliding; Ithaca, New York.

Daughter of a vice president of Yeshiva University, Brenner had moved from New York City to Ithaca to attend Cornell University, where she earned a bachelor's degree in social work in 1977. After graduating, she stayed in the Ithaca area, spending three years working with juvenile delinquents at the Family and Children's Service. "Tenacious" was how her colleagues described her. She'd go biking, hiking, and sailing with the kids, they said. She did everything in her power "to connect" with the youngsters and thereby try to save them from a life of crime and imprisonment.

In the fall of 1985, Brenner entered a master's degree program in architecture at Virginia Polytechnic Institute, in Blacksburg. It was there, at an organizational meeting of those interested in planning Virginia Tech Women's Week, an annual spring conference sponsored by the university, that she met Rebecca Wight, an alumna of Virginia Tech who worked in the local area. Brenner went to the meeting hoping to meet new friends and perhaps a new lover, having recently broken off a nine-year relationship with a woman named Anne.

At first sight, Brenner found Wight physically attractive, but there didn't seem to be any possibility of romance. Since Wight had been living with a man for several years, she was apparently a possible feminist friend for Brenner, nothing more. However, now a graduate student seeking an M.A. degree in business management at Virginia Tech, in 1986 Wight broke off her long-term heterosexual relationship, and in the spring of 1987 the women became lovers. Unfortunately, circumstances soon forced them apart. Once classes were over, Brenner returned to Ithaca to get a job, whereas Wight remained in Blacksburg. Over the summer, the two women visited each other occasionally and once went camping at Pine Grove Furnace State Park in Pennsylvania, located at the northern end of Michaux State Forest. Apart from these brief meetings, the two women were usually far apart from each other during the summer of 1987.

In August, Brenner left for Israel to take advantage of a prestigious six-month fellowship she had won to do research at the Technion. In Blacksburg, Wight began seeing a man, although Brenner didn't find out about Tony until she got back to the States in the early spring of 1988. At this time, Brenner also learned that Wight, who was now planning to enter a Ph.D. program, had decided not to apply to Cornell University. Instead, she was considering a program at the University of Oregon, even though she knew that Brenner had deep roots in the Ithaca area and that their relationship was unlikely to survive an extended coast-to-coast separation.

This was the situation when Brenner went to visit Wight in Blacksburg in late April 1988. The visit must have gone well, because a few days later Wight sent Brenner a postcard saying that the two had pulled up thorny weeds and the flowers they had planted last summer were blooming once again. Also, in a letter dated May 6, Wight informed her father that she was going to graduate school at Pennsylvania State University. Though she did not mention her relationship with Brenner, Wight added the following:

> And it is completely true that I have NO boyfriend in Blacksburg anymore; that was a short lived affair which ended for many reasons, including the fact that I got all these offers [to Ph.D. programs]. (He did not. He hasn't even been accepted here at Va Tech yet.) I doubt very much that any boyfriend will exist in my life for years to come, because my relationship with women and a few male buddies are all I need or want at this point of development.

This letter, along with the postcard to Brenner, suggested that the women were once again in love, which might have been a factor in Wight's choice of graduate school. Because Penn State wasn't too far from Ithaca, the two women could still have a future together.

After the April visit, the two lovers decided to return to Pine Grove Furnace State Park. They would meet at the park and camp somewhere on the A.T. The two women started out on Thursday morning, May 12. Brenner drove down from Ithaca in her white Toyota pickup, while Wight, coming from the opposite direction, was behind the wheel of her black Renault. They met at about 4:30 P.M. in the parking lot of the park. They hugged and kissed, but kept a low profile because some men who looked like park employees were at the other end of the parking lot. As

Brenner stowed her gear in the Renault, Wight looked over a topographical map of Michaux State Forest she had picked up from the campground headquarters. She noticed a local loop trail called Rocky Knob Trail that intersected with the A.T. It looked like a good one for a day hike, and it wasn't too far from an A.T. shelter that was only about two miles from Shippensburg Road. The two women set off in the Renault, traveling south on Pennsylvania State Route 233; they took a right onto Shippensburg Road and headed up South Mountain. At the top, they turned right on Ridge Road and began looking for a place to park. Luckily, at an intersection, they saw off to the right a small parking area with easy access to the A.T. They immediately parked their car, packed up their stuff, and hiked south on the Trail in the direction of Birch Run Shelter. As there were no road signs, they didn't know they had parked their car on a local state forestry road known as Dead Woman's Hollow Road.

II

Five shots had been fired, and five bullets had hit Brenner. With no place to hide, she could do nothing but wait for the sound of the next gunshot and the jolt of the next bullet striking her body. Wight was unhurt, but Brenner was already gravely wounded.

"[S]he realized that we had to take cover somehow, and she said, 'We have to go behind the tree.' There was a big tree right near where we had originally put our backpacks down."

"Near the center?"

"Kind of in the center of the campsite. Big, a big old tree."

The big old tree was a hemlock that stood in the center of the campsite that Wight and Brenner had discovered about 3:30 that afternoon. The campsite seemed perfect. Because it was off of the Rocky Knob Trail, the skinny unkempt man would never find them here. It was also alongside a stream that gurgled pleasantly on the gorgeous spring day. Beams of sunlight bounced off the water, their pale reflections shimmering against the bark of the trees. A bed of moss covered a flat area immediately adjacent to the stream.

"Did you proceed to set up camp?"

"No. It was early enough so we just sat down and ate a little something and talked with each other and thought we had lots of time before the sun would go down so we didn't put up the tent at that time."

"Did you set up a fire or start a fire?"

"We used the stove to boil water to make iced tea. It was very hot and we put the water that we had in one canteen in the stream to make it cold and we started to make iced tea and eventually put the plastic container that held the iced tea in the stream."

"To cool it?"

"[Yes. We then] drank some cold water and then we laid down a piece of the tent right near the stream to rest and lie down."

The two women were tired. They'd been hiking for three-and-a-half hours over terrain that had been pretty rough in places. The climb down Rocky Knob had been just as strenuous as the climb up. On the way down, Brenner became tired, and she asked Wight if they could rest for a while.

Wight was the more experienced hiker of the two. She had become serious about the outdoors long ago, before college, when she was living in Korea. Her father worked in the foreign service, and his job moved his family all over the world. By the time Wight was eleven years old, she had lived in Thailand, Laos, Brazil, Pakistan, and Afghanistan. Then, after a six-year stint in Washington, D.C., her father accepted an assignment in Korea in 1976. It was there at the age of seventeen that Wight started camping and hiking with friends. Soon she was climbing mountains and rappelling down cliffs, testing herself against the elements. A vigorous and adventuresome young woman had found her first passion: physical activity in the great outdoors.

Wight's attitude toward the physical challenges of the great outdoors mirrored her reaction to the challenges that life set before her. Her parents divorced in 1975, and her mother, who had a history of mental illness, committed suicide soon thereafter. The Wight children had to deal in quick succession with a divorce and the death of a parent. Rebecca, as the eldest child, assumed responsibilities that were beyond her years, such as caring for her two younger sisters, Evelyn and Judy. Leon, her father, was busy with his job and he sometimes drank excessively. Rebecca nonetheless coped with her situation. By the time she was a sixteen-year-old attending high school on an American army base in Korea, she had developed into an independent, self-reliant young woman.

After graduating from high school and returning to the States in 1977, Rebecca attended Virginia Tech. In 1979, she met Wayne, a man who enjoyed hiking and camping as much as she did. Eventually they fell in love and she moved in with him. Wayne started a camping goods store in Blacksburg, and Wight helped him with the struggling business, even though she was busy working toward and paying for her undergraduate degree. They took on life's challenges together until they went their separate ways in 1986.

Rebecca Wight had a zest for life. After she entered Virginia Tech's graduate program in business management in 1986, she wrote her father, then living in Washington, D.C., "I'm learning so much, it's incredible. I want to keep learning the rest of my life." Life in graduate school also presented Wight with her share of troubles, however. She was out of cash, the bank wanted to repossess her car, and she needed a new computer. Problems such as these, however, never daunted Rebecca. Her attitude toward life was reflected in what she told her father. "For me to be upset because the bank might repossess my car is absurd when I remember Bangladesh." Underneath Wight's concerns, worries, and regrets, there was a fundamental conviction that things would work out for those who worked hard.

The women had a bite to eat as they rested from their climb down Rocky Knob. They would soon have to begin looking for a campsite. Their map indicated that a stream ran along the southwestern edge of the loop trail.

"During all that time, had you seen anyone else at all?"

"Absolutely nobody."

"Had you heard anyone else, any noises in the woods that would seem as if there were people around?"

"Nothing. I completely believed we were alone."

"About what time would it have been when you laid down the piece of the tent and then lay down by the stream?"

"Possibly 45 minutes later."

"So we're talking 4:15, in that range?"

"4:15, 4:30. I am guessing a little bit."

The moss was beautiful but wet, so the two women spread out their waterproof tent. They stayed dry lying on it, but the cold wet moss underneath kept them cool on the hot day. Brenner got out some chocolate. She and Wight nibbled on it as they sipped their iced tea. The gnats were annoying, so they took off their shoes and rolled up in the tent to keep them at bay. Playful lovemaking began. Wight asked Brenner to take off her shorts. The lovemaking became more serious. Brenner asked Wight if she first wanted to pitch the tent. Wight replied, "No, let's stay out here."

A few seconds later, the first shot cracked the quiet of the mountainside. Screaming in panic, Brenner saw her bright red blood splatter on the green tent cover as her body jerked in reaction to the force of the small but flesh-tearing bullets. After the fifth shot, Wight cooly advised Brenner to take cover behind the large hemlock near the center of the campsite. Each had to take her chance and make a run for it. Brenner went first.

"I dashed for the tree and I made it, and Rebecca dashed for the tree and somewhere in there she got hit by two gunshots."

Brenner's dash for the tree had tipped off the shooter what Wight was going to do. Ready for her, he shot three times and hit Wight twice, once in the head and once in the back.

"What happened after Rebecca was shot?"

"We both got to behind the tree. It was absolutely terrifying, and we just tried to figure out what to do together."

The defenseless women realized that there was nothing to stop the shooter from walking right up to them and killing them at point blank range. The timing of the attack amplified their terror. The skinny, unkempt man with the rifle had come back, seen them making love, raised his rifle, and shot them. Brenner was hysterical, but Wight, despite her two gunshot wounds, was still thinking, still functioning.

"I was saying things like 'We got to get out of here.' 'We got to get help.' 'We got to get help.' 'We got to get out of here.' 'What are we going to do?' 'What are we going to do?' That kind of panic. We stayed behind the tree, and I said, 'What are we going to do? What are we going to do?' And Rebecca said, 'Stop the bleeding.'"

"Were there any shots being fired at that point?"

"No. So, I don't know how long it was, I took a chance and went out from behind the tree to one of the backpacks and grabbed a towel and some clothing to try and stop the bleeding."

"What did you do with that then?"

"I took the towel and I wrapped it around my neck really tight because I knew I was hurt and I knew I was bleeding there, but I didn't have any idea what was really going on."

"You essentially tried to make a tourniquet for yourself; is that right?"

"Right and for Rebecca. I gave her a bunch of clothing—a turtleneck and some shirts—and she wrapped them around her neck. But she was hurting real bad already then and so she wasn't moving around at all. She was just sitting by the tree, and I went back to the backpacks. Then I went back to get out sneakers and also to get some sweatpants because I hadn't been fully dressed at the stream. I had been wearing shorts and they were taken off, so I went back to the pack and got a pair of sweatpants, put them on, brought my sneakers over, put them on, and gave Rebecca her sneakers to put on, fully expecting she would be able to put them on, but she was having trouble by then and couldn't. She was hurting too bad and could no longer see. . . . So I helped her put them on."

"Your plan at that point was still for the two of you to try to get out and get help?"

"Yes."

Wight's physical condition, however, soon upset Brenner's plan. The bullet that had struck Wight in the head had fractured her skull. The one that had struck her in the back an inch or two to the right of her spine produced a small entry wound—only .6 cm in diameter—but as it moved through her body in a slightly upward direction, it had torn a 4 cm hole in her liver. Both lobes of this vital organ were destroyed, sealing Wight's fate.

"There was a number of different discussions—you know, her telling me that she could no longer see and that it hurt, and me trying to help her stand up, thinking that if I could help her get up she would be able to walk with me or lean on me, and trying a number of times to lift her body up. I was trying to lift her body up. I tried to resuscitate her when I thought she was starting to pass out. I shook her head to try and keep her conscious. I asked her to keep talking to me so she would stay conscious and keep relating—you know, keep conscious."

"It was obvious to you at that point Rebecca was hurt a lot more than you were?"

"Yes."

With Wight incapacitated, Brenner could no longer rely on her steadiness and calm judgment. Brenner had to face the horror alone. She had to make the decisions that would determine whether the two women would get out of Michaux State Forest alive. She had been shot five times, and the gunman was still out there in the forest that surrounded her for miles in every direction. It was enough to overwhelm almost anyone.

III

Brenner did not succumb to panic or despair, however. Her fear and terror did not depart, but she regained control of herself.

"I had thought I would die, and somewhere when I was holding that towel on my neck, I just all of sudden said, 'I can live.'"

Earlier, Brenner had told Wight that she thought she should go for help, but Wight had asked her not to leave. Now Wight was unconscious. Brenner thought she could still feel a pulse, but she wasn't sure. She reconsidered whether she should go. It was the hardest decision she had ever made in her life. If she stayed, there was nothing she could do to help her friend and it would endanger her own life. If she left, she might save herself and it would give Rebecca her only chance for staying alive.

"You made the decision that Rebecca couldn't go with you and you had to go get help alone. Is that right?"

"Yes. After trying to help her walk six or seven times, and after seeing that she couldn't see and every time I tried to lift her up, she just started to wheeze and couldn't keep her own body standing up—after I tried that as many times as I could bear, I decided that the only thing I could do was to get help and come back."

Brenner took a few minutes to gather what she needed for her escape. She retrieved her wallet from the pocket of her companion, who had carried it for her during their hike. She then grabbed the map of Michaux State Forest that Wight had earlier placed on one of the campfire stones under another rock. Last, because there were only a couple of hours of sunlight left, she searched for the flashlight that she knew she had put in her backpack. She couldn't find it. Not knowing where the shooter was, the thought of being alone in the woods without a light terrified her. She looked in the backpack again. There it was. Why she didn't find it the first time, she didn't know. It seemed to her that she had to do everything twice.

Wallet. Map. Flashlight. As she thought about whether she needed anything else, Brenner suddenly realized that she was cold. She had sweatpants on, but her T-shirt was drenched in blood and the sun was already descending. That's when she thought of Wight lying on the ground. Though unconscious, she might still feel cold. Brenner ran to the backpacks, got out Wight's sleeping bag, and carefully covered her with it. She then left the campsite without saying good-bye. There was nothing romantic about the parting. It was an escape, an escape to get help.

At first, Brenner felt an almost irresistible urge to go back. Whether it was fear of what lay ahead of her or love of what lay behind her, it seemed as if someone was physically pulling her back to the campsite. But Brenner kept moving forward. Step by step, she forced herself to keep going. She knew if she returned to Rebecca, they would both die in the woods.

"I left and started up the trail in the direction that would have completed the loop, which meant when I got to the [Rocky Knob] trail, I made a left turn and continued on the trail to complete the loop to get to that junction [with the A.T.] we originally talked about."

When Brenner turned left on Rocky Knob Trail, the A.T. was about a mile and three-quarters in front of her—a long way for a person with five bullet wounds. Though the trail broadened out at this point, it was gently uphill. Brenner wanted to run, but knew she couldn't. She was having trouble breathing because of all the blood in her mouth, and her arm throbbed painfully. Still, she kept moving, each step a moment of excruciating fright. She fully expected her assailant to step out from behind one of the many trees that surrounded her. She would never be able to get away from him. She was completely in his power.

Brenner came upon a Coke can in the middle of the path. Having seen no trash on the trail that afternoon, Brenner wondered, had the killer left the can for her to find? She suppressed the thought. She didn't want fear to get the better of her again and the can's presence made no difference for what she had to do. Though she was more scared than she had ever been before, her only chance for life was to keep walking.

"You made a turn on the Appalachian Trail?"

"No, I continued straight past—I didn't want to go on to the Appalachian Trail because I was scared."

Brenner could have turned right on the A.T. and retraced the route the women had taken that morning, ending up back at Birch Run Shelter. Instead, calculating that a forest road offered more safety than the A.T., she stayed on Rocky Knob Trail until it dead-ended into Ridge Road—the same state forestry road off of which the women had parked Wight's black Renault the afternoon before. Brenner turned right on the road and headed north toward Shippensburg Road, two miles away.

She was out from under the foreboding canopy of the woods. In the forest, each tree had been a potential hiding place and the darkening shadows of the early evening made the forest a hostile and intimidating place. The gravel road was better. Brenner could see where she was going, at least until the road disappeared around a bend or into the dusky gloom ahead. She resolved to take her chances on the road. For her, there would be no more trails or woods.

It occurred to Brenner that she might come across a house. If she did, should she break in? Would that make her situation better or worse? What if the man were in the house? He was always on her mind. Any option she considered triggered her fear that he would be waiting for her.

After walking for a couple of hours, Brenner began to feel more hopeful that she was actually going to make it to safety. Then she saw something out of the corner of her eye. Something had moved, she thought, in the trees on the left side of the road. Her newly recovered sense of security crumbled. She couldn't turn her head in the direction of what she had thought she had seen, because the two wounds to her neck, one on each side, were causing her terrific pain. She had to turn her entire body in the required direction. She then put her hands over her head and begged the unseen person not to shoot her. As she tried to communicate with whoever had made the movement she thought she'd seen, she edged down the road.

Nothing happened. No gunshot cracked the stillness. No assailant stepped out into the road.

Brenner moved on, her injured throat throbbing from her efforts to plead with whoever, if anyone, had moved in the woods. She couldn't believe how long it was taking to reach Shippensburg Road. One rise after another: there seemed to be no end to them.

Suddenly, Brenner saw headlights. What should she do? The driver could be her killer or her savior. There were no safe options for Brenner, only desperate choices that had to be made quickly. Brenner took the bloody towel from around her neck and waved it frantically.

A brown Blazer passed by. It didn't even slow down. Brenner was shocked.

"I guess they didn't realize I was in trouble."

The tail lights quickly disappeared and the sound of the Blazer died out. Once again, Brenner was alone on the forestry road, the night slowly closing in around her. Though the gravel was still dimly visible, the forest on both sides was shrouded in somber darkness. She forged on, expecting Shippensburg Road to appear at any moment, and yet after every turn of the forestry road, the dirty white ribbon of gravel stretched out before her and disappeared in the darkness ahead. Finally, after she'd walked more than three hours, she thought she heard the sound of a car passing on a road ahead. Then she was sure of it. A house appeared on her left. She considered breaking into it, but quickly rejected the idea. The man could be there waiting for her. She wasn't going to fall into any trap like that, not when a paved road was just a few yards ahead. She soon rounded a bend, and there it was: Shippensburg Road. She had made it out of the woods and, unbelievably, she was still alive.

What now? Since it was completely dark at this point, Brenner turned on her flashlight and studied her map. To the right, about five to six miles in an easterly direction, were the small communities of Bridgeport and Arendtsville. It wasn't likely that they would have much in the way of medical or police assistance. To the left, in a westerly direction, was the small city of Shippensburg. The problem was that on the map, Shippensburg looked to be at least seven or eight miles away.

Brenner knew she couldn't walk that far. She was exhausted, and her gunshot wounds were causing her intense pain. Her only option was to flag down a car. It was a rather lonely country road, but it wasn't that late, only about 9:00 P.M. A car would eventually come by. But if a car came, how was Brenner going to stop it? An hour earlier, the brown Blazer hadn't stopped, even though then there had been enough daylight that the driver must have seen her. Now it was dark.

Only a few minutes passed before headlights appeared in the west. Resolving to stop the oncoming car, Brenner stepped into the middle of the lane of the approaching car, extended her arm, and with her flashlight began making large circles of light. The car would stop or run her over. The vehicle began to slow down. Fearing that if she stepped aside the car might speed by her, Brenner stayed in the middle of the lane, signaling with her flashlight until the car came to a complete stop.

Brenner was then struck by the thought that the driver might be the gunman. Fearful, but determined, she went around to the driver's side of the car. Two teenage boys, two local kids, were in the old car.

The driver rolled down his window, and Brenner told him that she needed help, that she had been shot. Unexpectedly, the car started moving forward. The two teenagers were going to leave her, Brenner thought. They were going to abandon her on this lonely road. She screamed, demanding to know where they were going.

The surprised youngster driving the car replied, "We're just turning the car around."

Relieved, Brenner waited as Cory, the driver, turned the vehicle in the direction of Shippensburg. Chris, the other boy, got into the back to let Brenner have the front seat. They sped off, heading for the Shippensburg police station. Brenner immediately began telling the boys, over and over again, her name and that she had been camping on Rocky Knob Trail with another person named Rebecca Wight, who had also been shot. The boys repeated the information back to her. They wouldn't forget what she had told them, they assured her. They would be able to tell the police if she lost consciousness.

Cory drove fast. The speed frightened Brenner and she begged him to be careful. Cory said nothing, his eyes glued to the road. Chris was also silent. Two scared country kids who wanted to be helpful but weren't sure what to do.

Brenner couldn't stand the quiet. Now that help was getting closer, each adrenalin-packed minute of racing emotions and frightening impressions and recollections seemed like an hour to her. She needed a distraction, something to fill up her drawn-out sense of time.

She asked the boys to talk to her, but they didn't know what to say. One of them turned on the radio, but the music couldn't take Brenner's mind off the horror of what she had been through. The same thoughts, over and over again, tumbled through her consciousness when a moment of compassion interrupted her tortured mental state. Because she had difficulty swallowing, Brenner was spitting her bloody saliva into the towel she had taken from the campsite. Cory noticed what she was doing and pointed to a white plastic cup.

"Um, that's my spitting cup. I just started chewing a couple of minutes ago. There's not much in it. If you want to spit in it you can use it."

The unexpected offer reflected not only Cory's rough manners and origins, but also his underlying generosity and humanity. The boy wanted to help in any way he could. A few hours before, a stranger had tried to kill Brenner. Now, a young country boy, another stranger, had suggested that she use his spitting cup. Though touched by Cory's simple sweetness, Brenner declined his offer.

In ten to fifteen minutes, the boys and Brenner were in Shippensburg. They pulled into the driveway of the small building that housed the town's police station. A bearded man in a uniform sat on a folding chair, enjoying the warm night air.

Brenner got out of the car and told the man that she had been shot. He jumped up, ordered the two boys to stay where they were, and helped Brenner into the police station.

Brenner never saw Cory and Chris again. They were out of her life as quickly as they had come into it.

Inside the station, officers snapped into action at the sight of Brenner's bloody clothes and wounds. One officer called for an ambulance, and another called the state police. Brenner was directed to a swivel chair behind one of the two large wooden desks in the room. She sat down, and the officer in charge asked her the obvious question. What happened?

Brenner said she had been shot, but she emphasized and reemphasized that her friend, Rebecca Wight, had been shot, too, and that she was still out in the woods, hurt very badly. We have to go find her, Brenner urged, we've got to go get her now. There's no time to lose.

The officer told Brenner she wasn't going back to South Mountain. She was going to a hospital to get medical attention.

Brenner said she had to go along to make sure that the police could find Rebecca. She spread out her map and drew a circle on it where she thought their campsite had been. Looking at the map, the officers tried to figure out whether the shootings had taken place in Cumberland County or Adams County.

Brenner's exasperation boiled over. It made no difference which county. Rebecca needed help and she needed it now.

As a search party formed in the small police station, Brenner was still expecting to go along, even though her wounds were causing her quite a bit of pain. She had to brace herself for the stabbing sensation that accompanied each attempt to swallow, and she couldn't talk well, because her throat gurgled whenever she tried to say anything. But her wounds could be quickly stitched up, Brenner thought. The important thing was that she was conscious and alert. She was confident that she could lead the search party to the campsite. She at least wanted to try. She owed that much to the friend and lover that she had left in the woods.

Brenner's hopes were soon dashed. The rescue party left the station, taking along the map Brenner had drawn. A frustrated Brenner had to rely on people she didn't know to find Wight. Then the ambulance arrived, and a medic asked Brenner to lie down on a stretcher. Rather than going back to South Mountain to rescue Rebecca, Brenner was strapped to a stretcher in the back of an ambulance. After the terrible experience she had been through, she wanted to regain control of her life, but the opposite was occurring. Alone in a strange place without any friends to turn to, she had no choice but to trust strangers, both those who had gone off to find Rebecca and those in the ambulance who were now taking her vital signs and hooking her up to an IV as they sped toward Chambersburg Hospital, twenty miles away.

In the ambulance, Brenner's thoughts shifted from Rebecca's rescue to what was going to happen next. At the hospital, there would be questions. What should she tell the doctors and nurses? More important, what should she tell the police? Should she tell them the whole story?

Paradoxically, as the ambulance approached the hospital, Brenner's fears increased. To her fear of the unkempt man who had tried to kill her was added the fear of what the outside world would do to her. She felt she was out of the woods in one sense, that is, out of the immediate reach of the killer, but not out in another sense. She knew homosexual sex was a crime in some states. Was it in Pennsylvania? Maybe, if she told the whole truth, the Pennsylvania police would treat her as a criminal. She didn't know. Her uncertainty magnified her loneliness, distrust, and fear.

Brenner made a conscious decision. She would tell only the minimum. She would not tell anyone that she and Wight were lesbians or that they had been shot while engaged in lovemaking.

Brenner took comfort in the fact that she had friends she could count on, friends who were lesbians. Unlike the strangers who were coming into her life, they were people whom she could trust and rely on. Unfortunately, however, her friends were hundreds of miles away in Ithaca, New York. She would telephone them as soon as possible. That was the first step. She'd tell them what happened and they would come immediately—of that she was sure. They could be in Chambersburg in something like six hours. Their presence would be a big help. Especially her friend Anne. She would know what to do.

The other factor that buoyed Brenner's spirits was her mental condition. She didn't think she was in any kind of shock. She could remember what had happened to her, and she was thinking clearly about her options. Maybe, just maybe, Chambersburg Hospital could patch her up quickly so that she could help in Rebecca's rescue. Or perhaps she might be out of the hospital by the time her friends had driven down from Ithaca. Once with her friends, she'd be safe.

Brenner's plans, however, quickly went awry. When she arrived at the hospital at 9:40 P.M., the nurse wouldn't let her telephone her friends. She insisted that Brenner call her parents, which Brenner refused to do. She spoke briefly to a Pennsylvania state trooper. Then Dr. James Hurley came into the room, cut off her green T-shirt, briefly examined the wounds to her head and neck, and left the room. A nurse came in and told Brenner that a Life Lion Helicopter from Hershey Medical Center would arrive in twenty-eight minutes to take her to the trauma center.

Brenner was stunned. A trauma center!

When the Life Lion Helicopter arrived, the crew quickly strapped Brenner to a straight board using lengths of three-inch-wide tape and then fixed the board to a stretcher. Rolled-up towels were placed on both sides of her head, and her head was also taped down to the board. Brenner found herself immobilized and powerless. A female member of the crew warned her that it would be a noisy trip. Seconds later, the helicopter took off. It was six minutes before 11:00 P.M.

During her helicopter ride to Hershey Medical Center, Brenner rarely spoke to the medical technician at her side, but she tried to take in everything that was going on around her. She wanted to know what was happening so that she could make the right decision when it came time to make it. Maybe Chambersburg Hospital couldn't fix her up, but that didn't necessarily mean that she would have to stay long at Hershey Medical Center. Maybe she would be ready to be discharged by the time her friends arrived from Ithaca. But for that to happen, she had to get word to them. That was still her first priority.

After the helicopter landed on the hospital's pad, white-coated attendants expertly transferred Brenner to a gurney and wheeled her into the emergency room. Her vital signs were recorded. A doctor examined her wounds. X-rays were taken. It was now midnight. A chaplain arrived, and Brenner gave him Anne's phone number. He gently insisted that he should also call her parents. Brenner reluctantly gave in and gave him her parents' phone number. A consultation with an ear, nose, and throat (ENT) specialist was ordered. Two ENT doctors arrived about fifteen minutes before 1:00 A.M. They decided that a portable endoscopy, which would enable them to examine the interior of Brenner's throat, was necessary and that a surgeon should be called in. Brenner underwent the procedure and the surgeon, Dr. David Weigand, arrived at 1:15 A.M.

Weigand and the two ENT specialists discussed whether a special diagnostic test was necessary for them to understand the extent of Brenner's injuries to her throat. The procedure would involve taking X-rays of Brenner's throat while she swallowed a barium solution. The barium would show up on the X-rays and help the doctors determine more precisely how much damage the bullets to her face and neck had done to her esophagus. The damage that the bullets had caused to Brenner's mouth and neck area had to be surgically repaired, and the bullet fragments embedded in the back of her throat had to be removed. There was a small possibility that she would die on the operating table, her surgeon warned, but she really had no choice but to undergo the surgery.

For the first time, Brenner fully realized the seriousness of her injuries. She didn't like it, but she had to trust these strangers who were trying to help her. The barium-swallow procedure began at about 2:00 A.M. It was a small nightmare within the larger one that had become Brenner's life. In her condition, simply swallowing saliva caused her intense pain, but now she had to swallow a thick, unpleasant-tasting liquid that made her gag. Coughing, retching, spitting up blood, Brenner had to swallow the vile stuff and then wait for the click of the X-ray machine. She had to swallow and wait, and then swallow and wait all over again. She had to keep it up until the doctors thought they had all the pictures of her throat that they needed for surgery. The procedure took a full half hour of suffering.

When it was over, Brenner was exhausted. The terror of the shooting, the pain of her wounds, the anxiety of leaving Rebecca, the physical exertion of hiking out of the woods—all of it finally caught up with her. Physically and emotionally spent, she needed a break from the horror that had become her life. The anesthesia for her surgery came as a relief, letting her slowly fall into the comforting darkness of unconsciousness. Her Friday-the-13th was finally over.

The Suspects

I

On the night of Friday, May 13, 1988, Pennsylvania State Trooper Donald Blevins was looking forward to the end of his shift, an hour away, when the phone rang. As soon as he answered it, he knew that he would not be going home at 11:00. Two women had been shot on South Mountain. Trooper John Black from the Chambersburg station of the state police had just interviewed one of the victims—Claudia Brenner—at the emergency room of Chambersburg Hospital. Brenner had fled the scene of the shootings and was now on her way to Hershey Medical Center. The other victim—Rebecca Wight—was still on South Mountain. Blevins was to organize a search party from PSP Gettysburg and rendezvous with a group that had already left from Shippensburg.

The two search parties, along with two employees of the Bureau of Forestry they had called for assistance, met at a bridge on Birch Run Road at the northern edge of Long Pine Run Reservoir. Brenner's map gave the men a general idea of where to look for Wight, but finding her in the dark woods would not be easy. The two teams decided to split up. The Shippensburg team got back into their cars, returned to Shippensburg Road, turned left and drove about a mile up the mountain, took another left on Ridge Road, and drove south about two miles, stopping where Rocky Knob Trail dead-ended into Ridge Road. With Forester Merle Waltz in the lead, they walked quickly past the Appalachian Trail (A.T.) to the fork and proceeded down the southern loop of Rocky Knob Trail. The Trail was crowded with underbrush, but the Shippensburg party made good progress.

Led by Forester Gary Zimmerman, Blevins and the Gettysburg group hiked from the bridge directly into the forest in a northwesterly direction. The sky was clear, but the way was uphill and rugged. After about forty-five minutes, they finally reached the southern tip of Rocky Knob Trail and proceeded in the direction from which the Shippensburg team was presumably approaching. The two parties met a few hundred yards up the Trail. It was now about 11:40 P.M., about seven hours after the shootings, and Rebecca Wight was still unaccounted for. What to do now? Finding a person who was too weak to shout out or perhaps was unconscious seemed at that point to be an impossible undertaking.

Based on the location of the circle Brenner had drawn on a map of Michaux State Forest in the Shippensburg police station and the fact that the shootings had occurred beside a stream, Zimmerman and Waltz believed that Wight's location was most likely somewhere along Rocky Knob Run, a stream that ran parallel to Rocky Knob Trail about fifty yards to the south. The two foresters suggested that they should go on alone. They could make better time and they could easily call out if they found anything. The troopers, some of whom were worn out from the strenuous hiking, quickly accepted the plan, and Zimmerman and Waltz left Rocky Knob Trail in the direction of the stream. A few yards from it, they separated, Waltz heading up the creek and Zimmerman down. Shining his flashlight ahead of him, Zimmerman made his way slowly through thick underbrush and rhododendron along the northeastern side of Rocky Knob Run.

Suddenly, Zimmerman saw a shiny reflection. The light of his flashlight had bounced off something metallic, causing a flash. He looked intently at the reflection, trying to peer behind it, trying to make out what the object was. He kept his light trained on it as he carefully made his way forward, over fallen logs and around thickets of brush. The outlines of a metal camp stove gradually came into Zimmerman's view. Other items became visible as he shined his flashlight around the campsite. Behind a tree, Zimmerman made out the figure of a human body on the ground.

He called out to the troopers waiting on Rocky Knob Trail, "I've found something down here. I think I've got it."

Zimmerman stayed where he was until the troopers joined him. Then Blevins, accompanied by Larry Kerns, a medic, walked around the campsite to the spot where Wight was lying on the ground about five feet from a large tree. Except for her hair, she was completely covered with a blue sleeping bag. Blevins removed the bag, and Kerns felt for her pulse. There was none. Rebecca Wight was dead.

II

Blevins immediately secured the area to prevent contamination of the crime scene. At that point, he could do nothing but wait for daylight. Wight's body could not be moved until the coroner and a police photographer had arrived on the scene. In order to remove the body, some kind of vehicle also had to get down to the crime scene from Ridge Road, which meant that the foresters of Michaux State Forest would have to clear the 1.7 miles of the southern loop of Rocky Knob Trail enough to allow a jeep to traverse it. This job would have to wait until early morning. Because it would have destroyed more evidence than it would have uncovered, a search of the crime scene in the middle of the night would have been foolhardy. However, Blevins did notice a pair of panties lying on the ground a few feet from Wight's body.

"I wondered what those underpants were doing there," Blevins recalls. "I then checked to see if the victim had any underpants on. She didn't. And she looked like she had been hastily dressed. These facts and the location of the shootings were what made us first think that maybe the two women were lesbians. Of course, we didn't know for sure, but in my experience, women do not normally go camping without their men and they do not go camping in the middle of nowhere, three or four miles from any kind of help. It seemed obvious to me that these two women wanted to be alone, really alone. Why? Well, the most likely explanation was that the two women were sexually involved."

III

While Blevins waited for daylight at the crime scene, Trooper Denny Beaver was finishing up his shift some forty miles away at Troop H headquarters in Harrisburg.

"It was about quarter of twelve and I was ready to go home," recounts Beaver. "It had been a quiet night. I was then asked to go down to the Hershey Emergency Room. Two girls had been shot near Gettysburg. They didn't give me much information, but they did tell me that the other girl had died and that the two women were probably lesbians. They wanted me to interview the surviving victim."

Beaver arrived at the hospital at 12:35 A.M. and proceeded immediately to the emergency room, where Dr. Fred Fedok and Nurse Sherry Lauver were treating Claudia Brenner. Catching sight of the state trooper, Brenner asked him if the police had found Rebecca. Beaver replied that Wight hadn't made it. She was dead.

"One of the worst parts of being a police officer is having to tell people you don't know that one of their loved ones is dead. You wish someone who knew the victim would be there to do it, to make it somewhat easier, but so often it ends up that we have to do it and there is no easy way to tell someone something like that."

After Brenner regained her composure, Beaver asked her what happened. Listening to her tell her story, Beaver was impressed by Brenner's coherence but nonetheless had the impression that she was not telling him the whole truth.

"Yes, I knew that first night that she was withholding information," he says. "I'm pumping her for information and she is withholding some of it. At the time I thought she was protecting somebody else. The story she is telling me—a guy followed us into the woods—okay, it's possible, but let's look at the whole picture and she wasn't giving us the whole picture. There was a failure to communicate because there was a lack of trust."

IV

At Blevins's direction, troopers set up nighttime roadblocks on South Mountain and cruised the forestry roads of Michaux State Forest, looking for anything unusual. Since it was the standard practice of the state police that the first investigator on the scene became a case's chief investigator, Blevins was in charge of what would become one of the largest police investigations ever conducted in southcentral Pennsylvania. Of course, in the days ahead, many troopers would work on the Wight murder investigation, checking out the leads assigned to them, but whatever these troopers discovered would eventually be turned over to Blevins. Under the general supervision of Corporal Matthew O'Brien, supervisor of criminal investigations at the Gettysburg station of the Pennsylvania State Police, Blevins would evaluate the leads that came in and decide what to do next.

Blevins was well suited for the job he was about to undertake. Born in 1946, the brown-haired, brown-eyed West Virginian, of average height and build, had moved to Pennsylvania in 1967 and entered the state police academy in 1969. He now had nineteen years' experience as a trooper, including almost ten as a criminal investigator. The forty-two-year-old detective had been the chief investigator in five murder cases, four of which had ended in convictions.

"One of the easiest going guys you could ever meet" is how Blevins's associates describe him. He reminds one of the carefree lifestyle of the West Virginia mountains of his youth. "What the heck," he says, "I've often thought it would be neat to live back in the mountains, shoot rabbits for food. It would be a ball." But that's not the way Blevins has lived. His friends call him a "real workhorse" in the state police. "It's a mistake to let his style fool you," advises one of them. "Behind that easygoing, jovial personality, there is a very smart person who knows what he is trying to do and who's determined to get it. He is an engaging person who can easily establish trust and rapport with someone and then get that person to say what he wants him to say—a trait which has tripped up more than one criminal."

Blevins also seemed to have an intuitive feel for human situations. Probable theories about what happened in a given situation came to him naturally, yet he wasn't dogmatic or fixated on any particular theory or interpretation. "The most important thing in any investigation," Blevins was fond of saying, "is to keep your mind and your options open." Waiting at the crime scene that first night, Blevins thought about the little that he knew.

"The killer was probably someone who knew the victims. That was the most likely scenario. Normally people are killed by people who know them. We would keep all of our options open, but the investigation would begin there."

At about 4:00 A.M., Blevins could hear a team of Michaux State Forest workers working on Rocky Knob Trail, cutting down trees and shrubs to make way for a jeep to get through. As dawn began to break, Blevins and the coroner examined the dead woman's body. The victim was approximately five feet tall and had dark brown hair. She was wearing a pair of tight blue jeans, white sneakers with blue stripes, and three different shirts. One shirt had been wrapped around the victim's neck and knotted loosely in the front; the other two were a blue, long-sleeved work shirt and, under it, a white tank top with lavender flowers. Neither of these shirts was tucked into her jeans. They were pulled halfway up her torso, fully revealing her stomach. Blood was smeared on both hands of the victim and on her lower abdominal area. The police photographer, who also at this point was on the scene, took several photos of the dead woman. Blevins then turned the body over and saw a gunshot wound, perhaps the fatal one, right of center halfway down the victim's back.

"It was at this point that I saw a lot of leaves and twigs that were partway inside the back of her pants," he says. "You remember, I told you, the victim was not wearing any underpants. Anyway, all those leaves told me that she had had her jeans off. I had to think a while, to figure out why all those leaves and things were stuffed down in her trousers. Then it came to me. After she was wounded, the victim was probably lying on the ground and the other woman tried to pull the jeans up onto her. That would explain why all these twigs and things got inside her pants. But it meant that the victim had had her pants off when she was shot."

Wight's body was on one side of a large hemlock tree, and the campsite—which was closer to the stream—was on the other. A couple of backpacks were near the tree, and a tent fly was spread out between a gas camping stove and the stream. On the tent fly was a box of chocolate candy, a jean jacket, and a green plastic thermal cup with THE NATIONAL OUTDOOR LEADERSHIP SCHOOL printed in white letters on its side. Based on the amount of blood on the tent fly, Blevins concluded that at least one of the women had been shot while sitting or lying on it.

The jeep got to the crime scene at about 5:30 A.M. Wight's body was put into a plastic body bag and placed in the back of the jeep for transport back up to Ridge Road, where an ambulance was waiting to take it to Lehigh Medical Center for an autopsy. Since there was no extra room on the jeep, Blevins hiked back up to Ridge Road. Over a dozen state police personnel were rendezvousing at the intersection of Ridge Road and Rocky Knob Trail at 7:00 A.M. He wanted to be there to monitor what was going on.

V

Some sort of vehicle was needed to transport the troopers from Ridge Road down to the crime scene. Foreseeing this need, Blevins had asked Trooper Kenneth Zeisloft the night before to see what he could find. Zeisloft had called his old friend Larry Dillon, the fire chief of the Buchanan Valley Fire Company. Dillon, a man who loved cars and vehicles of all sorts, recommended a 1953 Dodge military ambulance he had recently purchased.

"They're the ambulances you see on MASH—you know, the TV show," Dillon says. "They're not very fast, but they're dependable, and inside one of them the cops would have some cover if the killer was still out there. I told Kenny about it and he liked the idea. The only problem, though, was that I didn't have any license plates for it. Kenny laughed and told me that he didn't think the police would mind. He asked if I could have the ambulance up on Ridge Road at 7 A.M. I said, 'Sure, I'll be there.' I got there about quarter til."

Blevins explained the situation to Dillon, and they loaded up the ambulance with troopers. Since only about seven could fit into the back at one time, Dillon had to make two trips to get all the troopers down to the crime scene. The trip took about twenty minutes one way.

"It was kind of wild," Dillon remarks. "There were potholes two or three feet deep, some full of water. But the old Dodge just climbed out of them. The tires on those things are huge. And we just squeaked through. More than once we were rubbing trees on both sides of the Trail at the same time. I made a couple of trips back and forth. Then I rigged some plastic sheets between trees so that the cops would have some place to keep dry if it started to rain. I got a fire going."

Dillon chatted with the troopers, since he knew many of them personally. "At first, the cops were very serious and a little nervous. They weren't so sure that the killer wasn't still around. Blevins didn't think so, but everyone was still a little jumpy. But after a few trips back and forth to Ridge Road, they loosened up. You know, those ambulances only have small windows in the back doors and the windshield. So, when I was driving, I told the troopers who were in the back, 'If you see him, let me know so that I can duck before you shoot.' You should have seen the firepower those troopers had. They were loaded for bear."

VI

With his newly arrived personnel, Blevins began a meticulous search of the shooting scene. Following standard procedure, the troopers began at the center of the campsite and worked their way outward in a circular fashion. They worked as fast as they could, searching the ground for footprints and other clues. Though undue haste could destroy evidence, they had no choice. Rain was in the forecast and it would destroy much of any evidence at the crime scene.

"Hey, I've got something here," yelled Corporal Robert Piscotty, one of the troopers from Harrisburg assigned to the search.

Blevins, only a few feet away, ran over and looked to where Piscotty was pointing. Next to a small tree, a blue knit cap lay on the ground with a pair of sunglasses peeking out of it. Two cigarette lighters and a black-handled knife were lying next to the cap, and twenty-five rounds of live .22 caliber ammunition were underneath it. It looked as though someone had carried the sunglasses, lighters, knife, and ammunition in the cap and these objects had fallen out when the cap had been placed on or fallen to the ground. In addition, within an eighteen-inch circle of the hat, Blevins counted eight spent .22 caliber shell casings. He quickly concluded that the knit cap belonged to the killer.

"How else could you explain the close proximity of the spent shells? Yes, all this stuff belonged to the killer. He gave us a whole nest of evidence to work with. I never thought we'd be so lucky."

After the evidence was safely collected, Blevins checked to see whether there was a clear line of fire from the spot beside the small tree to the tent fly.

"It was a very thick laurel thicket," Blevins explains. "I wouldn't be certain that I had found the right spot unless I could determine that the killer could see his victims. But when I looked, I found a picture window, in a manner of speaking, through that thicket. It was more underneath the bushes than anything else, but the killer could clearly see his victims on the tent fly."

Confirming to his satisfaction that the shots had been fired from the side of a small tree eighty-two feet northwest of the tent fly, Blevins speculated about the killer's psychological state.

"No killer who had kept his cool would have left all that evidence

THE SUSPECTS · 39

behind, and you've got to remember that he also left a live witness behind. He could have gone over to the victims and shot them dead. He had total control, but then he lost control."

The physical evidence found at the scene suggested to Blevins that the shootings were not the work of a professional killer or hardened criminal. Some average person committed this crime. Probably a man, he thought, because the eighty-two-foot distance separating the shooter from the victims suggested that a .22 caliber rifle had been used, and most women weren't proficient with that type of firearm. Most would not be able to hit moving targets with seven of eight shots at eighty-two feet. And since robbery was apparently not a motive for the shootings, it probably was a man known to at least one of the victims, a man unhappy about something one of them did to him, something that made him mad enough to kill.

"Perhaps the killer was mad about the fact that these two women went off camping alone together," Blevins remembers speculating. "A man could get really pissed off if his wife or lover ran off with a woman. I remember asking myself, 'Is that what we have up here?'"

VII

At about 11:00 A.M., Blevins took the evidence he had found at the crime scene back to the Gettysburg Barracks, a one-story brick building located one mile west of Gettysburg on Fairfield Road. Built in 1949 to house fifteen troopers, it was the first barracks constructed in Pennsylvania for state police to use. There Blevins met Harrisburg Troop H Commander William Hunter and Gettysburg Station Commander John Straka and filled them in on what he had discovered. They told him that Zeisloft had taken Wight's body to Lehigh Medical Center for an autopsy and that Beaver had interviewed the surviving victim the night before at the Hershey Medical Center emergency room and found her to be somewhat uncooperative.

Though he had missed a night of sleep, Blevins was not tired that Saturday afternoon. "A big homicide case is like that. You forget about sleep. You forget about food. You forget about everything, including your family. You're totally absorbed in the case."

Blevins told the desk sergeant to call his wife and tell her that she would not be seeing much of him in the near future. After grabbing a bite to eat, he and O'Brien climbed into a police car and headed back to South Mountain. Together they would supervise a general search of the area surrounding the crime scene.

About the time that Blevins and O'Brien were on their way back to South Mountain, Beaver entered Hershey Medical Center to interview Brenner a second time. He'd been assigned to liaison between the investigators in Gettysburg and Brenner, and the 6'1" cop with a weightlifter's body and a tough mental attitude was a perfect choice for the role. Brenner needed a strong, determined police officer beside her, because she was deathly afraid that her assailant would try again to kill her. Her fears may have been unwarranted, but they were real and the state police could not ignore them.

Because Brenner apparently wasn't fully cooperating with the investigation, Beaver could try to either win her trust or intimidate her into telling him everything she knew. If one kind of cop had been assigned the task of interviewing Brenner, the second option would have been immediately pursued. Beaver, however, was not the type of cop who could bully a reluctant victim. A strong masculine personality, Beaver truly cared for the innocent people he helped, the victims who found themselves, through no fault of their own, in trouble or danger.

When Beaver arrived at the Hershey Medical Center early Saturday afternoon for his second interview, he still had real doubts about Brenner. He suspected that she knew more about who had killed Wight than she was letting on. It was unclear to him whether Brenner was an innocent victim or whether she had crossed the line.

"When I went into the ICU," Beaver remembers, "there were people outside Claudia's room in the lobby area. Four or five people. They were all women. And when I saw all these women together, and with what I knew about the investigation, that lesbianism was probably involved, I'm thinking, what is this? Who are these people? This IS a homosexual relationship. And when I went into the room, there was a girl there with Claudia who identified herself as Anne Rhodes, Claudia's sister. I was immediately curious about the relationship between Anne and Claudia. I didn't believe for a second that she was a sister."

Beaver asked Brenner to retell her story, but Brenner had trouble speaking because her wounded tongue had swelled up overnight and she was wearing an oxygen mask as a result of having surgery on her neck early that morning. Noticing Brenner's discomfort, Beaver stopped the interview after a few minutes. He hadn't found any inconsistencies in her story, but his concerns were not alleviated.

"The only identification of the man she could offer was that he could be over six feet and was not heavy or skinny and that he had reddish hair to the bottom of the neck, straight and straggly. She thinks it was parted in the center. And she did not say anything about the love affair between Wight and herself. I still had the impression that Claudia and Anne were holding something back."

Late that same afternoon, Beaver drove down to Gettysburg and personally reported to Blevins and O'Brien, who had just returned from a fruitless search of the general crime scene area.

"I told them there was no trust and that Claudia and Anne Rhodes were very protective of what they were telling me, very careful," says Beaver. "I knew they were withholding information. At this point, we were wondering if Anne Rhodes was an old girlfriend. How did she get down here from Ithaca so quick? Could she have been involved? Could she have come down here to knock off the new girlfriend? Was Claudia protecting her? These were the questions that we had. Matt O'Brien wanted me to push to get this info, he wanted me to get into the homosexual thing. I thought at the time that I was building trust with these people and if I tried to push it, I was going to lose it. I told them, 'We can't push right now. She's not ready for it. Better to wait.'"

The investigators decided to play it Beaver's way for a couple days. Brenner could rest and gain strength over the weekend, and Beaver could nurture their relationship.

VIII

Members of Rebecca Wight's family arrived at the Gettysburg state police station on Sunday. Zeisloft drew the job of interviewing Wight's sister Evelyn, who told him that Rebecca had been bisexual, that she and Brenner had been lovers, and that Rebecca had recently broken up with a boyfriend. Unfortunately, Zeisloft unintentionally offended Evelyn by referring to the victims as "girls." Rather than make a bad situation worse, Zeisloft left the room, told Blevins what he had learned, and suggested that it would be better for Blevins to continue the interview.

Blevins tried to smooth things over with Evelyn, explaining that

Zeisloft had not meant any harm by calling the women "'girls." It was just his style and it was not an unusual one in Adams County, Pennsylvania. "Give us a little time to get to know you and to figure out what upsets you," Blevins told Evelyn. "The main thing is that we can't let this kind of thing get in the way of what we are trying to accomplish here."

Having regained her composure, Evelyn told Blevins that the break-up with the boyfriend had taken place about a month earlier and that he had been real "upset" about it.

The new information fit nicely with the evidence of the case and some basic police assumptions: jilted lovers sometimes kill; some men react violently—perhaps because they think their manhood is being called into question—if their lover runs off with another woman; men are more likely than women to be good with firearms; and a person who is not a professional criminal is more likely than a hired killer to leave evidence at a crime scene.

"Yes," Blevins thought, "we're going to take a close look at the former boyfriend."

IX

At first, the police suspected Rebecca's former boyfriend and Brenner's former lover more than they did a mysterious mountain man. Brenner's story about a scruffy guy with a gun just didn't seem all that credible to the troopers. They felt that perhaps Brenner had made it up to protect Anne by throwing them off the scent. On the other hand, the police didn't ignore Brenner's story completely. If she wasn't withholding information to protect Anne Rhodes, then perhaps the murderer was some strange mountain man.

Mountain men of various types are, after all, not all that exceptional in the South Mountain area. Like other mountainous regions of the United States, from the Smoky Mountains of Tennessee to the Rockies of Idaho and Montana, South Mountain attracts individuals who prefer the privacy and rough independence of a solitary life in nature over the dependencies and responsibilities inherent in modern civilized life. Many of these individuals are men who experiment on weekends and during vacations with a life of hunting, camping, and fishing, but also retain regular jobs in the American economy and maintain families and other social relationships. Others abandon society more or less entirely, living a life many would find nasty and brutish. Mountain men are therefore a diverse group. Certainly, it would be incorrect to assume that all or most of them are either criminals or psychopaths. Many are decent, law-abiding individuals who have simply chosen a different path. Nevertheless, it is undeniable that some mountain men have violent tendencies and predatory instincts. They are outlaws in the classic sense.

The name of one odd man who frequented the South Mountain area came up on Saturday, May 14th. Dick Carper, a forest ranger, told the troopers about Joe Banders, a thirty-eight-year-old white male from Arendtsville who had harassed women many times in the state parks of Michaux State Forest and on the A.T. The last incident had occurred in May 1987. Banders had approached two females and asked them to take his picture in the nude. For this incident, he had been cited for disorderly conduct and paid a fine of $300 and court costs.

Carper hadn't seen Banders for a year, but the funny thing was that he had seen his car on the evening of the 13th. He spotted the vehicle—a brown 1982 Chevy truck with a brown camper cap on the back—parked at a local access point to the A.T. Concerned, Carper took down the license plate number. If anything untoward happened on the trail that night, he wanted to be able to testify that Banders's vehicle was in the area.

When they heard about Banders late Saturday, Blevins and O'Brien didn't get overly excited.

"I, for one, was well aware of Banders," O'Brien recalls. "I knew this individual personally and I couldn't see him doing this shooting. He was peripheral because he was nonviolent."

The next morning at about 11:00, a more promising lead came in. Trooper Dennis Weible, from the Chambersburg station, called Blevins and told him that his station had investigated a one-car accident that had occurred near the shootings early on Saturday morning. The driver of the vehicle, a twenty-nine-year-old white male by the name of William Frank Brewster, had been taken to the hospital, and the vehicle, a 1978 Dodge Aspen wagon, had been towed to Don's Auto Body Shop. Late Saturday Don Crotty had informed the police that there was a .22 caliber rifle and ammunition in the car. As soon as the Chambersburg station found out that a .22 caliber rifle had been used in the Michaux State Forest homicide, troopers from that station took possession of the gun and ammunition, and Weible called Blevins.

On Monday the 16th, Brewster's wife, Jolene, coincidentally arrived at the body shop while troopers were searching the Dodge Aspen. Willing to answer questions, she told the troopers that she and her husband resided in Fayetteville, Pennsylvania, and that Bill worked at the South Mountain Restoration Center, though he had not worked toward the end of the previous week because he had been sick. On Friday, Bill had left their home at about 6:30 P.M. He'd probably gone drinking, his wife confided, even though he was under orders not to drink because he was taking a painkiller for his crippled leg, and indeed was taking more than what his doctor had prescribed. She hadn't seen him again until she visited him in the hospital on Saturday afternoon.

"Does he own a gun?"

Brewster's wife replied that he did and that she thought it was a .22 caliber rifle. "When he gets upset," she said, "he gets his gun and goes shooting." She didn't like guns and wouldn't let them in the house. Her husband kept his gun over at his brother's place.

"Did he have any reason to be upset last week?"

Well, yes, she admitted. Last Thursday she had told him that she wanted him out of the house by the end of the month. They weren't getting along, and she wanted to call it quits.

"What does he think of lesbians?"

Jolene said he hated them, though she had never known him to react violently. Once, for example, he had encountered some homosexual males at a party and he simply left without creating a disturbance.

The Chambersburg station thought they were onto something with William Frank Brewster, but the lead soon fizzled out. After Blevins obtained the rifle from Weible on Sunday, he drove up to the Harrisburg lab that afternoon, taking along Brewster's rifle and the bullet that the autopsy had retrieved from Wight's body. Sergeant Wayne Poust, a ballistics expert, glanced at the rifle and then closely examined the bullet that had killed Wight. It took only a few seconds for him to make up his mind. He told Blevins that there was next to no chance that Brewster's rifle was the murder weapon.

Disappointed, Blevins returned to Gettysburg on Sunday evening. By this time, Wight's former boyfriend had established that he was hundreds of miles away at the time of the shootings. In addition, Beaver had not yet made any progress with the surviving victim, and neither of the two local South Mountain men whose names had come up in the investigation looked promising. The tests conducted on the physical evidence found at the crime scene produced no valuable information, only the presence of white cat hair on the knit hat. Other members of the investigation team had spent Sunday patrolling the South Mountain area, asking motorists, bicyclists, and hikers the same routine questions. "Were you in the area on Friday or Saturday?" "Did you hear anything?" "Did you meet anyone?" "What did he look like?" "Was he wearing sweatpants?" "Was he carrying a rifle?" No worthwhile information had turned up. It had been a long, fruitless, rainy day on the Mountain. Only one incident relieved the frustration. Beaver, one of the three troopers riding horses brought in from the State Police Academy, caught a couple of guys stealing pine trees from the state forest.

"We saw these two guys coming around a corner; they saw us, and they ran back down in the woods and dropped four or five plastic bags, each with a pine tree in it. We caught the two and took their identification and told them to go back and replant the trees. We told them, 'We'll be in touch with you.' They're probably still waiting to hear from us. We had a good laugh, but we left the mountain disappointed that day. We may have solved the great pine-tree theft, but we had not made any significant progress in the murder investigation."

X

Beaver called Brenner late Sunday afternoon to let her know that the police were working on her case.

"This kind of day-to-day contact is necessary, even if you can't see the victim in person," explains Beaver. "I had to maintain daily contact so that she would start to trust me. Only then would she tell me what she knew."

Over the phone, Beaver could tell that Brenner was still suffering from an overwhelming fear that the killer would find out from the newspapers where she was and come after her in the hospital. Beaver didn't think it likely that the killer would try to pull off such a daring stunt, but he nonetheless called the Hershey Medical Center and arranged to have Brenner registered under "Jane Doe." The hospital would tell anyone asking for Claudia Brenner that no such person was in the facility. Beaver doubted whether the "Jane Doe" maneuver was necessary for security purposes, but he felt that it might help convince Brenner that she and the police were on the same side.

At about noon on Monday, he returned to Hershey Medical Center to interview Brenner for a third time. A trooper who would put together a composite picture of the mysterious mountain man Brenner had seen earlier on the day of the shootings accompanied him. The ID specialist brought an Identi-kit that contained overlays of different types of facial characteristics: hair lengths and types, foreheads, ears, noses, mouths, and chins. When Beaver walked into Brenner's room, he was encouraged at what he saw.

"Claudia was doing better. She didn't have the oxygen mask on anymore and she was able to talk. The first thing she did was show me a newspaper article from the Harrisburg *Patriot*. The article reported that the night before, Brenner had been secretly transferred from Hershey Medical Center to some undisclosed hospital for "security reasons."

Beaver says he grinned at the "news." His request to register Brenner under "Jane Doe" had worked better than he had anticipated. Evidently, after finding out that "Claudia Brenner" was no longer registered in the medical center, a newspaper reporter had concluded that the police had moved her. The killer, if he read the newspapers, would now never look for Brenner at Hershey Medical Center, and Brenner was under the impression that the police had "lied" on her behalf.

"Claudia thought we did it purposely and we never told her differently. Afterward, anytime a reporter asked, 'Where is she?', we would tell them 'No comment.' So we took advantage of a newspaper mistake, but our primary concern was for Claudia to develop trust and confidence in the police. We wanted and needed her complete cooperation. As of Monday, this had not yet happened."

In the third interview, Beaver probed for inconsistencies, but Brenner told the same story, adding a few new details. On the morning of the shootings, she said, Wight had told her that the guy in the lean-to looked like he had come to the Birch Run Shelter to do crossword puzzles. She also recalled that when she and Wight had left the shelter that morning, she had seen a red or maroon backpack lying in the lean-to beside the scruffy man. Later, when the man approached them as they were reading their map, she had noticed that he was wearing cheap-looking tan boots.

There were plenty of loose ends to Brenner's story, but, according to Beaver, that was normal. Victims of violent trauma tend to remember things in piecemeal fashion, and there is little or no coherence to the order of recall. Today Brenner remembered the backpack and the cheap tan boots. What new item she might remember tomorrow, if anything, was unknown. Her memory would come back in its own way. But the inherent consistency of Brenner's story began to have an impact on Beaver.

"By this time, on Monday, I thought her story was factual," he remembers. "She still was not telling us about her sexual orientation, but what she was telling us was true. There were many pieces missing, including who was the killer, but the pieces Brenner was giving us were falling into place."

Beaver therefore decided to forego the Identi-kit. For one thing, his fellow trooper was new at his job and Beaver doubted he had the experience, tact, and diplomatic skills necessary to work with Brenner and put together a good composite. Beaver had another, more important reason for canceling the composite, however.

"It was imperative that we get a good sketch, because now I'm convinced that Claudia is telling the truth and that she was right: the guy she saw earlier that day probably did do the shootings. So, I hoped that in a few days we could get a real artist in to do a high-quality sketch. Since I now thought that the guy Brenner saw was the killer, it was very important that the sketch be done right."

After Beaver left Brenner's room, he talked to some of the people waiting outside.

"Her whole family was there. They used the word 'family.' All of them were like sisters. Some of them even live together up in New York. At one of the visits, there must have been nine or ten, all women. No, no, there was one man with them. He was not real masculine or a tough guy. He was a person who, if you looked through a crowd, you would not pick him out. . . . He was there a few times, he was part of the family, but he did not have a whole lot to say."

From these conversations with the members of Brenner's "family," Beaver confirmed to his satisfaction that Anne Rhodes was an old girlfriend who had nothing to do with Wight's murder. He didn't have any hard evidence to back up his belief, but he was convinced nonetheless. He called Blevins and told him that he had canceled the composite sketch, and they briefly talked about bringing in a sketch artist. Beaver also told Blevins that Brenner had not admitted to the lesbian relationship.

"This upset them down in Gettysburg," says Beaver. "They wanted me to push it because they thought Claudia was hiding something or someone involved with the murder. They did not want to exclude Anne as a suspect, even though I was telling them there was no way she was involved."

XI

At about 6:00 P.M. on Monday, an anonymous call came into Troop H Headquarters in Harrisburg. A man said that Frank Candam of Duncannon, Pennsylvania, had been bragging that he had shot two girls in the Gettysburg area on Friday. Candam, the caller added, was "unbalanced and owned lots of guns." Within a couple hours of the anonymous tip, a trooper in the Duncannon area had found out that Candam was a 6′3″ white male between thirty-five and forty years old and weighed 165–175 pounds. He had dark brown hair that he wore long, below the ears. He drove a truck for a local trucking firm.

The next day, a trooper showed up at Candam's home and asked him his whereabouts on May 13th, but Candam had a well-documented alibi. He had been working in the Nesbitt area that afternoon and had hurt his back. A medical treatment report indicated that he'd left the Nesbitt Hospital at 2:37 P.M. He drove his truck back to Harrisburg and his employer confirmed that he'd parked it at 7:30 P.M.

"The conclusion," said Blevins, "was that Candam may be unbalanced, he may be unbalanced enough to brag about committing a murder he didn't commit, but it was absolutely clear he did not kill Rebecca Wight or wound Claudia. He was in the clear."

On Wednesday the 18th, troopers were still patrolling the South Mountain area, asking people whether they had seen anything strange the previous weekend. Trooper John Holtz stopped the vehicle of Paul Drixell on Ridge Road near the entrance to Rocky Knob Trail. From his driver's license, Holtz determined that Drixell lived in Shippensburg, was thirty-five years old and 5′9″ tall, weighed 210 pounds, and had brown hair and blue eyes. Holtz asked him a few routine questions, but Drixell began volunteering information.

"Do you know," he said, "that homosexuals frequent this area and they leave notes hidden under rocks by Shippensburg Road. I've read these notes on several occasions. Once I even left a note of my own. It said, 'I would like to use people like you for target practice.' Later, someone wrote a note back saying that I'm the lowest of low life and that a bastard like me ought not to be allowed to live."

Holtz called O'Brien over so that he could hear what Drixell was saying. Neither trooper knew what to make of Drixell's claims about letters under rocks, but his attitude toward homosexuals was decidedly hostile. After conferring with each other, the troopers asked Drixell if he would mind coming to the Gettysburg station on Friday so that he could tell them everything he knew about homosexuals on South Mountain. Drixell, glad to help out, said he'd be there and drove away.

When Holtz and O'Brien told Blevins about Drixell, the chief investigator was immediately interested.

"Yes, Drixell was a strong suspect," says Blevins, "primarily because of his relationship to guns and his anti-gay statements. And you got to remember that he said gays were hiding notes on the Mountain under rocks. When I heard that, I said to myself, 'This guy is a squirrel.' The key was the gun. If Drixell did it, he had to own a .22 caliber rifle. And if he owned such a gun, maybe he purchased it from one of the local gun stores. Our next step would be to check out the local gun stores."

The Drixell incident reminded Blevins that Merle Waltz, the forester who had helped the police find Wight's body, had told him the day before that he, too, had seen a scary-looking mountain man several months earlier. Waltz's recollection reminded Blevins of his cardinal rule. "You got to keep your mind and your options open. Maybe Beaver was right. Maybe Brenner was telling the truth."

XII

The value of Blevins's rule was confirmed later that afternoon, when Beaver called from Hershey Medical Center and told Blevins that Brenner had admitted that she and Wight had been lovers.

Beaver had begun the day on South Mountain, canvassing the homes in the area of the crime, but no leads had surfaced. One resident had seen a white pickup parked east of his place on Friday and Saturday, but he couldn't recall the make or model. The other six residents that Beaver interviewed had not seen or heard anything.

"It looked like it was going to be a very long and uneventful day for me," recalls Beaver, "until I was advised by radio that Claudia wanted to talk to me. Once I heard this, I immediately left for Hershey. Matt and some of the others were pressing me to push Brenner. I knew that time was running out on the way I wanted to handle it. Brenner had to come clean soon, or I was going to have to get tough."

"So, before entering Claudia's room, I approached Claudia's family—there were about four or five of them in the hallway—and I centered on Anne and got her off to the side and I said, 'Anne, you know, there are some things we have to talk about.'

"And she says, 'We have some things to tell you, too. Claudia wants to talk to you.'"

Beaver, sensing that things had come to a turning point, followed Anne into Brenner's room. After exchanging greetings, Brenner quickly came to the point: she hadn't previously told Beaver everything about the incident because she hadn't trusted him. After checking him out with a local attorney, she now felt sure that he was not going to give her a hard time and she was ready to tell the whole story. She and Wight had been lovers for about a year. Anne was not her sister, but a former lover from Ithaca.

Beaver felt an immediate sense of professional satisfaction. Because she trusted him, Brenner was for the first time going to tell him what really happened on South Mountain. His way of doing his job had been the right one.

"Claudia retold her story from the beginning, not leaving anything out. Some parts of the story I had already heard, but other parts were new. Claudia told me that before she and Rebecca had found out that there was a man at the shelter, they had walked down to a nearby creek naked and that Rebecca had also been naked when she walked to the outhouse. On her return from the outhouse, Rebecca told Claudia that she thought the strange man she had met had a 'hard-on.' Claudia also said that, before they left the shelter area, the man may have seen them kissing and holding hands.

"So, you see, the nudity and the kissing put a different slant on things. The same thing with the shootings. When Claudia told me when the shots occurred, it became much more credible, don't you see, that some strange mountain man had done the shootings. He shot them because he hated homosexuals."

Armed with this new information, Beaver immediately drove down to Gettysburg and talked to Blevins and O'Brien.

"I laid it out to the people in Gettysburg. As far as I was concerned, the interview had killed any version of the lovers-quarrel theory. The murderer of Rebecca Wight was a strange mountain man, just as Claudia had said."

Blevins was inclined to agree, but he wanted to hear Brenner's story himself. He and Beaver made arrangements to reinterview Brenner the following day. If she passed this test, the focus of the investigation would shift entirely to the mountain man theory.

"We were lucky," Beaver remembers, "that Blevins was the chief investigator on this case. If he had not been a caring person, we would not have had the success that we did have on that interview the following day. Claudia and Anne would have backed off if they had had to deal with O'Brien or Holtz. Don't get me wrong, those two guys are good cops. They are just a different type of cop. In policework, you need different personalities for different jobs. For that interview, we needed a trusting, caring person. That person was Blevins."

On Thursday morning, May 19th, Brenner once again "laid it all out" for Beaver and Blevins, and this time she allowed her account to be recorded on audiotape. There were no inconsistencies in her story, only new details that she had remembered from her last interview. The effect on Blevins was decisive.

"From that interview on, I had 100 percent trust in Claudia's idea that it was the guy they had met earlier. The encounters were too strange. Absolutely, it had to be the same guy. He had a rifle. He acted strange and he was in the area. Too coincidental. He was our man."

XIII

Beaver stayed in Harrisburg to meet with the sketch artist, while Blevins returned to Gettysburg. He found a message waiting for him. Trooper Ron Gettle from the Carlisle station wanted to talk to him about a mountain man. Blevins immediately called him. Gettle told him about a Shippensburg teenager who had told him she had occasionally seen a mountain man at her friend's house. Blevins instructed Gettle to set up a meeting with this girl.

"It was a little unusual. The girl was real scared. It all had to be secret. So when we went down to Shippensburg on Thursday evening, we parked our car a block away from her house and walked to her place. It was a small, dark room where we talked to her—kind of rundown and ugly."

The girl told Blevins and Gettle that she had a friend who worked with her at Kentucky Fried Chicken whose last name was Golden. She lived with her parents and two brothers on Sand Bank Road just west of South Mountain, and a mountain man used to visit the family. In fact, her friend had told her that this mountain man had been at their house the day after the murder.

"Do you know what he looks like?" Blevins asked.

"Yes," the girl said. "He is a tall person, with a thin face, and long brown hair. He's kind of dirty and messy and he always carries a gun around."

Before he asked his next question, Blevins thought about what he was doing. He didn't want to lead the girl in any direction.

"Tell me, does the Golden family have any pets?"

"Yes. They have a cat named Snow Ball."

"When I heard that," Blevins said later, "my heart went up to my throat. Rockets went off—Fourth of July. To me, this was the turning point of the whole case. That's when I said, in my own mind, 'This is it.'"

"Do you know the name of this mountain man?" Blevins asked the teenager.

"Sure. His name is Carr. Steve Carr."

The Manhunt

chapter three

I

Elated at what he had found out from the Shippensburg teenager, Trooper Donald Blevins ran an FBI check on Stephen Carr to see if he had a criminal record. If he did, there probably was a photo of him somewhere in the United States that Brenner could use to identify him as the man she had encountered on May 13th. Meanwhile, Trooper Denny Beaver and Sergeant Lewis Throwbridge of the New Jersey State Police, Special and Technical Services, Composite Drawing Unit, arrived at Hershey Medical Center. Having by this time developed a friendly relationship with Brenner, Beaver anticipated that he would function as a liaison between her and the artist.

"But Claudia surprised me. After I introduced Throwbridge to her, she kicked me out of the room," he recounts.

" 'I don't want you influencing me on this. I want to do it myself,' she says."

"So those two are in Claudia's room working on the sketch and I'm like an expectant father, out in the hall pacing, waiting. It took forever. I was expecting an hour, maybe two, but Throwbridge adapted his style to hers. If she went off on some tangent, he just sat back and waited until

Left: A police sketch drawn under Claudia Brenner's direction of the man she saw at Birch Run Shelter on the day she was shot. Right: A photo of Stephen Carr taken shortly after the shootings. Courtesy of Dennis Beaver.

she was ready to start again. They kept this up until finally, she said, 'It's him.' They didn't finish until four o'clock."

After photographing the sketch at the State Police Academy, Beaver raced to Gettysburg, knowing that other members of the team had already assembled a collection of photos. "I walked into the room and laid a Polaroid of the sketch on the table, and they had a bunch of pictures around it upside down. Then, all they did was turn them over. When they turned over one of them, they said, 'That's him.' "

The picture was a photo of Stephen Roy Carr that Florida officials had telexed to the Gettysburg station. The resemblance between Carr's picture and the figure Throwbridge had sketched under Brenner's direction was uncanny. The other pictures on the table, including one of Drixell, were quickly forgotten. Carr was the man Wight and Brenner had met earlier on the day of the attack, and the cat hair found on the blue cap was probably from the Goldens' pet cat.

Florida officials also telexed copies of Carr's criminal record and an outstanding fugitive warrant for his arrest. The fugitive warrant pleased Blevins because he could arrest Carr for murder only if he had "probable cause" that Carr was the killer, and not just the man Brenner had seen earlier that day. Blevins doubted that a few white cat hairs would be enough to arrest a man who could quickly disappear into the mountains if he became aware that he was a murder suspect. However, if Florida officials would agree to extradite Carr, Blevins could arrest Carr immediately as a fugitive from justice. A quick arrest might give Blevins incontrovertible evidence that Carr was the killer.

"A mountain man is not going to throw his gun away very quickly," explains Blevins. "With the fugitive warrant, we could arrest him on sight and then run a ballistics test on the weapon. If the bullet that killed Wight came from Carr's gun, then my job would be basically over. And even if we didn't find Carr's gun on him, the fugitive warrant would let us lock him up as we looked for it and any other evidence proving he was the shooter."

II

Florida's fugitive warrant did not tell Blevins where he could find Carr, however. On Saturday, May 21st, members of the investigating team showed the sketch of the man Brenner saw to hunters, hikers, and local residents. Several people said the sketch looked a lot like a local mountain man they knew as Steve Carr, but nobody knew much about this strange individual. He didn't appear to have a job of any kind. He might make a little money collecting deposits for bottles and aluminum cans discarded by motorists and hikers, but mostly he lived by hunting and fishing. He had a number of hideouts on South Mountain—a cabin against a rock face, a lean-to, a cave—all of them tucked away in the more isolated areas of Michaux State Forest. He also had an aunt and uncle by the name of Lucille and Gordon Luce, who lived on Sand Bank Road not far from the Goldens.

Blevins ordered a Special Emergency Response Team (SERT), Pennsylvania's version of a SWAT, to check out the hideouts, but the team found them empty. So, on Sunday afternoon, Blevins placed the SERT in a camouflaged line between the Golden house and South Mountain. If Carr tried to get from one to the other, the team would bag him without endangering civilians. If he didn't show up, the police would search the Golden place on Monday morning. If that effort also proved fruitless, a large-scale manhunt of South Mountain would commence immediately thereafter.

For the upcoming search of the Golden house, the leader of the SERT recommended a "dynamic entry." Members of the SERT would crash through doors and windows and surprise and immobilize everyone in the house before they had time to react. Blevins and other members of the investigative team were reluctant to take this approach. Although they, too, were concerned about the possibility that an armed Carr was holed up in the house, there was no real evidence that the Golden family was protecting him.

"To go busting into this family's house early on a Monday morning, who knows what might happen?" Blevins remarks. "An innocent person could easily get killed. On the other hand, if Carr is in that house, who's going to knock on the front door and shout, 'Police! Open up!' It would probably have to be me, and I did not like the way that sounded."

Delaying his decision about how to search the Golden house, Blevins gathered as much information as he could about the layout. He assigned the job of getting some photos of the house to Beaver and a fellow trooper, who took advantage of ongoing complaints about the phone service in the area.

"We got a telephone truck with a lift on it," Beaver explains. "There is another house about five hundred feet from the Golden place with a telephone pole right aside of it. I got in the bucket and took it up to the telephone lines. But then a man comes out of the house and asks, 'Hey, what are you doing?' I told him we had got some complaints about the service in the area and we were just checking it out. 'Well good,' the man says. 'I've been having trouble with my phone, too.' 'Okay,' I told him, 'We're working on it.' My partner finally was able to distract this guy, and I took out the camera and started shooting. When I was done, as I came down in the bucket, the man ran back into his house. A few minutes later, he came back out and said, 'Hey, thanks. My phone is working better already.' I answered, 'Forget it. It was nothing.' Back in the truck, me and my partner laughed about it as we drove away."

III

Late Sunday night, a trooper from the Carlisle station told Blevins that he knew the Golden family and doubted whether they were involved or would cause any trouble. Blevins weighed the need for the Goldens' cooperation, which he presumably would not get if the SERT damaged their home, against the danger that an armed Carr was in the house. In the end, he decided against a dynamic entry. The SERT would be available but kept in the background.

At 8:00 on Monday morning, eight police cars turned into the Goldens' driveway. A relieved Blevins saw Alice Golden outside her house. He quickly ran up to her and explained who he was and what was going on.

"It was immediately clear to me that these people had no idea of the situation they were in. I remember when I was talking to Alice Golden I could see behind her a camouflaged SERT officer in the trees about fifty yards away, his gun ready. But Mrs. Golden had no idea that he was there or that the police had staked out her house overnight. I was glad that she was so much in the dark, because it meant that Carr was probably not in the house and that there was no danger."

Mrs. Golden said she didn't want any trouble with the police. Yes, she knew Steve Carr. He was a friend of the family. No, he wasn't in the house. Yes, he "looked like" the sketch that Blevins showed her. She had last seen Steve early on the morning of Saturday, the 14th, at about 7:00. Yes, he owned a blue cap and a .22 caliber rifle, but Steve had told her that someone had stolen his gun. He had told her that the last time she had seen him. Yes, on that Saturday he had told her that. The rifle had been stolen, Steve had said, the day before. Yes, on Friday. On South Mountain.

Mrs. Golden went on to say that Steve had been upset that morning. Maybe it was because his rifle was stolen, or maybe it was because she and her husband didn't stay up to talk to him, but instead went back to bed. He'd said something like, "Fuck you people, you don't want to talk to me." She didn't know for sure what had been bothering Steve, but she knew something was going on.

Her son had stayed up with Steve, however, and talked to him in the kitchen for a half hour or so. He'd later told her that Steve had had tears in his eyes and that he had said, "I did something wrong." Carr also had asked her son, "Did you hear what happened on the flat last night? Two girls were killed."

"How do you know about Carr's gun? Did he bring it to your house?" Blevins asked Alice Golden.

"He wouldn't bring it into the house," she replied. "He would leave it by the back door when he came in. But Steve, my two sons, and my husband would often shoot at birds and targets in the backyard."

Blevins's ears perked up.

"If Carr shot his gun in the backyard, there might be empty shell casings back there that might match those found at the crime scene. I'd rather have Carr's rifle, but we can't afford to be choosy. If the shell casings matched, that would help to put Carr at the scene."

Alice Golden willingly showed the troopers where, a couple of months before, Steve Carr and her sons and husband had shot birds. The police searched the area carefully. They found four casings on a trail near the spot where the men had fired their rifles and additional casings in the yard behind and adjacent to the residence. One spent bullet was found at a dump near the rear of the property. A tree stump and a length of 2 x 4 lumber also appeared to have been used as targets. The police took them, along with the Goldens' rifle, into their possession.

Blevins also wanted to get some hair samples from Snow Ball. Zeisloft, who liked cats, held Snow Ball in his arms and stroked the cat as it nuzzled against his chest and arms. He walked away with clumps of white cat hair on his uniform. Later he carefully transferred as much of this hair as he could from his uniform into a plastic evidence bag.

The search of the Golden residence had been useful, but Carr's whereabouts remained a mystery. Blevins therefore decided to go ahead with the intensive search of South Mountain. The police set up a communications command post on Big Flat, a large field of state land adjacent to Shippensburg Road on top of South Mountain. About fifty state troopers were assigned to the effort. A dozen were on horses from the State Police Academy. The Maryland State Police Canine Corps provided thirteen search dogs of various types. Two Pennsylvania State Police helicopters were also made available.

The search was an intensive manhunt, but for Blevins it was a frustrating day. One irritant was the press. "I had to dodge reporters all day long," he remembers. "They had two satellite trucks up near Big Flat. Every time one of the reporters saw a police car, they'd be running out trying to interview someone. The whole day we checked places, things, people would call in sightings, we would go flying down the road with twenty cars. Then we'd get a call from somewhere else and we'd go zinging over there. The entire day was like that. It was maddening. One wild goose chase after another."

The ones who drew the really tough assignment were the SERT

officers. Their job was to provide security for the three dog teams and their handlers: two SERT officers per team. One regular trooper describes the nature of their assignment: "That has got to be scary. Running all over that mountain after those dogs. A lot of them were sucking air. And knowing all the time that if the dogs found Carr, he would know they're coming, because the dogs make so much noise. And Carr is a guy who has a gun and knows how to use it. No, I wouldn't want any part of that assignment."

Regular troopers also experienced their share of fear that day. Four of them, including Beaver, went over to the Luce place late in the afternoon. As they kept an eye on the premises, waiting for the dog teams to arrive, they noticed a migrant shelter a short distance away.

"There were eight modules there: one long building," Beaver recalled. "Each module had three rooms. They were boarded up in front, but each module was accessible through a window in the back. We thought, 'Is this kid hiding in one of these?' So, we went to each module, opened the back window, shined the light around, and one guy went in headfirst, while another guy covered him with a shotgun from behind. And we checked each module that way. We took turns going into the modules first, each taking his chance. Luckily, we didn't find anyone."

The first day of the manhunt ended at the Luce place. Here they searched a deep pit at the back of the property that Carr had dug and covered with a car hood.

"It literally was a room underground," Blevins says. "He had electricity from his uncle's barn, but because of the recent rains it was flooding out and the electricity was shorting out. So he left. When we were there that day, the dogs went crazy. His scent was everywhere, but he was not around."

The first day of the manhunt had ended in failure, frustration, and exhaustion. The dogs themselves were so tired that the handlers had to carry them back to their trucks. All of the men were physically spent. One of the horses died from a heart attack. None of the troopers could recall such a thing happening before.

IV

By Monday evening, Blevins thought he had probable cause to obtain a warrant for Carr's arrest for the murder of Rebecca Wight and the attempted murder of Claudia Brenner. First, there was the clear resemblance between the sketch made under Brenner's direction and the photo of Carr that Florida had telexed to the Gettysburg station. Second, scientific tests indicated that there was an 80 percent probability that the cat hair on the blue cap found at the crime scene was hair from Snow Ball. The ejector markings on the shell casings found at the scene matched those on some of the shell casings taken from the Goldens' backyard. A gun fired in that backyard was the same gun that had killed Wight and wounded Brenner, and it wasn't the Goldens' rifle. That test had come back negative.

Blevins and the other investigators also talked strategy that Monday evening. The manhunt was scheduled to resume at dawn the next morning. As they mulled over their options, one of the troopers floated the idea of publishing the sketch of the man Brenner saw in the local newspapers. It was a controversial suggestion, because if Carr saw his picture in the newspaper, he'd be gone. A consensus nonetheless developed to go ahead with the gamble of publishing Carr's name and Brenner's sketch. Would it work? Would someone call and tell the police where Carr was? Or would Carr see his sketch in the newspaper and disappear into one of the many mountainous regions of Pennsylvania?

V

"I was down by the creek when I first saw him," said Esther Weaver, a small, plainly dressed woman in her forties. "It was Wednesday, May 18th, about 5:30 in the afternoon. I was chopping down the burdocks that grow so thick down there by the creek. Well, it was then that I saw him. He was coming down the creek in a tub, one of those tubs that people use to mix concrete in. The water was high and swift.

"So I asked him, 'Aren't you afraid?'

"'No,' he says, 'I can swim.'

"And that was all that we said to each other. He floated by me and I thought he was gone. But all of a sudden, he was behind me. He must've come over to my side of the creek downstream and walked back to where I was working. But, like I said, all of a sudden I heard something and he was there behind me. He kind of scared me at first.

"I asked him, 'Can I trust you?'

"He said, 'Lady, I'd rather do you good than harm.'

"Then he asked if I would heat him a can of soup, because he hadn't eaten for a while because of the wet weather. With all the rain we'd been getting, he couldn't light a fire. I thought he was a fisherman.

"So I took my shovel and went up to the barn, while the man went to anchor his boat. He called the tub his boat. Chester and the boys were milking cows. I went in, where they were milking, and I said, 'Well, I guess I got myself into something. There's a man down there who wants a can of soup. I want you, Chester, to come up to the house.'"

Chester and Esther Weaver, along with their two sons, Curtis and Nevin, worked two adjacent farms on Creek Road near the Conodoguinet Creek in Cumberland County, Pennsylvania. Mr. and Mrs. Weaver resided with Nevin at the home place, located immediately to the northeast of the intersection of Bloserville Road and Creek Road. The farmhouse was on high ground about two hundred yards from the creek. Curtis and his wife lived next door to the east. The Weavers were a hardworking family and a religious one. A sign on one of the well-maintained farm buildings read, "Prepare to Meet Thy God."

"So," Esther continued, "he came up to the house and Chester talked to him while I heated his soup, made him a sandwich, and gave him a piece of pie. Cause he was hungry, you could tell he was hungry. Did he eat it outside? I don't remember offhand."

"No," said Chester. "He ate inside. He ate at our table." Chester, a man in his forties with a round, friendly face, paused to reflect for a moment, and then added, "Well, a man has a need, you know, why you just can't turn him away. Not the way he was, hungry and soaking wet."

"It was pouring down rain," said Nevin, a handsome, dark-haired twenty-year-old, the youngest of four Weaver sons. "We'd had two days of rain. The creek was bank full."

"So, you see," Chester continued, "he was wet and tired, and she," pointing to Esther, "asked me where we were going to put this man. I said, well, we have a cot down in the cellar. It's warm and dry down there and there's a lock on the door. I thought he could sleep there, so I asked him, 'Do you mind staying in the cellar?'

"He said, 'No. No.' He didn't mind at all. He'd be happy just to be out of the rain. So he went on downstairs and made himself comfortable.

"Anyway, I thought then that with this man in the house I'm going to stay home. We usually all go to the Wednesday evening prayer meeting, but I decided right then that I wasn't going to go that night. The rest went, but I stayed home. I thought I had to keep an eye on this person because I didn't know who he was."

The Weavers belonged to the Eastern Pennsylvania Mennonite Church, a fundamentalist Christian church whose followers live in strict conformity to what they believe is God's will. Unlike the Old Order Amish, Mennonites use electricity and drive cars, but, like them, they read the Bible literally and live and dress plainly. The men drive unadorned black cars and wear solid dark suits; the women cover their hair and hide their legs under long, colorless skirts. They also keep their distance from the sinful outside world. The local church is the central institution around which their lives revolve. The children attend church-affiliated private schools whose educational programs are largely shaped by the Bible.

"After the others had gone," Chester continued, "I was sitting here at the kitchen table studying my Sunday school lesson when he comes up the steps and asks me if he could have a cup of coffee.

" 'Sure,' I said. So, I got him his coffee and he sat down at the table and we got to talking.

"I was just wondering who he was and what he was doing, a little bit, you know. He told me his name was Mike Smith. He was camping. He didn't say anything about this, you know, what happened on South Mountain. We didn't know anything about that. We don't have a TV or a radio. We don't know the latest news.

"Anyway, we sat here and talked a while. He told me about his childhood and about getting in trouble with the law in Florida, stealing and things like that. Yeah, he told me those things and, well, it still wasn't right just to kick him out, you know. I had to take time and listen to him. We talked some more about this and that, but then, after a while, he said he was going down to go to bed. And I said, 'Hope you sleep good.' And that was it. He went to bed.

"But come next morning, it was still raining, so he said, 'Do you mind if I stay a few days more? If you don't want me to stay, if you want me to hit the road, I'll hit the road.'

"I said, 'I don't like to turn a man out into the rain. I'll be considerate of you and just let you stay.'

"Then he had another request. He said, 'My shoes aren't too good. If you would take me to town and get me a new pair of shoes, I'll stay and help you long enough to pay for the shoes.'

"Well, I said, 'It's raining and I ought to go to town anyway. I'll just take you along.'

"So we went to town. He didn't seem to be afraid to walk in public or anything like that. We went to one store and it didn't suit him. So we went to Super Shoes on the Carlisle Pike. There he found the kind of hiking shoes he wanted. I paid for them and he seemed to be happy. He seemed like a person who just liked to hike and camp. You know, I've heard of people hiking and camping all across the country. That's what I thought he was doing. Just living by himself for a while.

"Anyway, he had said that he would work to pay for the shoes I had bought for him, and he did that. It was still raining, off and on, but we started to build a grain bin. Then one day we poured concrete and he helped us with that. He worked good. He helped level it off."

"We also were fixing fence down here along the road," Nevin noted.

"That's right," Chester agreed. "And we were also fixing fence at Curtis's place."

"And helping out at Ethan's a little bit and out to Jason's one day," Nevin added. Ethan and Jason, the two oldest Weaver sons, operated farms in the nearby Newville area.

"That's right. He did quite a bit of work for us. He worked hard," Chester observed.

"Yes, he worked hard, but he didn't say much," Nevin said. "He was very quiet. Just working with him, you just didn't know what to make of him. He just sort of gave you an odd feeling, you know, having this man around. His hair was long and he had his whiskers. He sort of gave you an uneasy feeling, sort of."

"We did ask if we could give him a haircut," Chester remarked, "but he didn't want that. I told him the Bible says a man should not have long hair. I tried to impress that on him. 'If you would cut your hair and spruce up a little,' I told him, 'you'd be more attractive to society and you'd have more self-respect and self-esteem. Some things like that might even help your character, if you'd be willing to do some things like that.' Well, that just wasn't his way."

"Another thing about Steve is that he was always watching," Nevin added. "When Daddy gave him that first cup of coffee, he watched where

Daddy put the coffee jar. He was all eyes. He saw something, he knew where it was. He didn't forget. He was eyes. He saw every move you made. Believe me, he was sharp."

"A professional thief, you might say," commented Curtis, Nevin's reserved older brother.

"Yes, I think probably he was looking around to see if there was anything he might want to steal," Chester agreed. "He was eyeing up things. If he would have saw a gun or something like that, he might've taken it and took off.

"But Steve didn't get a chance to take anything because on Saturday I told him that we were going to church on Sunday and I asked him if he wanted to go along.

" 'Well,' he said, 'Well, yes, I think I'll go along with you. Been a long time since I've been in church.'

"I didn't want to bring him into the house," said Esther, "so I told him that in the milkhouse there was water and soap and that I'd see that he had a towel. If he was going to church, he was going to have to take a bath."

" 'We won't bother you,' I told him," Chester said. " 'We'll get you soap and a towel and you can clean up a little and you can go along with us to church tomorrow.' "

"I told him that we could give him other clothes, but he said, 'But Esther, God doesn't care what you wear, does he?'

"I said, 'If your clothes are clean, no.'

"Well, he said, 'Okay, fine.'

"But really, I did some washing for him. He hardly had any clothes. One change of clothes. That's all."

"Yes, that's right," Chester agreed. "She washed his clothes, and he went along to church that Sunday. But that's where he got . . . , well, a deacon at church, Laban Zimmerman, saw him, and of course other people saw him too."

"Most people already knew about him Wednesday evening," Nevin observed. "We told people about him at the prayer service that night. Then come Monday evening, Daddy, you didn't show up for the board meeting at the Mennonite school, and the other board members were wondering why and so they got to discussing this man amongst themselves."

"That's right, that's the way it was," Esther declared.

"And as they were discussing this man, they decided that someone should look into it."

"Laban told me," Chester remembered, "that he couldn't sleep Monday night. He said he was worried about our safety, with this man in our house, so he went to the police station on Tuesday morning."

"He asked them, first of all, whether they were looking for anybody," Nevin noted. "He told them there was a man who came down the creek and no one knew much about him and he was just wondering, in case they were looking for somebody. I don't know for a fact whether Laban knew about the murder on South Mountain when he went to the police station. I really wonder about that."

"I'm not sure about that either," Chester admitted.

"Anyway," Nevin continued, "When Laban asked them if they were looking for anyone, they said, 'Yes, we are. You come on inside.' And they took him inside and they showed him this picture and they asked him if he could identify that person.

"Laban said, 'Yes, that's the man. I know where he is.' "

VI

On Tuesday, the day Steve Carr's photo appeared in the local newspapers, the manhunt resumed at first light without Blevins, who had left for Gettysburg to get a warrant for Carr's arrest for murder, attempted murder, and other charges. The dog teams, horse patrols, and helicopters were once again out in force, trying to pick up some fresh lead of Carr's whereabouts, when a call came into the communications command center on Big Flat. Laban Zimmerman, a deacon of a local Mennonite church claimed that Carr was staying with the Chester Weaver family on Creek Road. Trooper Holtz and Corporal O'Brien immediately sped off to the Carlisle station to talk to Zimmerman, while Beaver, Frank Donnelly, and a couple of other troopers raced to the farm site. Their orders were to seal off the road that ran past the two Weaver farms. Beaver, at one end of Creek Road, was angry.

"Donnelly and I were being pushed away from the arrest," he recalls. " 'Don't go near it,' we were told. 'We're bringing in the SERT. They're going to make the arrest.' Now our nose is out of joint. We've been following this thing from the beginning, and we knew he was there. The officers on the other end of Creek Road could see a tractor out in the field driven by the Weaver father, and this kid was with him. We knew he was there and we couldn't go get him. We had to wait for the SERT team.

"As we were waiting, a car pulls up with Weaver's son and his wife in it. He asks, 'What's going on?' and we tell him that we're looking for someone. He says, 'There's a guy staying with my mother and father. He's over at my father's farm.'

"So, I tell him, 'Yes, he's the one we're interested in.' Then I ask him if there is any way for us to get to his farm without being seen by anyone at his father's farm.

"He says, 'Yes, there is a rolling ridge between the two farms. You could drive to my farm and no one at my father's place would be able to see you.'

"Well, I told this to the supervising officer on site, Major Jim Hazen, and I asked him if we could go over to the son's farm, climb the grain bin, and surveil the place. We could then radio back and tell him what was going on.

"The Major said, 'Okay, go ahead and do it. But don't do anything else. If you screw up, it's my ass.' "

Beaver and Donnelly drove to the son's farm, parked their unmarked police car in a large machine shed, and climbed the bin. They couldn't see anything. The tractor that had been out in the field had disappeared. A few minutes later, a car turned into the driveway of the son's farm, forcing Beaver and Donnelly to scramble to the ground.

"If Carr had been in that car and we weren't ready for him, there would have been hell to pay, but it was a false alarm. It was the elder Weaver and his wife. Mr. Weaver talked to his son for a few minutes and then left again with his wife. The son then told us that Carr would be coming over to his farm in a little while. His brother and Carr were going to bring some heifers over and put them in his barn."

"What luck," Beaver exclaimed. "Donnelly and I could set a trap for Carr. He would be coming over in a few minutes and we could nail him. I radioed the new information back to Major Hazen. O'Brien and Holtz must have overheard my report, because they drove in and pulled their car into the same machine shed where we had parked our car. They then tried to close the door, but it wouldn't close the whole way. The bottom of the door was a couple of feet off the ground."

O'Brien and Holtz stayed in the garage, while Beaver considered what he should do.

"I knew if they were bringing heifers over to put them in the barn, they would probably come along the side of the barn, so I picked the milk house," Beaver recounts. "I had a shotgun. Donnelly went into the house and picked a spot in the kitchen, near the back door. Then we waited. The trap was set.

"But before Carr arrived, another car comes whipping in, stones flying. It pulls behind the machine shed and two guys get out. They were the SERT guys, all loaded up. One tries to roll under the partly opened door of the machine shed and gets stuck. Holtz and O'Brien are trying to pull him in as the truck with Carr in it is heading down the driveway. The other Weaver son is driving and Carr is in the passenger seat.

"When the truck pulls up and stops, the Weaver boy who was driving gets out and his other brother—the one we had been talking to—tells him he wants to talk to him. That left Carr alone. By this time, he's gotten out of the truck and is walking alongside the barn, heading toward the barnyard.

"He's coming right down toward me. And I'm waiting for the trap to spring and it's not springing. And he's getting closer and closer and closer and I don't see my guys. I think, 'If I don't step out now, he's going to be past me and then we will be chasing him.' So I stepped out—and I still didn't see any of my guys—and I had a shotgun and I put it right on his chest and said, 'Move and you're dead. Get down on your face.'

"He went right down. Donnelly came running over and cuffed him behind his back and it was over. It was about 11:30 A.M."

Donnelly informed Carr that he was being arrested on a fugitive-from-justice warrant and advised him of his constitutional rights.

O'Brien and Holtz walked over and took charge. "Are you Stephen Roy Carr?"

"Yeah," the handcuffed man replied.

VII

"It might have looked to Steve, when he was arrested, that we had a plot set up for him, but we didn't," Chester Weaver insisted. "We didn't have a thing to do with it."

"Curtis went and talked to him afterwards," Esther recalled. "Tell what you said."

"Well," said Curtis, "he was laying on the ground. I came up to him and said, 'Sorry this has happened Mike, but I want you to know, we didn't turn you in.' He didn't say anything back, but he heard me."

"But Steve didn't seem to show any bitterness or resentment towards us at any time, even after he was caught, not that I can recall," remarked Chester. "We went down and visited him in Adams County Prison a number of times."

"We visited him every Sunday afternoon while he was there," Curtis noted. "Not always us, but someone from our church."

"Yes," Chester agreed, "we talked to him about what happened, the whole thing. I told him I just thought that it was God's hand working, protecting us and caring for us.

"And Steve said, 'I believe too that it was. I'm glad I'm caught. It relieves me of a lot of . . . I might have gotten into more trouble,' he said. 'God stopped me there at your place and God used you to stop me.'"

VIII

Beaver placed Carr into the backseat of a police car and sat down beside him, keeping his hand on him at all times. O'Brien and Holtz jumped into the front seat and they drove to the Carlisle station. On their arrival, Beaver waited with Carr in an interrogation room. Carr had not been out of his sight since he had put him down. At about noon, O'Brien came in.

"Holtz and I are going to do the interview," he said.

Beaver was surprised. He saw no reason why the interview couldn't wait until Blevins got to Carlisle, since he was the chief investigator of the case who had the warrant for Carr's arrest for murder. Technically, it was true, the arrest at the Weaver farm had been based on a fugitive warrant, but Beaver knew that O'Brien and Holtz would be going after incriminating statements about the murder.

"At the time, I thought to myself, 'I don't like the way this is being done. You should wait for Blevins. But if you guys want to make your bones, you go ahead.' My preference at the time would have been to go straight at the murder. They knew the man had committed the murder, and they were going for that evidence, but they went off on a tangent that he was arrested for theft in Florida. But I'm a trooper, not a corporal. O'Brien was the boss. I just kept my mouth shut."

Beaver left the room, and Holtz and O'Brien began their interview of Carr at 12:04 P.M. Forty-five minutes later, the interrogation was over. Having admitted that he had shot the two women in a hunting accident, Carr agreed to take the police to the gun.

"When Carr said he was willing to take us to the gun," O'Brien says, "we did not waste any time. We dropped everything and went."

As O'Brien, Holtz, and Beaver, with Carr in tow, were going out the door, they unexpectedly ran into Blevins. O'Brien said, "Come with us. He's going to take us to the gun."

Without saying a word, Blevins climbed into the driver seat of the police car. O'Brien, Holtz, and Carr got into the same vehicle, while Beaver and another trooper jumped into a different car and followed.

"Reporters were everywhere," Blevins recounts. "We get started and the media follows us—dozens of cars, kind of like a caravan. We get on Interstate 81 and head south and soon we're flying down the interstate trying to get away from the media. It's kind of funny now, but it wasn't then."

Along the way, there was no formal questioning of Carr, just conversation about the weather and the beauty of the South Mountain area. The police wanted to keep Carr talking and keep his mind off how much trouble he was in. Carr eventually told Blevins to get off Interstate 81 and head east on Shippensburg Road in the direction of Big Flat. He then informed the troopers that he had buried the gun under a stump near the power line that ran along the left side of Shippensburg Road. On Carr's command, Blevins stopped the vehicle and all four men got out.

Carr pointed to a stump about seventy-five yards away, while Beaver kept the media at bay. Blevins climbed a steep embankment, took photographs of the stump, and then moved it aside. There, underneath some soil, he found a disassembled rifle wrapped in plastic.

Not wanting to contaminate the evidence, Blevins did not unwrap the rifle, but instead turned it over to Beaver, who would take it to the crime lab in Harrisburg. The officers and Carr left the scene. O'Brien and Holtz took Carr back to the Carlisle station, while Blevins first dropped Beaver off at his car on Big Flat, where he had left it that morning; Blevins arrived back at Carlisle a few minutes before 3:00 P.M. He had a brief conversation with O'Brien and Holtz concerning what Carr had told them. It was only then that Blevins found out for sure that Carr had admitted to pulling the trigger. Blevins reacted warmly to the news.

"The first goal in a murder investigation," says Blevins, "is to get the suspect to admit he pulled the trigger. That is a major threshold. Once he says that, you sit back in your chair, relax, and play with him. Anything more after that is a Christmas present—icing on the cake."

Blevins decided to conduct his own interview of Carr. As the chief investigator in the case, he wanted to know firsthand what exactly Carr was confessing to. In addition, there was Beaver's concern that Carr had been arrested on the fugitive-from-justice warrant but interrogated about the murder of Rebecca Wight.

"I thought the best way for me to fix the situation, if I could, was to tell Carr that he was being arrested for murder and get him to confess all over again. I knew that the story about an 'accident' had been given to him. 'If it is an accident, we want to know so we can get your side of the story.' Then you get him to say that he did it. Then the next move is to get him to say things indicating that it was not an accident. That's the way it's done. And this guy could not keep his story straight. It kept changing as we gave him the option of changing it, seemingly to his benefit. Then, the worm turned."

At 3:10 P.M., Blevins advised Carr of his rights and told him that he was being arrested for murder in the first degree, murder in the third degree, attempted murder, and two counts of aggravated assault. Carr immediately asked if there was any chance that the first-degree murder charge could be dropped. Blevins could see that Carr was still hoping that the police would swallow his story about a hunting accident. Not wanting to discourage Carr's thinking along these lines, Blevins tried to deflect the question in a way that would not prompt Carr to ask for a lawyer.

"Sorry Steve, that would be hard to say. I don't make those decisions. I would have to talk first to the district attorney before I could really give you accurate information about that."

Carr mumbled in reply that he understood.

Blevins then asked Carr what happened on May 13th. Carr gave the same story that he had given Holtz and O'Brien a few hours earlier. He shot the women in a hunting accident. In less than half an hour, Blevins ended the interview. He had heard all that he needed to know, and Carlisle District Justice Paula P. Correal had arrived at the Carlisle station to arraign Carr on the fugitive-from-justice warrant and the other charges. Because the media followed the officers' every move, it had been easier for the district justice to come to the station than for the police to take Carr to her office. Afterward, Blevins, Holtz, and O'Brien drove Carr to the office of District Justice Harold R. Deardorff in Fairfield, Adams County, where he was again arraigned. Then the three troopers took Carr to the Gettysburg station to be booked and fingerprinted. They left Carr in the hands of Adams County Prison authorities at about 6:30 P.M.

While Blevins, Holtz, and O'Brien drove Carr around, from Carlisle to Fairfield, from Fairfield to the Gettysburg station, and from there to the Adams County Prison, they engaged him in seemingly casual, friendly conversation. In these exchanges, Carr unintentionally undermined his claim that the shootings had been an accident. Any chance that he could avoid first-degree murder charges evaporated as he chatted with the troopers.

"The real problem for Carr and many other defendants," Blevins observes, "is the casual conversation. During the interrogation itself, they are more careful. But when you're just chatting with them, they start to think that you're their buddy. And I am their friend, or I at least try to be, no matter how much I hate and despise the person for what he did. If you treat him with contempt, you're not going to get anything out of him. And that's the job. Get the confession, get the information out of him. But when it comes time to testify, I tell the jury or the judge exactly what the guy told me. It's my job."

The next morning, Blevins went to the Adams County Prison to reinterview Carr. Once again he advised Carr of his constitutional rights, and Carr signed a Rights Waiver Form. Blevins then asked Carr if he would be willing to provide samples of head and facial hair. Carr agreed to do so, even though Blevins warned him that the evidence collected could be used to convict him of the charges against him. After the samples were collected, Blevins asked Carr about his background: where he had been born, the schools he attended, his criminal record in Florida. When the subject of the interview shifted to the events of May 13th, Carr muttered that he'd better talk to an attorney.

Blevins immediately stopped his questioning, put his pen in his pocket, and closed his notebook.

"At that point, I knew we were finished with him," he says. "Had to be. We could not talk to him again until he talked to his attorney and he would never talk to us again once he talked to an attorney. I left the prison. My job was basically done."

The Lawyers

The setting for the Stephen Carr case was Gettysburg, Pennsylvania, a borough of approximately seven thousand people situated twelve miles east of South Mountain. Although small, Gettysburg is well known as the site of both the Battle of Gettysburg and the Gettysburg Address, in which Abraham Lincoln proclaimed that our nation was "conceived in liberty and dedicated to the proposition that all men are created equal." Between 1.5 and 1.7 million Americans travel to Gettysburg each year to visit the six-thousand-acre National Military Park and the Gettysburg National Cemetery. The park's official map and guide inform visitors that Lincoln's speech in 1863 "transformed Gettysburg from a scene of carnage into a symbol, giving meaning to the sacrifice of the dead and inspiration to the living." In the 1990s, Gettysburg retains its role as a symbol of sacrifice and inspiration in the struggle for freedom and equality. Americans who tour Devil's Den, Little Round Top, the Peach Orchard, the Wheatfield, and the High Water Mark cannot help reflecting on the contemporary meaning of Lincoln's words and what transpired here long ago.

Coexisting with Gettysburg the symbol is Gettysburg the reality, the seat of Adams County, Pennsylvania, where murderers, rapists, thieves, and other violators of the state's criminal laws are brought to justice daily. Here, as elsewhere around the United States, the key roles in the criminal justice system are all played by lawyers: the district attorney, who tries to prove beyond a reasonable doubt that the defendant is guilty of a crime; the defense attorney, who attempts to create a reasonable doubt; and the judge, who umpires the contest in accordance with an established set of rules. The presumption is that the innocent will not be separated from the guilty and the guilty will not receive the proper punishment unless these "role players" do what they are supposed to do. Lawyers working within the criminal justice system, however, have their own personal agendas, values, and identities that inevitably affect how they perceive and fulfill their professional responsibilities. The mesh of personality and professional duty in the criminal justice system is an interesting subject if only because it reveals the often elusive and sometimes delusive character of human ideals.

I. Roy Keefer, District Attorney of Adams County

Adams County had a new district attorney (DA) in May 1988. His name was Roy Keefer, and he had just taken office in January 1988. No one had run against Keefer, perhaps because he'd had the inside track for the job. He'd been an assistant DA for five years, and the people of Adams County value experience. "If it ain't broke, don't fix it!" is a principle they know and respect. Keefer had paid his dues, and the local community had confidence he could fulfill the DA's responsibilities, including the difficult one of deciding when to seek the death penalty in a case of aggravated first-degree murder. By mid-May, Keefer had two such potential capital cases scheduled for trial in October. One, against Barry Laughman, had been pending when he took office, and the other was the investigation of the murder of Rebecca Wight, in which he knew early on that if an arrest was made, the case would be a potential death penalty case. Accordingly, during his first six months as DA, Keefer had to consider how he would go about deciding whether to seek the death penalty. His personality had a significant impact on the policy he selected.

Keefer describes himself as a competitive person, having adapted for the courtroom the competitive instincts he developed playing basketball and running track in high school. Even at the relatively young age of thirty-four, Keefer had a lot of confidence in his prosecutorial skills. He liked the thrill of courtroom battles and the pressure of thinking on his feet, matching wits against another lawyer, and his large, 250-pound frame, draped in the typical dark suit of the lawyer, cut an imposing figure in front of a jury. There was an intensity about it that Keefer found exhilarating.

"What I'm talking about is sort of like what you see in a big ACC [Atlantic Coast Conference] basketball game. Now, my team is North Carolina. After my Dad and Mom moved down to North Carolina, we all became big fans of Dean Smith's Tarheels. You can see for yourself," he says, pointing to a display of books and memorabilia behind his desk in his office in the Adams County Courthouse.

"The message here is hard work, a game plan, discipline, and cool-ness under fire," he explains. "You got to have some talent too, no one doubts that. But the key is to be able to think and keep your wits about you at the choke point. That is what Dean Smith has been able to do down in North Carolina. He doesn't break the rules, at least I don't think he does. But within the rules, he does whatever he can to win. If the rules permit a four-corner offense, he uses it. He's looking for any advantage he can find. I try to do the same in my work as a prosecutor."

Uninterested in a career of wills, contracts, and trusts, Keefer had joined the staff of the Dauphin County Public Defender's Office in Harrisburg, Pennsylvania, after he graduated from the Dickinson School of Law in 1979. Here he learned his trade, but he quickly became disenchanted. "I had a real problem with working to get guilty people off. I knew that the system was supposed to work if everyone did their job, but after a few months in the Public Defender's Office, I could see that that was not happening. There were no innocent people being convicted, at least none that I knew about, but there were guilty people getting off and I was helping bring about that result. I couldn't live with that, so I got out of defense work as soon as I could."

Keefer admits that people become lawyers for a lot of different reasons, but he insists that the DA's office attracts those who are more committed to public service and the ideals of the criminal justice system. He still recalls the first time he watched *To Kill a Mockingbird* when he was a boy. In this classic movie, a lawyer named Atticus Finch (played by Gregory Peck) defends a black man unjustly accused of raping a young white woman. An all-white jury knowingly convicts the innocent man, who soon thereafter dies while attempting to escape from prison. Bob Ewell, the young woman's father, tries to take revenge on Finch by attacking his two children. The lawyer's neighbor, a kind but reclusive young man by the name of Arthur "Boo" Radley (played by Robert Duvall), comes to the aid of the children and kills their assailant. The movie upholds the ideals of the American criminal justice system at the same time that it shows how vulnerable the system is to prejudice, bigotry, and arbitrariness. It is still, many years later, Keefer's favorite movie. A romantic at heart, he watches it at least four times a year and he understands his own professional life in terms of it.

"The one thing a prosecutor is sworn to do that no one else in the system is sworn to do is justice. My role is to see that justice is done. For example, when the sheriff decides at the end of the movie not to charge Boo Radley, when he says that Bob Ewell's death was an accident, what you see that sheriff doing is what prosecutors do everyday—they do justice. It's his decision as to what justice requires, and it shows that a prosecutor does have a lot of discretion. It is built into the system. And I think by being sworn to do justice, as opposed to just prosecuting cases, prosecutors are encouraged to use that discretion so that justice can be reached."

Keefer sees no incompatibility between prosecutorial discretion and justice. Their decisions should, of course, be principled, but prosecutors quite properly decide whether to file charges or drop cases. At the same time, Keefer personally has a problem with exercising such discretion in the area of the death penalty. The difficulty arises from his deep commitment to his religion.

"I am a Lutheran, so I do have some problems with taking another person's life. I'm not sure the death penalty is effective for anything. I'm not sure that it deters anything, and I'm not sure retribution is a valid reason for anything. It seems to be just a dressed-up name for revenge, and I personally cannot endorse vengeance. Of course, if my daughter, friend, or wife was killed, I'm not sure that I wouldn't say in that case that I want the death penalty. But that doesn't make the death penalty right. In any case, I personally can't be responsible for choosing the ones who will face the death penalty from the ones who will not. That's a Godlike decision."

It may seem puzzling that Keefer sought the job of DA if he couldn't take the responsibility of making life-and-death decisions, but he thinks he has come up with a workable method of balancing the conflicting demands of his private and professional lives.

"When I took this job, I swore that I would perform my responsibilities to the best of my ability, and that means I must follow the law of Pennsylvania. Sure, I have some moral problems with the death penalty, and I have to deal with them. In my own case, I have decided to handle these problems by strictly enforcing the death penalty statute. This statute lists what are the aggravating factors that make a murder-one [first-degree murder] case potentially subject to the death penalty. If I have a murder-one case and there is arguably an aggravating circumstance, then I'm going to ask for the death penalty. That's the way I live with the moral quandary. By following the letter of the law, it's not really me making the decision."

Many prosecutors across the United States have felt comfortable deciding not to seek the ultimate punishment in a potential death penalty case that contains one of the aggravating factors required by statute, perhaps because one or more mitigating factors were also present. Pennsylvania's sentencing code (42 Pa.C.S.A., Section 9711, (e)) identifies eight such mitigating circumstances:

1) The defendant has no significant history of prior criminal convictions.

2) The defendant was under the influence of extreme mental or emotional disturbance.

3) The capacity of the defendant to appreciate the criminality of his conduct or to conform his conduct to the requirements of law was substantially impaired.

4) The age of the defendant at the time of the crime.

5) The defendant acted under extreme distress . . ., or acted under the substantial domination of another person.

6) The victim was a participant in the defendant's homicidal conduct or consented to the homicidal acts.

7) The defendant's participation in the homicidal act was relatively minor.

8) Any other evidence of mitigation concerning the character and record of the defendant and the circumstances of his offense.

Relying on these mitigating factors or others not listed in the statute, a Pennsylvania prosecutor could "do justice" by exercising the discretion entrusted to him or her and not seek the death penalty in a case authorized by law. Keefer's moral and religious commitments, however, make it impossible for him to exercise such discretion in capital cases. On his watch, any case of aggravated murder is a death penalty case.

The irony is that Keefer's way of resolving his moral-professional dilemma would result in more death penalty cases in Adams County than there would be if he allowed his personal doubts about the death penalty to influence his decisions. He wouldn't let his personal doubts influence his decisions because in 1988 he didn't want to "play God." Avoiding the anxiety of "Godlike" decisions was more important to him than avoiding the infliction of a punishment that in his own opinion had no legitimate purpose.

There are, of course, purely strategic reasons why many prosecutors like the death penalty. First, the death penalty is different from a prison term. It gives defendants an additional incentive to plea-bargain their case, that is, agree to plead guilty to a reduced charge or penalty. Defendants who plea-bargain might think they're getting a "bargain," but the reality may be that the prosecutor has manipulated the death penalty sanction to ensure that they get what they deserve without the public's having to pay for an expensive and time-consuming trial. Keefer concedes that some prosecutors use the death penalty in this way, but he insists that he personally has never done so, calling such tactics "unscrupulous."

Once Steve Carr was arrested, Keefer could proceed with his prosecution only if he concurred with the police's judgment that there was "probable cause" that Carr was responsible for the shootings. In this "charging" capacity, Keefer functioned as a grand jury, evaluating whether there was enough evidence to "present" a case that Carr was guilty to a petit jury. The issue for the prosecutor, according to Keefer, was not whether the jury *would* convict, but whether it *could* convict. Accordingly, whereas a petit jury at a trial must consider the credibility of witnesses, Keefer takes the evidence and what witnesses say at face value. He's concerned only with whether the testimony supports the conclusion that the defendant probably did the crime. According to Keefer, if the jury could convict, the prosecution should go forward, even if it's a death penalty case.

"I try, quite frankly," replies Keefer, "to analyze a death penalty case the same way that I would approach any other case. If it's a presentable case, I take it to the jury. I let the jurors (or the judge if it's a bench trial) sort it out. If the jury finds the defendant guilty and sentences him to death, that's just the way it is. I also argue to the jury that a death penalty case does not change the burden of proof. If I have proven beyond a reasonable doubt that the defendant did it, then the jury should convict, even if they are not certain of the defendant's guilt. Just because it is a death penalty case does not mean that the burden of proof is suddenly guilt beyond all mathematical certainty."

Keefer clarifies his position by referring to the fact that Blevins had come to his office seeking an arrest warrant for first-degree murder for Carr before his arrest and confession.

"As Blevins and I pieced the case together, it was pretty clear that the same person the women had seen earlier that day had stalked or tracked them. This kind of stalking or tracking was pretty good evidence of an intent to kill, which makes it first-degree murder. Later that day, when I found out that Carr confessed and that we had his gun, all doubts disappeared. I was pretty sure we had the right guy before, but now there was no doubt. But the confession and the discovery of the gun did not influence my decision on the death penalty. That decision had already been made for me. The physical evidence gave me probable cause that Carr was the murderer, and the statute determined whether I was going for the death penalty."

As soon as Keefer had enough evidence that a jury could convict Carr of aggravated first-degree murder, Keefer knew it was going to be a death penalty case, because he would not allow any other factor to influence his decision: not the preferences of the surviving victim or the deceased woman's relatives, not the media, and not public opinion. The local media's coverage of the high-profile case was intense, but Keefer insists that neither the media nor organized political interests had any effect on him.

"Maybe it's my naiveté, but I didn't feel any media pressure," says Keefer. "I didn't feel pressure to do one thing as opposed to another, just because the media was there. The same thing can be said for the gay and lesbian groups. From my perspective, no organizational groups were pushing either one way or the other. Perhaps—in fact, I know—the media and the groups were on the sidelines watching, but I felt nothing. We were able to make the decisions about the case based on the law, not outside pressures."

The Carr murder case caught the local media's attention in part because rumors immediately began to circulate that the two women were lesbians. Such speculation titillated the local community, but there was no large public demand for the death penalty in the Carr case. According to Keefer, however, what the public wanted had no bearing on how he carried out his professional responsibilities.

"A prosecutor has to exercise his own judgment on how to apply the law. He can't become the prisoner of what some local group thinks. Remember the prosecutor in *To Kill a Mockingbird*. He knew the black man did not rape the girl, but he failed to stand up to local community sentiment. He went along with the prosecution of an innocent man. That's what can happen if a prosecutor becomes a prisoner of the local community. An innocent man can be punished, or a guilty one can get off. That is why a prosecutor must make his decisions according to the law, not according to how the local community perceives the case. It might be difficult to do in some cases, but that's his job."

Despite the apparent senselessness of Carr's crime, the people of Adams County were not screaming for his blood. The murder had not been part of a robbery. It had not been an act of jealousy or revenge. The way Keefer understood it, "The only reason Carr shot those two women was because they were lesbians. About that I have no doubt in my mind. He shot them because he just couldn't stand watching them together. He couldn't take it."

Such irrational crimes are perhaps worse than other types of homicides because they serve no purpose other than ventilation of hatred, prejudice, and bigotry. From this perspective, it may make sense to execute a homophobic murderer. Keefer knows prosecutors who would proceed accordingly, and he has no criticism of them. Yet, Keefer emphasizes that he could not seek the death penalty on that ground alone, because a motive of hate is not an aggravating circumstance as defined by the Pennsylvania death penalty statute.

"Yes, I think it's valid for a prosecutor to consider whether a murder is a hate crime, but that's not something that I personally consider, because of my feelings in regard to just following the letter of the law," explains Keefer. "That is something I try very hard not to allow to come into my consideration. I want it to be black and white. Here's the statute; here's the evidence. Does it fit? If it does, the decision is made. The decision is ultimately made by the case and the law, not by me. So, if you look at the death penalty statute, what's in it is a grave-risk clause. It's item number seven [see box]. If a person intentionally kills another and at the same time exposes another person to a grave risk of death, then the

---

42 Pa.C.S.A., Section 9711, (d)

(d)   Aggravating circumstances.—Aggravating circumstances shall be limited to the following:

(1)   The victim was a fireman, peace officer or public servant concerned in official detention, as defined in 18 Pa.C.S. Sec. 5121 (relating to escape), who was killed in the performance of his duties.

(2)   The defendant paid or was paid by another person or had contracted to pay or be paid by another person or had conspired to pay or be paid by another person for the killing of the victim.

(3)   The victim was being held by the defendant for ransom or reward, or as a shield or hostage.

(4)   The death of the victim occurred while defendant was engaged in the hijacking of an aircraft.

(5)   The victim was a prosecution witness to a murder or other felony committed by the defendant and was killed for the purpose of preventing his testimony against the defendant in any grand jury or criminal proceeding involving such offenses.

(6)   The defendant committed a killing while in the perpetration of a felony.

(7)   In the commission of the offense the defendant knowingly created a grave risk of death to another person in addition to the victim of the offense.

(8)   The offense was committed by means of torture.

(9)   The defendant has a significant history of felony convictions involving the use or threat of violence to the person.

(10)   The defendant has been convicted of another Federal or State offense, committed either before or at the time of the offense at issue, for which a sentence of life imprisonment or death was imposable or the defendant was undergoing a sentence of life imprisonment for any reason at the time of the commission of the offense.

statute makes it a death penalty case. That's the provision on which I based my decision to seek the death penalty for Carr. Carr intentionally killed Wight and exposed Brenner to a grave risk of death. The fact that it was a hate crime was irrelevant."

Keefer concedes that someone could argue that Carr did not "knowingly create" a grave risk of Claudia Brenner's death. He instead intentionally tried to kill her. A strict reading of the Pennsylvania statute therefore might not necessarily support Keefer's decision to seek the death penalty in the Carr case.

"The way out," Keefer explains, "is to see that we have court decisions holding that a multiple murder can satisfy the requirement of a grave risk of death. These decisions say that if a killer intentionally kills one person, then kills another, he has in effect put the second person at grave risk. It's like a threshold requirement. The killer must intentionally kill at least one person plus something more. If the killer does more than the minimum, by killing a second person, Pennsylvania courts have said that the killer can face the death penalty. I think the same kind of argument can be made if a person kills one person and attempts to kill another. That person has done more than the threshold requirement of exposing a second person to danger. I didn't have any cases that explicitly said that I could seek the death penalty, but I didn't have any trouble with that conclusion. And I think the courts would have backed me up on that. I think they would have said that Carr fit the statute and that's why I sought the death penalty."

Thus this prosecutor who wanted the law and the evidence to separate homicide defendants who would face the death penalty from those who would not ultimately had to make the call himself, because the law ran out. The very fact that Keefer felt that the courts would have "backed up" his decision to seek Carr's execution reveals that Keefer was out in front of the law. His effort to distance himself from deciding whom to subject to the death penalty is of course understandable, especially because his religious commitments compelled him not to "play God." A heinous murder like Carr's, however, demands a proper prosecutorial response. Keefer's decision to seek the death penalty for Carr therefore illustrates the uneasy tension that can arise between professional responsibility and human personality.

II. Defense Attorney Michael George

In Adams County, the job of defending Steve Carr normally would have gone to Roy Keefer's counterpart, Jeffrey M. Cook, the local public defender, but Cook was already defending Barry Laughman and he felt that one death penalty case at a time was all that he could handle. So Cook asked if a private attorney could be appointed to the case. Soon thereafter Michael George agreed to take on the responsibility of Carr's defense.

George was a young lawyer, only thirty years old. He had graduated from the Dickinson School of Law and joined the Gettysburg firm of Campbell and White only a few years before. He had a polite, soft-spoken demeanor, but underneath he was smart and aggressive, and he possessed the mental toughness that would be needed for the job of defending Carr. It was to George's credit that in just a few short years he had developed among the Gettysburg bar a reputation as a capable criminal defense lawyer. His professional idealism was one reason why his peers were confident that he would do more than an adequate job of defending Carr. In contrast to Keefer, George had seen innocent people convicted and punished.

"When I defend some criminal," George explains, "I don't do it just for him. I do it for me, for you, and for everybody else out there on the street, including the judge and the DA. If I start making the decision—'this guy is trash and he doesn't deserve a defense' and I roll over—then I compromise the whole system, because it's no longer a trial by a jury of peers, but a defense attorney making the decision. The adversarial system works well. It's not 100 percent perfect; it can't be. But when you see that innocent person go to jail, you begin to see what it all means. Too many people out there think it doesn't happen, but it does. So, when I get the guilty person off the hook, what I'm doing in my own mind is trying to make it less likely that some other innocent person will be punished. I really believe in the old principle. I'd really rather see ten guilty people walking free for one innocent person being punished. And I will work like hell to get those ten guilty people off for the sake of that one innocent person. That's what I take my job to be."

George's philosophy of hard work and commitment to professional and personal ideals reflects his upbringing and the work ethic of White

Oak, the steel town near Pittsburgh where he grew up in a large Catholic family. Of course, in the blue-collar towns of western Pennsylvania—the home of Joe Montana, Dan Marino, and Joe Namath—football is king. Most kids who have any kind of size and speed dream of a college and pro career. George himself played the high school game, and he still has the look of a football player: 6′2″, over two hundred pounds, an athletic body, though a few pounds overweight. And George's personality still has that football player's "edge." His soft voice only magnifies the impression of a strong-willed and determined individual.

George is not sure why, but as far back as he can remember he always wanted to be a lawyer. It was while attending Dickinson School of Law that he decided to specialize in criminal law. After graduating in 1986, he accepted the offer extended by Bob Campbell and John White to join their firm in Gettysburg, and he says he has never regretted that decision. More than 50 percent of his work has been criminal defense, and he's loved it.

"When the story about the murder on South Mountain hit the news, I knew that it might end up on my desk. I knew how busy the Public Defender's Office was and what lawyers in town were up for a job like this, and I knew what lawyers could do it but wouldn't want to. So I followed the case in the newspapers."

Even before he was asked to take over Carr's defense, George considered what he'd do if he were asked. A death penalty case was an all-consuming thing. To supervise the investigation, draft the necessary motions, and prepare for the pretrial hearings and the trial itself, George would have to sacrifice many hours that he would otherwise spend with his family and friends. It was a big commitment, but that was not George's major concern.

"The biggest problem was the possibility of failure," says George. "Would I be able to handle it. The scuttlebutt around the courthouse was that it was going to be a death penalty case. Certainly my read on it from the beginning was that Keefer was going to try and fry this guy. So, when I was asked if I would do it, before I said yes, before I even met with Carr, I asked myself, 'Would I be able to handle it? What guilt was going to follow me if this guy gets convicted and gets the death penalty. Do I understand the ramifications of what I am getting involved in?' "

One factor that influenced George's decision was his own personal doubts about the death penalty itself. He doesn't think the death penalty has any special deterrent effect, and he sees retribution as nothing more than vengeance. An additional concern, in George's view, is that the death penalty cannot be applied fairly. After all, the decision to seek the death penalty is made by the DA—an elected official.

"Now, Keefer has a lot of different responsibilities, but one thing he has to deal with is the public's perception. In that way, I think that some decisions to seek the death penalty are political to some extent. And one has to remember that all of our decisions depend upon who we are and where we come from—our experiences. To the extent that such factors subconsciously influence Keefer's decisions to seek the death penalty, and I suppose they do influence his decisions no matter how objective he tries to be, to that extent they're going to affect his objectivity. Now is that fair, having political and subconscious factors determine who is going to face the death penalty and who is not?"

Whether he "hypnotized" himself or not, George is unsure, but in the end he took the job of defending Carr. It was a lucky day for Steve Carr. The state had an obligation to supply him with competent counsel, but, with George, Carr got a defense attorney who would, if only to avoid the guilt that would surely follow failure, fight hard to save his life.

"A death penalty case is a war," asserts George. "I had to do everything in my power to get Carr off, everything, that is, within the law. There is the public perception that defense lawyers will violate the law to get their guilty clients off. It is my belief, however, that criminal defense attorneys generally have just as high a moral standard as lawyers in other fields of law. The great majority of us don't present false testimony before a court, we don't allow perjury, nor do we create or taint evidence. Those are the rules that most defense attorneys respect and live by. We will do everything we can within the rules to win, but we don't violate our legal obligations. In a death penalty case, it's a war, but it's a war conducted according to rules."

George was going to fight hard for Carr, but that didn't mean that he could or would trust him. This lack of trust between criminal defense attorneys and their clients is one of the least understood aspects of the criminal justice system.

"That first day I saw Stephen Carr, he didn't trust me one bit. I could see it on his face 'Who is this now that they're sending to talk to me.' Hell, he doesn't know anything about who I am. But I had to break through that barrier, he had to trust me, he had to realize that I was the only one that stood between him and the electric chair. My point is that anyone who wants to be a defense attorney must be able to do this kind of thing. He must be able to build a relationship with some very undesirable people. Steve Carr, for instance, looked like a person you would hesitate to get close to, yet the system wasn't going to work unless he trusted me."

The opposite, however, does not hold true. Though defense lawyers must inspire their clients' trust, they must never trust their clients. George explains the paradox.

"When something goes wrong, it's always the attorney's fault. 'My attorney didn't tell me that,' is what many defendants will claim. So, to protect myself from that sort of thing, whenever I had something important to say to Steve Carr, I always had another person with me to verify what was said. I also have to protect myself against claims that I asked the defendant to commit perjury. By lying in this way, the defendant gains some leverage with the DA. For his testimony against the defense lawyer, he can bargain for a better deal in his case. My point is that you can't trust defendants because many of them will turn around and bite you if they get a chance. The job is often a lot like petting a rattlesnake. You're trying your utmost to be the rattlesnake's friend at the same time that you're very worried that the damn thing will bite you."

In death penalty cases, the ambivalent nature of the relationship between defense lawyers and their clients places enormous stress on the attorneys. They may be waging a "war," but they're waging it for someone they don't trust and often despise. It's no wonder that many lawyers avoid defense work.

"It is a psychological strain to work so hard for someone you don't trust. I find it a little strange myself. But the way I keep going is to remind myself that I am first and foremost representing the law and the potentially innocent person. I work hard to get the guilty person off because I want to make the system work, make it work so that as few innocent people as possible are convicted. That's how I keep going."

In his own estimation, George is a man who would, for the sake of all the innocent people who in the future might find themselves caught up in the criminal justice system, wage war on behalf of a man he would "hesitate to get close to." Obviously, what his client did or deserved was not the controlling variable in George's calculus. His focus was on the abstract injustice of punishing the innocent. In the service of justice in the abstract, Geroge would knowingly sacrifice actual justice in the concrete case. It was his job, one for which few persons are well suited.

III. Judge Oscar F. Spicer

The people of Adams County elected Oscar F. Spicer to the bench of the Court of Common Pleas in 1977. He was forty-six years old at the time and had spent the better part of his life in Adams County, much of it as an attorney laboring in the local courthouse. Born in the tough mining community of Harlan, Kentucky, he had migrated with his extended family to Adams County in 1942, right after the attack on Pearl Harbor brought the United States into World War II. Having endured the Great Depression, and troubled about what the future might bring, the Spicer family turned to the security of agriculture, buying farms between the small towns of New Chester, Heidlersburg, and Hunterstown a few miles northeast of Gettysburg. Charles Spicer, Oscar's father and a lawyer in Kentucky, purchased a thousand-acre farm near Biglerville, a peaceful place far removed from the turbulence that plagued the American economy and society just before World War II.

"My Dad might have been a very fine lawyer down in Kentucky, but he was a helluva poor farmer in Adams County," says Judge Spicer. "Everything about farming was difficult. My father had thought about farming the way the English do—sort of like gardening. Well, it wasn't that way at all, not in Adams County. The other farmers were so handy and experienced. They could sharpen the blades for their grass mowers right out there in the fields. We, on the other hand, could spend the whole morning trying to get the blade sharp and we just couldn't do it. We didn't know how."

Oscar himself never contemplated a life on the farm. He graduated from Biglerville High School in 1949 and immediately went to the University of Pennsylvania. Four years later, his undergraduate degree in hand, he joined the navy. For most of his three-year stint in the navy, law was the furthest thing from his mind. He was taking things day by day and had no firm plans for the future. Then one day something "just happened."

"I didn't get into law, I don't think, because my father was a lawyer.

In my experience, kids don't want to do what their parents do. It just happened in my last year in the navy. We were in port, and by chance I heard that the LSAT was going to be given the next day. I took the test for the hell of it. I didn't plan or prepare for the test at all. I sent my scores to the University of Pennsylvania Law School, and they accepted me. So, you see, it was all a matter of chance. I took the test on a whim and wound up a judge."

Judge Spicer's account of how he found himself in law school mirrors his perception of much of life and the role that the law plays in human affairs.

"So much of life is fortuitous. So much of it is a matter of luck and happenstance. You can't predict it. You can't control it. The law is like that, too. Take this Carr case for an example. Think of the odds of this sort of thing happening, the odds of two educated women running into a guy like Carr out there on the top of South Mountain. In a way, that's the most striking thing about this case. That's the real story. A set of circumstances brought those women there, and a completely different set of circumstances put Carr on the scene. The result, violence erupts. No one could've predicted that. That's the way so much of life is. In some way, each of us is a puppet in a story that we do not know or understand," says Judge Spicer.

After law school, the twenty-eight-year-old lawyer spent a year practicing law in Chester County before returning to Adams County in 1961, where he did pro bono work for indigent defendants. Soon thereafter, Judge W. C. Sheeley convinced the county commissioners to set aside $1,800 per year for a part-time public defender and appointed Spicer to the position. In 1967, Spicer ran for DA and won. For the next ten years he prosecuted those who committed crimes in Adams County. When Judge Sheeley retired in 1977, Spicer, with sixteen years of experience, was the natural choice to replace him. In the mid-1980s, a second judgeship was created in the Adams County Court of Common Pleas, and Spicer became president judge. In this capacity, he has presided over many of the serious felony cases in the county, including the Stephen Roy Carr case in 1988.

Most judges are bright, practical people, well versed in the law and amply endowed with basic common sense. Oscar Spicer is all of these things, and more. An aesthetic sensibility and artistic talent have led him to write a novel, mold ceramic figurines, paint, and craft silver jewelry. He also helps produce local musical comedies, for which he pens lyrics that make the Gettysburg community howl with laughter. In addition, he is deeply literary.

"I've read a great deal of legal philosophy," he says matter-of-factly. "It's always been a great interest of mine. Plato. Aristotle, of course. Hobbes. I've tried to appreciate what these great minds had to say."

A conversation with Judge Spicer is enough to prove his claim true. References to Shakespeare, Montesquieu, Mark Twain, and Joseph Conrad come easily to him, suggesting that he has integrated what he has read into his personality. It's one of life's "fortuities" that sleepy Adams County has an artist and scholar for a judge.

At the same time, Judge Spicer is a very practical man. Perhaps it was his early unhappy years on the farm, where things have to work or the farmer goes broke. Perhaps it was his responsibility for administering the court, trying to save a few dollars here, a few dollars there. Whatever the reason, Spicer is a man who focuses on the bottom line. He believes that a judge should never let colorful or sophisticated legal arguments obscure what's at stake.

"To tell you the truth, I used to admire rhetorical and philosophical judges until I became a judge. Then I began to wonder. Take Oliver Wendell Holmes, for instance—his glowing allegorical descriptive writing. I used to think it was wonderful. It is great reading, great prose. But sometimes the writing seems to blur what the holding is more than it enhances it. An example is when Holmes talks about the law as a tree. The law has its branches and its limbs, etc., etc. The danger with this is that the mind starts to think in terms of symbols and metaphors, not in terms of the realities of a case."

For Judge Spicer, law has a practical purpose: to achieve in any particular case a fair result based on the law and a community's sense of justice. A judge works within this framework. His or her job is to apply the law to the case at hand, but often the finer points of the law require the judge to consider the general community's values. A judge's personal values are of no help in this endeavor. Rather, says Spicer, they are a constant temptation to bend the law to individual prejudices, a temptation that a judge must always resist.

"It's very difficult to do sometimes. In a case just this morning, I tried very hard to restrain my sense of outrage. I told a man that I was sentencing that he really deserved a ten- to twenty-year sentence for what he had done. I ended up giving him seven to fifteen—which is a substantial sentence. The minimum was five to ten. It's a constant battle within myself, but I feel strongly that I don't want to let my feelings interfere with my role as a judge. As a judge, I have to look at the broad picture. What is happening in this commonwealth? Would a person in Adams County be treated basically the same way in Cumberland County for the same type of crime, the same kind of conduct? If the law is going to be fair—and that is its goal—then judges have to restrain their personal beliefs and any peculiar views of their local communities so that criminals who commit the same kind of crime are treated fairly across Pennsylvania."

A case in point is his view of the death penalty.

"Personally, I don't care who knows about my personal views about the death penalty. It's always been my attitude. I've said it to people. But I am not sure whether it ought to be put in print. Putting it in print might give some ignorant person the wrong impression. He might think I made some ruling because I personally don't think much of the death penalty when in fact I made the ruling for some other legitimate reason, perhaps because the law specifically required it. But I guess one way to fight the delusion that judges are just applying their own personal moral codes is to try to educate people as to what a judge's job is all about. So, as long as it is clear that what I personally think about the death penalty has no impact on my work as a judge—and I try very hard to project a completely neutral image as to the death penalty or anything else—maybe there is no harm in discussing it [in print]. After all, I'm not ashamed of what I think. I've told people, and many people down here in Adams County know where I stand on the issue."

Judge Spicer is not conscientiously opposed to the death penalty. A prisoner already serving a life sentence who makes a game of killing prison guards ought to be executed, he believes, just to put an end to the game. But according to Spicer, this kind of murderer is the exception, not the rule. In the standard case, he doesn't see the utility of imposing the death penalty.

"For what purpose? It has never been shown to have any deterrent

effect. Take policemen, for example. There have been studies of policemen who shoot their spouses. Here you have people who are involved
with prosecuting murder cases and many of them favor the death penalty.
Yet, they get into a huge argument with their spouses on a Saturday night
and they take their service revolver and shoot their wives. Where is the
deterrent effect? If the death penalty is not going to deter these policemen,
is there much reason to think that it will deter anyone else?"

Another problem that Judge Spicer has with the death penalty is the
"whimsical" way it is applied. Referring to Jeremy Bentham (1748–
1832), the English utilitarian philosopher and legal reformer, Spicer
argued that deterrence requires the certainty of equal punishments.

"If you don't punish everyone the same, the deterrent effect is
washed overboard, because anyone who thinks about the punishment—
though most won't even think about it—will figure that he's one of the
exceptions, one of those who will be treated more leniently. That's just
human nature. We now try to limit the discretion in death penalty cases
by using a list of aggravating and mitigating factors, but it's not eliminated. All we have done is channel the discretion into a different reservoir. And as long as there is discretion, there will be whimsical results and
the deterrent effect of the death penalty will be undermined."

Judge Spicer's last concern is a practical one. Death penalty cases are
usually about three times as long and as expensive as murder cases not
involving the death penalty. Also, the burden that a death penalty case
places on the jury is often not appreciated by the public. A long death
penalty case can cause a juror all sorts of family problems. Spicer uses the
term "fallout" to describe the practical problems that are caused by the
death penalty. He sums up his position succinctly:

"My own personal opinion is that the death penalty is inefficient,
whimsical, and very costly, and I think it reflects poorly upon a society
that imposes it. It's a simplistic solution to a very complex problem.
Unthinking reaction. Playing to emotions rather than reason. Frankly, I
don't think any civilized society is going to persevere if it relies primarily
upon it."

Judge Spicer has often wondered why rural counties like Adams
County don't seem to have as many death sentences as metropolitan
counties. Though the people of Adams County, he thinks, are generally

in favor of the death penalty, when they serve as jurors they rarely sentence a person to death. Spicer has wondered whether he is in part responsible for this paradoxical result.

"I sometimes wonder if I unconsciously reflect a negative attitude toward the death penalty and that is why Adams County juries rarely sentence anyone to death. This has been one of my closest concerns. So, in death penalty cases, including the Carr case, I go out of my way to be completely neutral. A judge has to be very careful."

Judges can properly perform their role, Judge Spicer believes, only if they conscientiously suppress their private views and biases for the sake of their public function. Members of the local community must help judges in this effort by treating them with the respect that the office deserves. In the main, the residents of Adams County act and behave in the requisite manner, says Spicer.

"The people of Adams County, in general, are not a demonstrative people. For instance, during the Carr case, I am sure that there was a lot of joking going on about what those women were doing, people joking privately with each other, friend to friend. But there was not much of a public reaction. And certainly people did not joke about it with me. That would have been improper, and most of the people around here know that. That's why, when I got this letter from this woman, it just astounded me. And I think it would have astounded most people in Adams County, to tell you the truth. Not because of what it said. Many people were probably saying similar things to each other. What astounded me was that this woman had the effrontery to direct the letter to me! Here, I'll show it to you. Take your time and read it."

> *Dear Judge Spicer,*
>
> *Reading the morning paper, [I saw] a recap of the event involving Stephen Roy Carr. Two things have been going through my mind and the minds of many Christians I've talked with. 1st, Our Lord destroyed an entire city because of homosexuality and tells us in Romans Chapter 1 how he feels about this sin. Innocent people are dying of AIDS because this sin has been allowed. 2nd, Why were[n't] indecent charges brought against Claudia Brenner? Are people allowed to run through the woods naked and indulge in a sin so terrible that even God turns on [it]? This country was founded on the Bible but we are all failing God by not keeping his laws. Would you have wanted your wife or children to have*

witnessed two women having sex? Any parent would feel like destroying such horrible people. Think about it. Has this man really committed such a terrible crime? Our Lord did just what he did. I do not believe in murder but I think it's time America wakes up and does something about homosexuals. The world is coming to a fast end just because people have let sin rule the laws. Mr. Carr was at church shortly before he eliminated sin. What was taught in that sermon? Maybe he felt he was doing just what the Lord did. When the Bible is used for oaths next time in court, stop and think, "Are the words contained therein really obeyed"?

Thank you for being a judge. I know it isn't easy but I know you do your best for all America.

[Name Withheld]

The letter came from a woman who lived in Fayetteville, Pennsylvania, a town just west of Michaux State Forest off of Route 30. Her references to God's destruction of Sodom and the verse from Romans declaring that practicing homosexuals deserve death implied that she felt Carr was only doing God's work when he shot Rebecca Wight and Claudia Brenner.

"Most people in Adams County would think that this kind of letter is clearly the wrong kind of thing to send to a judge. It's so unusual, but here it is. It says something about this case. It shows there was a lot of undercurrent out there about what Steve Carr had done."

The letter upset Judge Spicer, because he felt that local community sentiment, of whatever variety, should have no influence on how he resolved the legal issues that would arise in the Steve Carr case. Though some of these issues would require him to consult community sentiment, it would be the sentiment of the community of all Pennsylvanians, not just the people of Adams County. Of course, there was no easy and objective way for Spicer to discern the social attitudes of Pennsylvanians. It's arguable that his subjective feelings and prejudices would inevitably affect any such assessment and would thereby unavoidably introduce a fortuitous element into Carr's death penalty case. The fact that a judge wary of local sentiment and prejudice was going to preside over the case was itself a fortuitous event.

IV

In late May 1988, the stage was set and the roles were cast for the trial of Steve Carr. Roy Keefer, the Lutheran prosecutor, intended to go after

Carr with everything he had. He didn't believe in the value of the death penalty, yet he was purportedly seeking it for Carr on the basis of the law so that he could avoid the anxiety of making a Godlike decision. On the other side was Michael George, a champion of innocent defendants who was going to wage war on behalf of a man he'd "hesitate to get close to." Both attorneys were competitive, ambitious individuals. Presiding over the contest was the erudite Judge Oscar Spicer, who, despite his perception of life as a stream of chance events, was determined that the game be played fairly, in accordance with the rules and values of Pennsylvania. Ironically, not one of these three lawyers who would play pivotal roles in the Carr case was a firm supporter of the death penalty.

The Preliminary Hearing

I

As soon as Michael George accepted the job of defending Stephen Carr, he called Stanley R. "Skip" Gochenour, a private detective who worked out of Harrisburg and was one of the most experienced homicide defense investigators in southcentral Pennsylvania. George knew that in a death penalty case Judge Oscar Spicer would provide the defense with a publicly paid investigator, and he wanted his friend Gochenour for this role. "Skip's the only layperson I know," says George, "who can read a police report and then tell you what really happened. He can do that because he knows cops. He knows cops because he was once one."

In the early 1970s, Gochenour left a graduate program in criminal justice to join the Northern York County Regional Police Department so that he could gain some real-world knowledge of police investigations. However, about the time he was ready to return to school for his doctorate, the York County DA asked him if he would take over an independent investigation of a local criminal defense lawyer who was suspected of being a part of a burglary ring. A normal police investigation would have tipped off the lawyer.

"Soon after my investigation was complete, I got a call from a lawyer who was defending a Puerto Rican against a murder charge. The murder had taken place in a tavern. The police arrested this kid who had been in town only two days and charged him with it. Then I found out that there had been thirteen people at the bar at the time of the shooting and that the police had only interviewed four of them. It took me about a half an hour to locate the other nine witnesses by using the telephone book. The key inconsistency was the location of the Puerto Rican in the bar. There was a powder mark on the back of the victim's head at the point of the bullet's entry, about the size of a nickel, which meant that the shot had been fired from two or three inches. The killer had to have been right beside him. But, you see, the witnesses that I interviewed put the Puerto Rican thirty feet away. Based on the information that I had come up with, the charges against the Puerto Rican were dismissed and the guy who did it was arrested. That was my first homicide case and it started me on my career as a homicide defense investigator. Now, my office handles about one homicide case per month."

Gochenour, a short, stout man in his late thirties with reddish brown hair and a serious demeanor that contrasts sharply with his somewhat leprechaun-like appearance, has no qualms about his profession. In his view, the basic premise of the criminal justice system is the presumption of innocence. The state bears the burden of proof and the defendant has a right to a lawyer, a right that Gochenour believes evolved from the practice of medieval champions' fighting to the death to prove the innocence of those they defended. The idea that physical combat could decide who was telling the truth has been abandoned, but, according to Gochenour, the system is just as adversarial as it ever was. Lawyers and defense investigators are champions who fight with their minds, and a murder case is the ultimate form of intellectual combat.

The most famous homicide case that Gochenour ever worked on is the one that became the subject of Joseph Wambaugh's *Echoes in the Darkness*. William Bradfield and Jay Smith were convicted of killing Susan Reinart and her two children, but only Smith was sentenced to death. During the summer of 1988, as they tried to get Smith's conviction overturned, Gochenour and Smith's attorney, William Costopoulos, discovered that the police had hidden or misplaced evidence that was exculpatory for Smith.

"Well, this story about the police hiding evidence in the Smith case was just starting to come out about the time that Adams County was prosecuting Steve Carr," says Gochenour. "And guess what? A cop whose name had come up in the Smith case reappeared in the Carr case: John Holtz. He was a cop who had this uncanny ability to get confessions from defendants. Other people couldn't get a word out of a suspect. Holtz goes in, and fifteen minutes later he's got a confession. A real wonder boy. Well, my dealings with him in the Smith case made me immediately suspicious of how Holtz got Carr to confess. After Mike got the case, we went down to Adams County Prison to visit Carr on May 26. He was quite a sight. Long, shaggy hair. He really was a mountain man. First thing I told him was to cut all that shit off. At least he could look presentable. Well, it didn't do any good. Next time I saw him with all his hair cut off, I told him to grow it back. He had these weird bumps on his skull."

Gochenour explains that he and George were very careful during that first interview, because they didn't want to destroy the possibility that Carr could be a witness in his own defense. If Carr told them something in that first interview and they later confirmed that it was true, Carr couldn't testify differently on the stand. They could not knowingly let Carr commit perjury.

"I didn't ask him what happened," Gochenour states. "I asked him what he told the police. That's a very different question. If he later changes his story about the facts of the incident, that's fine, because during that interview he was only telling me what he told the police. I learn something about what happened and Steve is not locked into any particular story. Another thing, by asking Steve what he told the police, he doesn't have to defend himself to me. I don't want him to lie to me about what happened. I don't want that psychological barrier between Steve and me and I need to know what he told the police, anyway. And as Carr tells us what he told the police, I watch him closely. I ask him to tell it to me again. At some point, this guy is going to look at me while he's telling me what he told the cops and by his manner I'll know that this is where he's lying. This way I find out something about what happened without having Steve tell me what happened. Maybe it's not a lot, but it's something. That's the way you conduct that first interview. As I said, you're very careful."

During the interview with Gochenour and George, Carr went through his story of what he told the police three times. In the first version, Carr admitted that he saw the two women at Birch Run Shelter that Friday. They were both naked, but at first he thought one of them was a man. When he went to get water for his coffee from a nearby stream, he saw one naked person on top of another. While he was drinking his coffee, he saw the two naked people kissing each other and walking down to the creek holding hands and carrying towels. After a while, they returned to their tent. Then, the one he thought was a man went to the outhouse. It was at this point that Carr discovered that "he" was a "she." Later, after the women had packed up their things and left, Carr met them again at a trail intersection. Carr asked them if they were lost and told them he had a map. One of the women replied, "No, we're not lost, are you?"

Carr's second version of the morning's events was a bit more complicated: He claimed that the women had to have known that he was at the shelter. He had a campfire, he was making a lot of noise, and their tent was only a few yards from the wooden lean-to he occupied. Early in the morning, a naked woman left the tent and walked around the campsite. After she returned to the tent, Carr put more wood on his fire and looked through the open flap of their tent and saw one naked body on top of another. The same naked woman again left the tent, but was soon joined by another naked person whom Carr took to be a male. The naked couple kissed, walked around the area, went to the stream together, and then returned to the tent. A naked woman then went to the outhouse, and Carr masturbated behind the lean-to. On her way back to the tent, the woman talked to Carr for a few minutes.

After she left him, Carr went down near the tent, concealed himself, and looked in. He saw two females engaged in oral sex. Afterward, when the two females came out of the tent, Carr was behind the lean-to masturbating again. Then he saw the woman he had always thought was a female go into the woods to a place where she and he were in full view of each other. There, he saw her "going to the bathroom." Carr said "she showed me everything" while she was looking straight at him. After this, the women packed up their things. As they were taking down their tent, one of them looked right at Carr and pulled down her tank top, exposing her breasts. Then the women waved to Carr and said good-bye to him. Carr waited fifteen minutes and followed them. He met them at the intersection and asked them if they were lost. They responded that they were not.

Carr's third account of what he told the police focused more on his earlier life. He told George and Gochenour he had engaged in sexual intercourse with only two women in his entire life: when he was twelve years old, he had intercourse with a fifteen-year-old female; eight years later, he had sex with a woman who was staying over at his friend's house. In both enounters, the woman had initiated the sexual activity. When he saw what the women were doing that morning, he thought they were "putting on a show for him." He followed them, hoping that he would get another look at "the show."

Carr's three versions of what he told the police raised questions in the minds of George and Gochenour. Did the women do all the things that Carr claimed they did? Was the tent close enough to the shelter that the women had to have known that Carr was there, or, since Carr wasn't at first able to determine the sex of one of them, was it a considerable distance away?

Neither George nor Gochenour is willing to say explicitly whether Carr told them he had admitted to the police that he had shot Claudia Brenner and Rebecca Wight. They did indicate, however, that there were at least three possible scenarios of what Carr had said to the police about the shootings. The first was that Carr had told them it was a hunting accident: He saw a small deer standing in some mountain laurel. He first saw only the legs of the deer. Moving closer, he saw the head of the deer and fired several shots. He then heard girls screaming. Scared, he packed up and left the area.

The second scenario was basically the same as the first, with the addition that Carr had told the police that he couldn't tell them what really happened, because he was a fugitive.

It can be assumed that the following, third scenario was prompted by George's and Gochenour's unwillingness to believe that so many shots could be fired from a single-shot gun and two different people be hit so many times in a hunting accident. In reaction to their skepticism, Carr would only say that he'd told the police, "I think I shot them. I don't know why I did it." One of the females was sitting up against a tree and the other one was "eating her." "I heard a little voice that told me to shoot them now. I shot them, I shot, and I shot." Carr first shot the woman leaning against the tree, and then he shot the other female. "I saw them in my front sight each time I shot."

The women screamed, "That's enough!" and ran behind some mountain laurel. Carr could see them moving around. He then packed up and left the area. Afterward, he saw one of the women again. The "voice" told him to shoot her, but he couldn't do it. Later still, from behind a dirt pile, he observed the same woman looking at a map. He then headed toward Big Flat, an area of state land adjacent to Shippensburg Road.

"So there you have three scenarios of what Carr told the police about the shootings," Gochenour observes. "I can't tell you which, if any, of them Carr truly said [to the police], but even if I could, you still wouldn't know what the real truth was. Finding out what happened in a murder investigation is very difficult. Fifteen people look at a tin can and you get fifteen interpretations. Just imagine the different versions you can get when there's been a murder. So the bottom line was that we did not have much concrete information going into the preliminary hearing. All we had were Steve Carr and the newspaper accounts. Steve was talking to us, but he didn't trust us and what he was saying was inconsistent on some points and vague and ambiguous on others."

II

On June 13th, George filed a motion with Judge Spicer for an independent, publicly-paid, psychological examination of Carr's mental health. The exam would determine whether Carr was competent to stand trial and whether the defense would have expert testimony available if it decided to use a mental infirmity defense.

"You didn't have to be Sigmund Freud," George remarks, "to see that Carr was not your average person. I personally didn't think he was crazy, but that was not my call. So, I asked for the exam and I requested a specific psychiatrist—a guy by the name of Robert Sadoff. He was an expert on human violence, especially violence that had a sexual component to it."

Dr. Robert L. Sadoff, clinical professor of psychiatry at the University of Pennsylvania, is a nationally known forensic psychiatrist who has testified as an expert witness at criminal trials. He is the author of two books and many professional journal articles, including "Sexual Violence," which appeared in the *Bulletin of the New York Academy of Medicine* in 1986, and "Violence: Roots and Remedies: The Perspective of the Forensic Psychiatrist," which was published in the *Bulletin of the American Academy of Psychiatry and Law* in 1988. In these articles, Sadoff defends the role that psychiatrists play in criminal courtrooms and expresses his regret that the law often does not give forensic psychiatry the credibility that it deserves.

The next day, George prepared a letter to Dr. Sadoff in anticipation of a favorable ruling on his motion, but Judge Spicer surprised him. The judge agreed to pay for a psychological exam of Carr but turned down his request for Sadoff, whose fee was $200 per hour. Since George never sent or signed the letter, he today neither affirms nor denies the statements made therein. The letter may nonetheless throw light on what Carr was telling George and how the latter viewed Carr's crime and psychological health.

> Dear Dr. Sadoff:
>
> . . . [Carr] has resided in the mountains of Adams County near the Appalachian Trail. Over the majority of that time he lived in a hole in the ground. . . . Basically, he lived on whatever he could find from the ground or hunt. He also saved aluminum cans which he would turn in for money and thereafter buy food. He has indicated that he has a substantial drug problem including cocaine and methadone. I suspect that in addition to his hunting and can collecting, he was supporting his drug habit through theft and burglary. . . .
>
> . . . As he describes it, they [the victims] began teasing him and putting on a show for him. Thereafter, this display went on for the remainder of the afternoon. He claims they were dancing nude in the stream for him, that at various times they would come over and rip open their blouses and show their breasts in front of him; and, on at least one occasion, one woman stood in front of him, squatted down and urinated and defecated in front of him. He claims that they saw him and in fact knew that he was masturbating as he watched them.
>
> Mr. Carr claims that later in the evening, after he had followed the women for awhile, they again stopped [hiking] and began having physical involvement. He states that at some point, as the women were again putting a show on for him, he heard a voice in his head say "shoot them." Thereafter, he fired what appear to be eight (8) shots killing one of the

women and seriously injuring the other. For your information, from the beginning until the end of his contact with these women, he had his rifle with him.

Mr. Carr's appearance is obviously unattractive. It clearly reflects the serious mental and emotional problems which this individual suffers from. During the course of my conversation with him, Mr. Carr stated that "all I ever wanted out of life was just to be normal." When asked what normal meant, he claimed "you know just a job, any job, and a girlfriend." Thereafter he related that throughout his formative years, he was always referred to as "freak," couldn't get a girlfriend and no one would hire him. . . .

P.S. I neglected to mention above that the prison officials have informed me that they believe Mr. Carr to be suicidal. Also, they informed me that there have been incidents when Mr. Carr has woken up in the middle of the night screaming.

Whether this unsigned, unsent letter provides any insight into what happened on South Mountain is debatable. If it is even partially accurate, however, it suggests that a lonely, frustrated, psychologically disturbed man killed Wight and wounded Brenner.

Carr's psychological exam was important, because it could have a bearing on three legal issues: incompetency to stand trial, mental insanity, and diminished capacity. For Carr to be declared incompetent to stand trial, a psychiatrist would have to testify either that Carr did not understand the charges against him or that he could not help in the preparation of his defense.

In regard to insanity, Pennsylvania follows the M'Naghten Rule. A psychiatrist would have to testify that at the time of the shootings, Carr either did not know what he was doing or, if he did know what he was doing, did not know that it was wrong. For George to plead that Carr fit this narrow definition of insanity, Carr would have to admit that he pulled the trigger. In June, George was not prepared to make any such concession.

Diminished capacity is a partial excuse that reduces but does not eliminate culpability. In some states, defendants in any type of criminal prosecution can present evidence that they have a diminished capacity to conform their conduct to the law. Diminished capacity in Pennsylvania, however, is confined to cases of first-degree murder and the excuse is much narrower than in some other states. The rule in Pennsylvania is that a judge should allow into evidence psychological testimony regarding a homicide defendant's diminished capacity only if it is directly relevant to whether the defendant could intentionally or deliberately kill someone. Intention and premeditation are necessary mental elements that the commonwealth has to prove in every case of first-degree murder. Accordingly, if a judge lets this kind of testimony into a trial and the jury believes that the testimony establishes that the defendant did not have the mental capacity necessary to kill someone "intentionally" and/or with "premeditation," the jury can return a verdict of third-degree murder. Therefore, in Pennsylvania, though diminished capacity is often referred to as an excuse, in reality it's another way of saying that the commonwealth did not prove all that it had to prove to get a first-degree murder conviction.

"The results of the psychological exam would have a direct bearing on our strategy," George explains. "The 'right' kind of results would give us more options; the 'wrong' kind would reduce the number of cards in our hand and make it more likely that Carr would not escape the death penalty. That's why I was a little disappointed with the judge's decision to go with the local psychiatrist. Sadoff was no hired gun, but he was generally sympathetic to the idea that mental and physical illness should have a role in determining criminal responsibility. The mentally ill should not be held to the same standard as the mentally healthy—that was his approach. He also had a national reputation. That might have been very important with a jury. Just because some psychiatrist testifies that Carr was insane or didn't intend to kill anyone, doesn't mean that a jury has to believe it. But, at $200 per hour, Sadoff was too expensive. A local psychiatrist by the name of Larry Allen was going to conduct the exam. I wasn't very happy about that, but Judge Spicer did say that if Allen recommended that Carr should get an additional exam, he would be open to that request."

III

The preliminary hearing, District Justice Harold Deardorff presiding, that would decide whether there was enough evidence to hand Carr over for trial began about 1:30 P.M. on June 23rd in the new Adams County Courthouse on Baltimore Street, one block south of Lincoln Square, in

Gettysburg. This large, modern brick building, which opened its doors in 1979, is adjacent to the old Adams County Courthouse, which is listed in the National Register of Historic Places. Long ago, hundreds of men had died in the old courthouse, when it was turned into a hospital after the bloody Battle of Gettysburg. In this same building, a jury in 1964 convicted Elmo Smith of first-degree murder and sentenced him to die in the state's electric chair. Smith was the last person to be executed in Pennsylvania before the 1966 U.S. Supreme Court decision that established a national moratorium on the death penalty. The Supreme Court reauthorized the death penalty in *Gregg v. Georgia* in 1976, and in 1988 it was possible that Steve Carr would be the first person executed in Pennsylvania since Smith.

Certain that there was more than enough evidence to hand the case over for trial, Keefer used the hearing to undercut Carr's hunting-accident version of the homicide and to showcase his star witness: Brenner. On direct examination by Keefer, Trooper Holtz testified that during his interrogation, Carr admitted that he owned a rifle, a knife, and a pair of sunglasses but claimed that all these items were stolen from him on May 13th while he was napping on the Appalachian Trail. Holtz said he then told Carr that he had some good news and some bad news for him. The police had recovered these items for him, but they had been recovered at the scene of a murder. At this point, Holtz testified, Carr started to cry, and he cried even more when he was told that one of the victims lived. A few minutes later, Carr admitted that he accidentally shot the women, Holtz said. Carr shot at a deer, heard the girls scream, got scared, ran away, and hid the gun under a tree stump.

"That was more or less the substance of the confession itself," Keefer reports. "I then asked Holtz about a conversation that he had with Carr later that day after they had gone out and picked up the gun."

> Keefer: During the further course of your contact with Mr. Carr that day, did he make a later statement? Specifically, did he make a statement during the time of transportation?
>
> Holtz: He did.
>
> Keefer: What was that statement, please?
>
> Holtz: At this time Mr. Carr was asked if he really saw the girls kissing. Carr said the girls were lesbians. Carr said after he

set up his camp at the creek, he saw the girls. They were engaged in a lesbian act, Carr said, and I quote, "They were eating each other."

Keefer: Did he mention anything about deer during that statement?

Holtz: No, sir.

"I ended my direct examination of Holtz in that way to show that Carr's story of a hunting accident was simply ridiculous," explains Keefer. "He had to have known he was shooting at two women, because he said he saw them engaged in sexual activity. I did the same thing with Trooper Blevins. I asked him whether he had ever determined whether there was a clear line of fire from where the eight spent shell casings were discovered at the scene of the shooting to the place where the two women had been shot."

Blevins: Yes, there was a clear sight.

Keefer: Was that sight through bushes, overtop of bushes, or primarily underneath the bushes?

Blevins: More underneath than anything. It's a very thick laurel thicket, but from where I determined that the shots were fired, [to] where the victims were, there's a picture window in a manner of speaking, through that thicket, that they would have been very visible. . . .

Keefer: Would it be fair to say that the entire area is no more than about two feet off the ground?

Blevins: The entire area is no more than, if you were to fire higher than two feet you would probably hit thicket. Two feet would be the maximum.

Keefer: Trooper Blevins, do you know of any two-feet-tall deer?

Blevins: None that I am aware of.

Blevins's testimony underscored the incredible aspects of Carr's version of the incident.

Keefer knew that George, during his cross-examination of Brenner, would ask questions about her relationship to Wight and about their activities on the morning and afternoon of the shootings. He decided not to object to almost any question that George might ask, because he didn't want it to look as if the prosecution was hiding anything or that the women had done anything wrong or illegal. Keefer was reasonably confident that Brenner could handle the pressure of talking about the personal and intimate aspects of her relationship and conduct in open court, with the press and everyone else there. He nevertheless tried to help her out on direct examination, by asking her open-ended questions that let her address these sensitive issues in her own way, before George cross-examined her.

> Keefer: At some point, Claudia, did you and Rebecca make plans to come here to Adams County in the spring of this year?
>
> Brenner: About a year and a few months ago, Rebecca and I became involved in a relationship that included a romantic component, a sexual component and an interpersonal friendship component, and from last March until her death we were involved in that kind of intimate relationship. We were involved in a lesbian relationship where we kept in touch throughout my journey to Israel and upon my return.

In a similar way, Keefer's questions gave Brenner an opportunity to explain that she and Wight were naked on the morning of the shootings only because they thought no one else was around. They put on clothes as soon as they found out otherwise.

The toughest part of Brenner's testimony dealt with the shootings, but even in describing these she kept her composure. When they set up their camp by Rocky Knob Run, the women thought they were completely alone in an out-of-the-way area of Michaux State Forest. Keefer asked Brenner what happened next.

> Brenner: What happened was when we were laying down, and as I described to you, we were involved in a relationship together, so we were affectionate together. There was talking. There was laughing. There was kissing. There was playfulness. There was making-love activity. There was sexual activity and it was very enjoyable. There was sun

shining and the stream beside the campsite. It was as if any couple was enjoying an afternoon together by a stream.

"What Claudia was trying to do," Keefer notes, "was to put the lesbian sexual activity into a context that would not seem so foreign. The two women were like any other couple enjoying an afternoon by a stream. That's why I say that Claudia did such an excellent job on the stand. She could talk about her relationship with Rebecca in a way that made it seem natural, nothing out of the ordinary. I thought this was going to be a big asset with the jury. So I wanted to make sure that Mike George knew what he was going to be up against at trial. That's what I mean when I say I wanted to use the preliminary hearing to showcase Claudia."

According to Keefer, George tried to fluster Brenner, but she answered his questions without hesitation or embarrassment, even the one concerning whether she and Rebecca were putting on a show for Carr, a question that actually upset Brenner badly. From Keefer's perspective, there were two ways to interpret George's purpose in questioning whether the women had teased Carr. One interpretation was that the defense was trying to turn the local media and community against the victims by suggesting that they were outwardly teasing Carr with their sexual orientation. If in fact that was what George and Gochenour were attempting to do, Keefer thought that it constituted unethical professional conduct. A defense attorney should not intentionally ask questions that create in the public's mind false impressions of the victims. Keefer readily admits, however, that if Carr told George that the women teased him, he had the duty to ask such questions, even if there was little or no reason to believe that any teasing had taken place. The question of whether this cross-examination was unethical conduct or professional duty turned completely on what a suspected murderer told his lawyer, even if what he told him was an obvious lie.

"I think if Carr told George that the women teased him, he was obviously lying, but then George would have had the right to test these waters, if you will, with that line of questioning. He would have to test those waters to see if they would be a fertile avenue for the defense at the trial, to see if it made any sense to challenge Claudia's testimony by putting Carr himself on the stand. Of course, Claudia's performance on the stand took that option away from the defense. Like I said before, she did a great job."

IV

Knowing that a trial in the Carr case was a foregone conclusion, George tried to probe the strength of the prosecution's case during the preliminary hearing. The key question was whether he could destroy or undermine Brenner's credibility.

"On my cross-examination, I was going to press Brenner on whatever she had already admitted to on direct examination. I wanted to get her full story on the record. That meant a full story as to how many times the women were naked and how many times they were engaged in lesbian sex. I wanted the graphic details. All of them."

George wanted these graphic details because they might be relevant to the defense of provocation. The classic case of provocation is a man's finding his wife in bed with another man. The theory is that the husband is so overcome with emotion and passion that he is no longer capable of cool reflection when he pulls out his gun and kills the lover. Instead, the victim is partly to blame, because he is doing something that he shouldn't have been doing—sleeping with the guy's wife. When the law looks at this kind of case, it says that the husband has done something wrong, but the crime committed is voluntary manslaughter, not first-degree murder.

"With a voluntary manslaughter conviction," George points out, "there wouldn't be any death penalty. At most, the husband would get ten years. With good behavior, he'd probably get paroled in five. So, you see, provocation doesn't get a person off the hook completely. It only takes him off a big hook and puts him on a smaller one."

If the provocation argument was going to work at all, Brenner and Wight had to appear partly responsible for what had happened. As cruel as it sounds, George had to point the finger at Brenner and say, at least indirectly, "It's your fault. You did it to yourself." He began with the public nudity.

George: The morning of May 13th, you say that you got up at sunrise . . . and you were the first one out of the tent?

Brenner: Correct. I just went out to go to the bathroom and went right back inside of the tent.

George:	And you had no clothing on; correct?
Brenner:	Correct.
	. . .
George:	At some point then Rebecca got up and left the tent to go to the outhouse?
Brenner:	Right, correct.
George:	At this point Rebecca again didn't have any clothing on?
Brenner:	Correct. We completely believed we were alone until the point when Rebecca came upon the defendant.
George:	When she went up to the outhouse, how long was she up there?
Brenner:	Four or five minutes maybe. A few minutes.
George:	Were you inside or outside the tent?
Brenner:	I think I had started to boil water on the stove outside the tent.
George:	Again you were naked?
Brenner:	Right.
	. . .
George:	When she came back from going to the outhouse she did not have any clothing on; correct?
Brenner:	Correct. Sneakers.
George:	To the best of your knowledge, while she was speaking with this person, she was completely naked?
Brenner:	Correct.

George returned to the issue of nudity three times in his cross-examination, because he didn't think many women living in Adams County would walk around a campsite naked, even if they thought they were all alone in the woods. He hoped that Brenner's testimony left the impression that something was wrong with these two women.

For the same reason, George could not ignore Brenner's and Wight's sexual orientation. "I had to get it on the record," he explains, "and I wanted it to look like these two women were bold with their lesbianism, that they didn't hide their lesbianism from anybody, including my client. The more sexually reckless the women appeared, the better for Carr."

George: Inside the tent, I assume that you and your friend were being intimate again?

Brenner: Inside the tent prior to Rebecca going to the outhouse, we didn't see anyone and we were being intimate.

George: Kissing, rolling over each other, making love?

Brenner: The things that people who are in love do with each other.

            . . .

George: After she came back from the outhouse, it is true that you two began fondling each other?

Brenner: I believe that at some point during the rest of the morning, which was about two hours long, there were times when we embraced or kissed as people who love each other do. . . .

George: After she had informed you that there was somebody else present, you still went on, as you say, caring for each other, fondling each other, kissing each other?

Brenner: I would say we had breakfast and we were in the area of the campsite for another several hours and proceeded with our lives. Which sometimes included embracing and kissing, which didn't mean we were laying outside of the tent together.

George: Kissing, embracing, were you feeling each other?

Brenner: Excuse me?

George: Were you feeling each other?

Brenner: Feeling?

George: With hands, yes.

Brenner: Not to any great extent at that point.

George: Were you aware that my client was in the area at this point?

Brenner: I believed him to be minding his own business in his lean-to.

The specific words George used to ask Brenner questions coincided with his purpose. While Brenner described the sexual activity generally and in an uplifting sort of way—as "the things that people who are in love do with each other"—George tried to get her to accept more specific, less ethereal descriptions, repeatedly asking whether the two women had been "fondling" or "feeling" each other. Brenner, of course, resisted George's efforts to deromanticize the two women's intimate activities on the morning of the shootings.

George notes an interesting discrepancy between Brenner's and Carr's versions of what happened that morning. Brenner admitted that some sort of sexual activity had occurred in the tent before Wight went to the outhouse, but Carr said that he had also observed the two women engaged in sexual activity after Wight had returned.

"An interesting discrepancy. Who's telling the truth, I don't know. I will say, however, that at the time of the preliminary hearing, it occurred to me that if Brenner had testified that the two women had sex at a time when she admitted that she knew Carr was there, then people might really begin to wonder about these two women. In other words, if the women were making love after the outhouse visit, Brenner might have had a motive to lie about it. It would not be in her interest to present herself as a person who would engage in sex while some person she described as strange and creepy was wandering around the campsite."

George agrees that Carr could have lied about when the sexual activity took place but doubts that Carr would have known that he could marginally improve his lawyer's ability to argue provocation by placing the sexual activity after the outhouse visit, instead of before. According to George, that kind of thinking was simply beyond Carr. Carr had a motive to lie but not the wits to know how to. "Like I said," George concludes, "I can't see it. I tend to believe Carr. I tend to think the women had sex after Rebecca went to the outhouse, after the women knew Carr was hanging around."

Apart from whether the women engaged in sexual activity after the outhouse visit, Brenner did concede in her testimony that she and Wight were publicly kissing and embracing each other after they knew of Carr's presence.

"Now maybe Brenner and Wight knew that Carr was there prior to this time. That's a separate question," says George. "But why would they be kissing and fondling each other in front of Carr? I don't want to seem like a prude, but would you do such things in front of some guy who looked like a mountain man? So why did they act that way? I was glad that Brenner was not shy about describing what she and her lesbian friend were doing that morning. My goal, quite frankly, was to put the two women into a poor light. Brenner made my job easier because she was a proud advocate of lesbianism. I tried to do the same thing in regard to what the women were doing in the afternoon."

George: When you got to the second campsite, was it at that point that you undressed again?

Brenner: We had something to eat. We sat by the campfire. We talked. We made iced tea. We drank cold water. . . .

George: At some point you undressed, correct?

Brenner: At some point my shorts came off and I was not fully dressed.

George: How about Rebecca?

Brenner: She was fully dressed, except for her sneakers, the entire time at the campsite. At the second—

George: She was fully dressed while she was shot?

Brenner: Correct. With the exception of her sneakers.

George: Your shorts came off. She was fully dressed.

Brenner: Correct.

George: What actually were you doing?

Brenner: As I described to Mr. Keefer, we were engaged in making love. There was some oral sex involved. There was kissing. There was rolling around playfully and there was affection connected with making love.

George: Would you define oral sex for me?

Brenner: Oral sex is when one person has their mouth on someone else's genitals.

George: And Rebecca had her mouth on your genitals?

Brenner: Correct.

George: In fact, isn't that when the shots took place?

Brenner: To be perfectly honest with you, I am not certain if her mouth was on my body when the shots took place, but there was—that activity was shortly prior to the shots.

According to George, Brenner "didn't want to give the slightest impression to anyone that she had done anything that she was ashamed of. So she laid it all out there." But George doubts whether Brenner considered how what she was saying would be perceived by the people of Adams County, the people who would serve as jurors in the upcoming trial. In George's opinion, "the great majority of Adams County folk would be disturbed, if not disgusted, by what they heard at the preliminary hearing."

It's possible that Brenner's testimony helped George establish a defense that Carr didn't deserve. That was not Brenner's intention, of course, but the criminal justice system at times makes victims pay a price in this way for telling the whole truth.

From a legal point of view, Carr's claim of provocation would have a better chance if the women had actually done something to him. Accordingly, George asked Brenner whether any teasing had taken place. Because of what Carr had told him, George was very curious as to what Brenner would say.

George: At some point, did either you or your friend lift your shirt and sort of show?

Brenner: No.

George: No?

Brenner: No, absolutely not.

. . .

George: Where did you urinate at?

Brenner: Just about the same place I did the first time, which was just in the opposite direction of the lean-to in the brush a little ways.

George: At any time after you put your clothing on until you left, did you undress in any way?

Brenner: I don't think so. I think at one point when I was lying down I might have let my stomach get the sun's rays, but I didn't take off my shirt.

. . .

George: At any point during that afternoon, to your knowledge, did either you or Rebecca put on a show for my client?

Brenner:	No.
George:	At any time during that day did you, to the best of your knowledge, or Rebecca intentionally tease my client?
Brenner:	No.
George:	At any point during that entire day did either you or, to the best of your knowledge, Rebecca purposely reveal any part of your body to my client?
Brenner:	No.

Brenner's denial that she and Wight had teased Carr in any way created another potential conflict of fact about what had happened on South Mountain. Carr said some teasing had occurred; Brenner said the opposite. It seemed that one of the two was lying.

"To this day I don't know for sure which one is telling the truth," George reflects. "There are only two people alive who know what happened up there on that Mountain—Brenner and Carr. I don't know which one is lying, but I do have my suspicions. In any case, by asking those questions about nudity, lesbianism, and the 'show' at the preliminary hearing, I was planting a seed, a suggestion in the mind of the prosecution and the public. I gave the prosecution something to worry about and the public something to think about. Of course, my ultimate goal is to affect the jury, and the prosecution knows that. Keefer has to start wondering whether people on the jury will have already made up their mind from the press reports of the preliminary hearing that, for example, the two women had teased Carr."

George describes his tactic as a form of "posturing" or "bluffing." He insists that in homicide cases, both the defense and the prosecution engage in this kind of activity and it is perfectly justifiable.

"That's why we had to get all the steamy facts of what had happened up on South Mountain out before the public. Sort of let what happened simmer in the public's imagination. In a way, we wanted to get the local folks talking more about the lesbianism than the murder. The general strategy was to shape public opinion in such a way that we would have a better chance that the jury would take our claim of provocation seriously. Some folks might think that this kind of tactic is not right. That I'm misleading the court and the public. But you have got to remember that I'm only asking questions. What people do with these questions is something I'm not responsible for. And you can't forget that this was a death penalty case. I had to do everything in my power to save this guy's life. I had to do everything short of going over the line. And that I did not do. I did not knowingly introduce perjured testimony. Maybe Brenner and Wight did tease Carr. To this day, I still don't know for sure. So why can't I ask Brenner if she teased Carr? Especially if it's going to save Carr's life?"

V

At the hearing, George also explored whether there was a chance that Carr's confession could be thrown out on the ground that it had been obtained in violation of Carr's Sixth Amendment right to a lawyer.

"The way it is now," George observes, "if police officers interrogate a suspect and get information proving that he did it, as they did in the Carr case, then later, perhaps at a preliminary hearing, it's the police officer's word against the defendant's about whether or not the defendant had asked to see a lawyer during the interrogation. In my experience, when that question comes up, cops are going to say, 'No,' and the defendant will say, 'Yes.' I've seen this dozens of times. Then it's the old question— who are you going to believe, the police or a murderer? At that point, the cards are really stacked against the defendant. Maybe the defendant's right to an attorney *was* violated—you don't know—but the evidence shows pretty clearly that he did the crime, and knowing that the guy is guilty makes it a lot easier for most people to just assume that the police are telling the truth and that the suspect never asked for a lawyer. A defense lawyer has to fight this kind of reasoning all the time."

Carr had told George and Gochenour that he had asked for a lawyer two or three times during his interrogation but the police hadn't given him one. George didn't know whether he was telling the truth, but he did know that Carr had been through Florida's criminal justice system three separate times. Somewhere along the line, according to George, he certainly should have learned that a defendant should never talk to the police without a lawyer present. Yet, after his arrest in Pennsylvania, he purportedly didn't ask for a lawyer, not even after he knew he was a suspect in a murder investigation. In these circumstances, George and Gochenour had to consider the possibility of a bad cop. The cop they were suspicious of was Holtz.

"On direct examination," George reports, "I noticed that Holtz was referring to some pieces of paper. So, when I stood up to cross-examine him, I asked if I could read what he was referring to. Keefer agreed and gave me a copy. It was Holtz's police report of the confession itself. That was my first look at the report, right there in the courtroom."

George carefully read the report before he asked Holtz a series of questions that included repeated references to whether Carr had asked to see an attorney. By going back again and again to this question, George was indirectly attacking Holtz's credibility. He then focused on why Carr had never signed a written confession or a formal statement and why the confession hadn't been taped. "Why not?"—was the sort of impression George wanted to leave.

George:	Officer, at 12:04, you advised my client of his Miranda rights. Was this recorded in any fashion? Tape recorder?
Holtz:	No, sir.
George:	Video camera?
Holtz:	No.
	. . .
George:	After my client gave you the statement which you read here today, did you show that statement to him?
Holtz:	No.
George:	Did he make any handwritten statement in his own writing?
Holtz:	No.
George:	Did you request him to sign at the bottom of that statement that that in fact was his testimony?
Holtz:	No.
	. . .
George:	Was what was said at the Carlisle Barracks recorded, copied, preserved in any other way outside of what you and Corporal O'Brien wrote down in your notes?
Holtz:	Just that and our recollection.
George:	And your recollection?
Holtz:	Yes.

George: Were any notes kept during that period [of transporta-
          tion to and from the gun]?

Holtz: No.
          . . .

George: Over your fourteen years as an investigator, have you
          attended any seminars on interrogation?

Holtz: Yes.
          . . .

George: At these seminars, are matters discussed such as taking of
          notes while conducting an interview or interrogation?

Holtz: Note taking, yes.
          . . .

George: Allowing the alleged defendant to read his statement after
          he's made it?

Holtz: If you take a formal statement from him, yes, you would
          ask him to read it and sign it.

George: This isn't a formal statement?

Holtz: Certainly not.

George: Did you ever take a formal statement from my client?

Holtz: No.

George: I have no further questions.

George's cross-examination of Holtz left an impression that the full truth
about whether the police had respected Carr's right to an attorney had
not come out at the preliminary hearing.

Holtz's testimony on direct examination indicated that he had tricked
Carr into inadvertently undermining his story that the incident had been
a hunting accident. During cross-examination, George thought he saw an
opening to help substantiate Carr's version of the shootings.

"You see, Holtz had testified that he had asked Carr if he had really
seen the girls kissing and that Carr had said he had seen more than that.
The prosecution assumed that Carr was saying that he saw the women
engaged in oral sex at the time of the shootings, but that's not exactly
what Carr said. He said after he set up his camp. Now Carr had already
told us that he had seen the women engaged in sexual activity in the

morning. So, I tried to get Holtz to admit that maybe Carr was talking about what he had seen in the morning. He set up his camp in the morning, then he saw the women. If Holtz would admit that maybe Carr was talking about what he saw in the morning, then it became more plausible that Carr had shot the women in a hunting accident. But Holtz saw immediately what I was trying to do. We went around and around on the issue."

George: Officer, that exchange which I just mentioned about seeing the girls kissing, seeing the girls making out, to the best of your recall, that was an exchange relating to what occurred on the morning of May 13th and not in the evening of May 13th?

Holtz: Not at all. Not at all. I asked Carr, "Now tell me did you really see the girls kissing?" He began to laugh and he said that he did. That was after he set up his camp along the creek. Now you have to remember in the morning he did not set up any camp along the creek. He was at the Birch Run Shelter. He told us after he shot what he thought were deer, he went back to his camp which was set up along the creek, packed up his stuff and left. When he made that statement, there was no doubt in my mind [what] he was talking about. He saw the girls engaged in a lesbian act and that's when he shot them.

George: Officer, did he say what camp he was at, or did he just use the word "camp"?

Holtz: "Camp next to the creek" is what he used.

George: I believe there was testimony [that] there's a creek along both areas?

Holtz: You remember what he said now, he went back to his campsite and picked up his stuff. He was camped next to the creek. When he was at Birch Run he was in the shelter itself. I believe the testimony was [that] there was a creek and that was a distance away at the bottom of the hill at the Birch Run center. . . .

George:	Officer, you asked him if the girls were really kissing, and you were referring, at least from what I understand, to what was going on that evening. Where in your report prior to that does it say that my client said those girls were kissing on that evening?
Holtz:	It doesn't say they were kissing that evening.
George:	That was just a general, "Did you really see the girls kissing?"
Holtz:	That was a statement I made to him, a question I was going [to use] to get in[to] what happened that evening, and he made it very easy for me. I said, "Did you—tell me the truth, did you really see the girls kissing?" He went into [it] much further. He said he saw much more than them kissing.
George:	When you asked that question, what time period were you referring to that the girls were kissing?
Holtz:	I just asked that question to start the conversation again. I didn't mention any time period. I am just telling you what was said and his reply.

"As you can see," George recalls, "Holtz and I exhausted the subject of what Carr meant when he said what he said. You can take a look at the paragraph in Holtz's report yourself. Here it is."

After CARR was arraigned at District Magistrate DEARDORFF'S office, he was transported to the Gettysburg Station. During this trip, CARR was asked if he really saw the girls kissing. CARR said the girls were lesbians. CARR said after he set up his camp at the creek, he saw the girls. They were engaged in a lesbian act. CARR said, "They were eating each other." It should be noted that according to the surviving victim, at the time of the shooting, both of the victims were laying down. The surviving victim said she was naked from the waist down and WIGHT had her head resting on the surviving victim's thigh. CARR also said he knew the police were looking for him. He heard that the police were showing his photograph to people last Tuesday (05/17/88) and he decided to leave the area. It should be noted that CARR'S identity did not become known to the police until Friday, 05/20/88.

"Interpreting this language can be pretty subjective," George continues. "At a minimum, it goes to show how important one little line in a police report can be in a murder case. Maybe all that Carr meant, when he told Holtz that he saw the women engaged in more than kissing, was that he had seen the women having sex in their tent on the morning of May 13th. You can decide for yourself."

At the conclusion of the hearing, District Justice Deardorff denied bail for Carr and ruled that the commonwealth could proceed to trial on all the charges. The hearing was adjourned at about 4:15 P.M.

The Suppression Hearing

I

July 1–3, 1988, marked the 125th anniversary of the Battle of Gettysburg. The National Park Service, the people of Gettysburg, promoters, and the many visitors who came for the commemorative events celebrated the occasion with fanfare. There was a large reenactment of Pickett's Charge, not on the battlefield itself, which is considered sacred ground by the Park Service, but on a nearby farm, so that the reenacters would not in any way insult those who had died in 1863. There were also lectures and demonstrations of what military life was like during the Civil War. One of the more memorable events was the relighting of the Eternal Light Peace Memorial, located about a mile north of Gettysburg. In 1938, Franklin Delano Roosevelt had lit a gas flame and, along with eighteen hundred Civil War veterans, dedicated the memorial to "Peace Eternal in a Nation United." In the 1970s, the National Park Service had converted the gas light to an electric one. Realizing its mistake, the Park Service relit the original gas light at the 125th anniversary of the battle.

Soon after the celebration was over, Defense Attorney Michael George filed a motion with Judge Oscar Spicer to confine Dr. Larry Allen's psychological examination to the question of Steve Carr's competency. In the motion, George claimed that Carr "is substantially unable to understand the nature or object of the proceedings against him and is unable to participate and assist in his defense" and argued that Spicer ought to confine Allen's exam to the incompetency issue. Allen would be facing a potential conflict of interest, George reasoned, if he were both the defense's expert in determining Carr's state of mind at the time of the shootings and the court's expert in determining Carr's competency to stand trial. George explains what he intended to accomplish with his motion:

"The idea was to figure out a way to dump the local psychiatrist. Because of information that Skip Gochenour had picked up through prison scuttlebutt, we didn't expect to get a report out of Allen that would help Steve. It wasn't that I really thought that Carr was mentally incompetent to stand trial, but I'm not an expert. And by requesting that incompetency hearing, I had a reason to ask Judge Spicer to confine Allen's job to the incompetency issue, letting us then ask for another psychiatrist to figure out Carr's mental state at the time of the shooting. That was the real exam that we were interested in. The other one was just a dodge, a maneuver to get rid of Allen."

Judge Spicer was not fooled, however. He granted the incompetency hearing but refused the request for an appointment of a court expert. It was the defense's job, not the court's, to find out whether Carr was mentally incompetent. At the upcoming hearing, George would have to "prove incompetency by clear and convincing evidence." If the local psychiatrist testified in a way that made it impossible for the defense to meet this burden, that was not Spicer's concern.

"We didn't pull it off," Gochenour admits. "Spicer saw through what we were trying to do. But he's also the kind of guy who would have sat there and smiled and said, 'Nice try.' "

II

Whenever George talked to a reporter about the Carr case, he always asked for a copy of the story, so that he could keep track of whether the slant that he was trying to put on the case was getting out to the local community. One reporter covering the Carr case attached a note to a news article he passed along to George.

Mr. George:

Here is a copy of the story that you requested. You were asking after the hearing last week if we were going to include the lesbian aspect in our story. As you can see, we decided it was an important part of the case and used it accordingly. If you disagree with how we covered the case, I'd be happy to hear from you. . . . At any rate, thanks for your help.

The story quoted George as saying, "I certainly think that provocation can take many different forms" and concluded that "the lesbian relationship will become an integral part of the case."

"You see," George comments, "that last statement is not my statement. I never said that lesbianism would become an integral part of the case. That's the reporter's conclusion, not mine. So, do you see how the system works? The reporter wants a story, I want to shape the story. The newspaper wants to sell newspapers; I give the reporter something that sells, but I give him something that sells in a way that helps my client down the road. On his own, the reporter adds his own conclusions. [Prosecutor Roy] Keefer reads the story and he's got to wonder what I got. Do I have something or am I bluffing? This sort of posturing isn't like filing legal motions or briefs, but it too is a part of what a defense lawyer does. He uses the press to affect how his client is perceived and how the prosecutor looks at the case."

George received a letter harshly critical of his tactic of manipulating the press to his client's advantage:

Mr. George:

I have read . . . of your plan to make the lesbian relationship of Stephen Roy Clark's [sic] victims an integral part of your defense of him, and I want you to know I consider such tactics reprehensible. . . .

Raising the issue of provocation at all in a brutal crime like this is just as sleazy and Neanderthal a tactic as it used to be in defending rapists. It is at least a mark of the growth of our legal system and our consciousness that such tactics are seldom used nowadays by intelligent and responsible lawyers.

Your plan to victimize Brenner because your client reacted like a mad animal to her love for another woman leaves me wondering about your own motives. You may be telling yourself (and others who ask you why you're doing it) that you're just giving Mr. Carr the best possible de-

fense, to which he is entitled under the law. Could your action be, instead,
an expression of and a rationalization for your own homophobia? . . .

"This letter," George explains, "indicates the kind of visceral reaction a defense lawyer has to put up with. No one with a thin skin should get into this business. You're often perceived to be as bad as the guy you're defending. These people compared what I was doing in the Carr case to what lawyers do in rape cases. Well, I was once defending a guy accused of rape and someone anonymously sent me a naked doll with pins stuck into it: one where the doll's heart was, one in the groin area, and one in the side, I guess where the liver is. Can you believe it? It was a damn voodoo doll and the clear implication was that whoever sent that doll thought I should be dead. This is the kind of stuff you get into as a defense attorney. You got a wife and kids and here's some guy threatening you only because you're doing your job."

III

On July 14th, Gochenour met again with Carr at the Adams County Prison. Carr told him he went back to find the women in the afternoon, because he thought he could "get something off of them." Since in the morning one of them had stood there naked "as if it were nothing," he felt they might be receptive to his sexual advances. If not, he resolved "to have them one way or the other." But when he arrived at the women's campsite, he heard "a voice say 'kill them, kill them now.'" At first the voice was faint, but then it got stronger and stronger. Carr thought to himself, "What is going on?" His head started pounding and the voice got louder and louder. He had heard such voices before, when he was high on cocaine and committing burglaries in Florida. A voice would tell him to go in and take all he wanted. At the campsite, Carr heard such a voice, but he couldn't remember picking up his gun and shooting the women, and he did not know why he shot the women.

Carr also told Gochenour that he had been raped twice in Florida prisons. In one instance, several inmates made him perform oral sex on them and laughed at him afterward. He was then sent to the O Unit, a section of the prison that Carr said was reserved for homosexuals. There he was raped again by three other prisoners. Carr also recalled an altercation outside of prison. He approached a couple of prostitutes and they beat him up. This image flashed through his mind right before he shot Rebecca Wight and Claudia Brenner at the campsite.

Gochenour's July 14th interview did not clarify why Carr shot the women. Did the prison rapes lend any credence to Keefer's view that the shootings were a homophobic hate crime, or did Carr's statement that he wanted to have sex with the women indicate that the shootings were a sex crime? These different interpretations of the crime had a common denominator: an association in Carr's mind of sex with violence. Men had raped him, and women had beaten him. Both experiences could lead to a depraved outlook on human sexuality: one compatible with the possibility that the image of the two prostitutes flashed through Carr's mind when he shot Brenner and Wight. His rifle—itself an instrument of violence—perhaps functioned as an extension of his sexuality.

IV

Dr. Allen's first interview with Carr, which potentially could have uncovered the motive of Carr's crime, was on July 19th. Gochenour arrived at the prison at the scheduled time of 9:00 A.M., but Allen didn't show up until 10:30.

Hiding his irritation, Gochenour quickly briefed the psychiatrist, telling him that Carr believed that the women knew he was there from the beginning of the morning, while Brenner claimed that they were not aware of him until Wight came back from the outhouse. Carr would not describe in any detail what happened at the time of the shootings, and refused to say why he shot the women. He trusted no one, not even the members of the defense team. Even with plenty of time at his disposal, Dr. Allen would probably have had difficulty establishing rapport with Carr. As it was, Allen was constantly looking at his watch and seemed to be a man in a hurry.

At about 10:40 A.M., an unhappy Carr was brought into the room. He sat down, pulled out a cigarette, and lit it while Dr. Allen introduced himself and the other people in the room. "When Allen saw the cigarette," Gochenour recollects, "he told Carr to put it out. Carr stiffened, sat upright, and glared at Allen. He demanded to know why he couldn't smoke. Allen said that he didn't like smoking. Carr stared at Allen for several seconds, frowning, obviously disgusted and agitated. He finally put the cigarette out, but he was clearly pissed off."

During the interview, Carr withdrew into himself, answering most of Dr. Allen's questions with only "yes" or "no." There was no exposition, few details, little meaning. About a half hour into the interview, Carr seemed to relax somewhat, but about ten minutes later Allen terminated the interview because he was expected at another facility.

On July 25th, Dr. Allen's second interview of Carr began around 9:35 A.M. Carr looked as though he had just awakened, but he seemed in good spirits. He lit a cigarette, and this time Allen made no objection. Allen asked Carr about his childhood. Carr related that when he was quite young he had suffered a serious injury to his head. Also, after he had stolen some old coins from his father and sold them for cash, his father had beaten him severely. His mother was very religious. She would read from the Bible whenever she caught him doing something he shouldn't be doing, like smoking cigarettes, but then he would at times catch her smoking. This kind of behavior confused Carr. Once, when he was about twelve, he found her kissing an older friend he had brought home. Evidently his mother cared more for one of his friends, Carr concluded, than she did for him.

It was evident to Gochenour that when Carr talked about himself he always came back to the same experiences: his mother kissing his friend, his father beating him, his classmates teasing him. These experiences were the landmarks of Carr's life, defining who he was and what made him tick. Some real insight could be gained, Gochenour believed, if someone would encourage him to talk about these experiences in depth. But Dr. Allen would ask a question and then move on. At about 10:10, Allen asked Carr to identify five large cities and to count backwards from thirty by threes. A few minutes later, Allen dismissed Carr. His psychological examination was over. After Carr left the room, Allen turned to Gochenour.

"He said," Gochenour recollects, "that he thought that Carr was severely anti-social, that he tended to act out his anti-social personality by engaging in criminal activity such as thefts and violence." In the same way, Dr. Allen argued, Carr followed the women—perhaps to have sex with them, but he shot them instead. It was just another way for him to express his basic anti-social personality. Gochenour told Allen that his explanation made no sense. "If Carr wanted sex, why didn't he go into the camp armed with his weapon and demand sex from them? It made no sense to kill the women if sex is what he wanted." Allen conceded that he did not know why Carr shot the two women, but he stuck to his diagnosis that Carr had a violent anti-social personality.

Gochenour reminded Dr. Allen that kids had picked on Carr and teased him. Maybe Carr got into fights because of what he had been subjected to, not because he had a violent personality. Allen conceded that name-calling and teasing could provoke even a well-adjusted child into violence. Gochenour suggested that the thefts could be explained in a similar way. Perhaps Carr stole simply because he needed the money for food and clothes, not because he was inherently violent. Allen conceded that he did not have all the answers.

The dispute between the psychiatrist and the criminal defense investigator was a fundamental one. According to Dr. Allen, Carr was a person who enjoyed hurting other human beings; that's why he was in fights, that's why he stole things, that's why he shot the two women. He might be mentally ill, but he was not insane, at least not according to the M'Naghten definition of insanity. He knew what he was doing when he engaged in violence, and he knew what he was doing was wrong. Knowing that he was hurting someone was part of the thrill, part of the kick. Allen therefore was of the opinion that Carr intentionally shot the two women. In contrast, Gochenour tried to ascribe Carr's anti-social actions to something outside of himself. The kids who called him names provoked Carr into fighting, Carr's social and economic deprivations caused him to steal, and the women on South Mountain did something to Carr to set him off. Carr didn't have an anti-social personality. His anti-social actions were instead the product of a hostile and indifferent society. Society was to blame for Carr's action.

Dr. Allen was adamant. His report to George would say that Carr was competent to stand trial, that he was not insane, and that there was insufficient evidence for a diminished-capacity defense. Gochenour exploded. If Allen filed such a report, taking away from the defense any possibility of a diminished-capacity defense, he and George would ask Judge Spicer for an open hearing on Allen's psychological examination of Carr. At this hearing, Gochenour would testify on everything that he had observed. If Allen wanted to avoid such a public spectacle, Gochenour warned, he should not file a report, but write George a letter recommending a second psychiatric examination of Carr.

Several days later, George received such a letter from Dr. Allen. It contained no references to Carr's competency, sanity, or diminished capacity but only a recommendation that a second psychiatric opinion should be sought. Perhaps Allen had second thoughts about his initial diagnosis, or perhaps he wanted to avoid a public hearing on his professional competence.

"Soon thereafter we got a letter from Judge Spicer," Gochenour recalls, "telling us that we should check out two local psychiatrists who had once done forensic psychiatry: Dr. John Hume and Dr. S. Philip Laucks. Well, I knew Hume from earlier cases. He was a forensic psychiatrist who knew how to keep his personal prejudices out of his work. Next day, we got in touch with him. He agreed to take the job at $100 per hour."

V

On July 26th, Carr was formally arraigned before Judge Spicer. Keefer read the formal information charging Carr with first-degree murder, third-degree murder, attempted murder, and two counts of aggravated assault. Spicer then asked Carr whether he was pleading guilty or not guilty, but Carr said nothing. In the jargon of the law, he "stood mute" and George entered a plea of not guilty on his behalf.

As the legal consequences of standing mute were basically the same as pleading not guilty, tactical considerations explain Carr's silence at his arraignment. About to undergo another complete psychological evaluation by Dr. Hume, Carr still had a chance of being declared incompetent to stand trial. The defense did not want to do anything at the arraignment that would undermine this possibility. A plea of not guilty would implicitly leave the impression that Carr understood the nature of the charges against him. It could therefore be said that by standing mute Carr really did understand very well what was going on around him, but, ironically enough, by standing mute he helped substantiate the conclusion that he legally did not understand. Such paradoxes are not uncommon in a courtroom. What is factually true and what is legally true are often two different things.

VI

On Friday, August 12th, Keefer, George, and Judge Spicer met in chambers to discuss whether pretrial publicity had made it impossible for

Carr to get a fair trial in Adams County. Spicer was concerned that a change of venue (moving the trial to another county) or venire (bringing in an outside jury to Adams County) would be time-consuming and expensive. He therefore requested that if George was going to file a motion for either, he should do so as soon as possible.

Over the weekend, George reviewed all the newspaper accounts of the incident that he had collected, including those that described Carr pejoratively as a "mountain man" and those that referred to his confession and criminal record. "On the one side," George notes, "there was the negative impact that these newspaper accounts would have on potential jurors. If the defense was successful in its effort to have Carr's confession, gun, and hair samples ruled inadmissible, could a juror who had read newspaper accounts about them really decide whether to convict Carr only on the basis of evidence admitted into evidence at his trial?" Though worried about this question, George nonetheless concluded that the advantages of staying with an Adams County jury outweighed the potential danger of unfavorable media coverage.

"The one thing that I could not get out of my mind," George says, "was that the local people did not think much of homosexuals. If the Carr case went to trial in Adams County, it was almost a virtual certainty that not one member of the jury could completely identify and sympathize with the victims. So, was it more important for us to have a jury untainted by pretrial publicity or a jury unsympathetic to the victims' lifestyle? In the end, I became convinced that the pretrial publicity probably posed no problem for the defense if the local community was as conservative as I perceived it to be. Indeed, the more the case became identified with lesbianism and gay-rights, the more likely it became that Carr would escape the death penalty or be convicted of a reduced charge, perhaps third-degree murder. Voluntary manslaughter was a stretch, but even that possibility could not be ruled out."

It seems fair to say that one reason George didn't think any of Carr's jurors would "completely" sympathize with the victims was that, in his opinion, there were few homosexuals or gay-rights supporters in Adams County. The chances were slim that any of them would be called for jury duty in Carr's case. Moreover, in such a close-knit community, the political views or sexual orientations of some of the local gay activists or homosexuals would be public knowledge. Accordingly, any activist or homosexual who survived George's questioning during jury selection and found him- or herself on the jury would likely be a person whose sexual orientation or ideology was generally unknown. The person would have been living "in the closet" and would perhaps want to remain there. Such a person could sympathize with Carr's victims but might not be willing to articulate forcefully such sympathy to fellow jury members who had the values of conservative Adams County. It therefore seemed a "virtual certainty," in George's view, that the jury who would decide Carr's fate would be a group of people with values generally unsympathetic to homosexuality.

On Monday, August 15th, George wrote a letter to Judge Spicer informing him that he would not, at this time, be filing a motion for a change of either venue or venire. Though there had been some "improper influences," George concluded that their significance paled in comparison with the virtues of the people of Adams County. "I believe that the people of Adams County are honest and just people who will be able to set aside any improper influences in giving my client the fair trial to which every human being is entitled."

"What I'm doing here is really pretty obvious," George explains, "at least to lawyers. I wrote this letter to Judge Spicer, but I also filed a copy of it with the clerk, thereby ensuring that local newspapers would come across it and publish its contents. Since I had decided to go with a local jury, I wanted the good people of Adams County to know what I thought, which was that they would be honest and fair to my client."

In his letter and in this later explanation of it, George did not say whether the people of Adams County would be fair to his client's victims, but it seems that he expected or hoped for the opposite. His assessment perhaps indirectly reflected the bifurcation of the town of Gettysburg. On the one hand, it's a tourist town, full of motels, restaurants, shops, and gas stations. The townspeople who control this sector of the local economy don't wish to offend the diverse people who come from all over the world to visit the battlefield where Lincoln spoke his famous words. On the other hand, Gettysburg is a small urban center of a predominantly rural and agricultural county. The values that pervade the county, including much of Gettysburg itself, are conservative, family-oriented, and based on religion. There are thirty-four well-attended churches in the municipal area, indicative of the religious devoutness that counterbalances the secular cosmopolitanism of the local tourist industry. Usually the two sides of the Gettysburg community get along well, but tensions have occasionally risen to the surface. In the summer of 1988, it was unclear whether the Carr case would have a negative effect on Gettysburg's symbolic image.

VII

On August 16th, George sent Keefer a "request for discovery," initiating the process by which the prosecution would inform the defense of certain types of evidence that it had in its possession. In Pennsylvania, disclosure in a criminal trial is governed by Rule 305 of the Commonwealth's Rules of Criminal Procedure. This rule requires the prosecution to turn over certain types of evidence, such as evidence that is exculpatory for the defendant, and gives it the option of declining to disclose other types of evidence, with the process subject ultimately to the presiding judge's discretion. George's request contained twenty-five items.

Keefer's page-and-a-half answer to George's request for discovery was filed on September 7th. Of the twenty-five items, Keefer refused to turn over twelve on the ground that the evidence in question was "not discoverable." In particular, Keefer refused to hand over any evidence regarding the sexual or other physical interaction that occurred between Brenner and Wight during the weekend of May 13th, 1988. In his view, George and Gochenour "were on a fishing expedition to see if they could get the commonwealth to help them set up some sort of undeserved provocation defense." Regarding the thirteen other items requested by George, Keefer disclosed eight and denied that the commonwealth had any evidence of the other five types.

"I know that Mike filed a motion that suggested that he was not satisfied with what I had sent over in the Carr case," says Keefer, "but he was just protecting himself against a later charge that he was incompetent. I don't think he really thought that I didn't give him everything he was entitled to. I think it was just a C[over] Y[our] A[ss] motion. That's all it was."

VIII

"When I got the stuff that Roy sent over in the discovery process," George remarks, "for the first time in that case, I was really pissed off. In my opinion, Roy did not disclose all that he should have. For example, I asked whether the commonwealth had any statements made either by Brenner *or by any of the family members of the victims* that some person other than Carr had shot the two women. Roy's answer was not fully responsive. He said that the commonwealth had in its possession no statements from Claudia Brenner that some person other than Carr shot the two women, but what about the relatives of the victims? Did the police have any statements from them that someone other than Carr might have been responsible for these shootings? That was my question, and I am still convinced that Carr had a legal right to see such evidence if it existed."

George also noted that the state police's file on the Carr case exceeded ninety-two pages but Keefer turned over only about half of them, and many of these pages were substantially edited. Paragraphs were missing, and dates and names of the police officers who filed the reports were whited out. In addition, Keefer had refused to give the defense the police's handwritten notes of Carr's confessions and Brenner's interviews. George thought the failure to divulge the notes was serious, because they would arguably be the most accurate representations of what Carr and Brenner actually told the police.

"One last thing," adds George. "We had good reason to believe that Brenner had participated in a photo lineup on May 20th, while she was still in the hospital, but Keefer had provided information only on the three lineups she had participated in on June 16th—a full three weeks later. We had the right to know the results of that first lineup, because, if she screwed up the first lineup, then maybe all the later ones weren't based on her own recollections of the incident. Maybe they were instead based on her seeing newspaper photos of Carr when he was arrested. So, on June 16th, when she identified Carr as the guy she saw on the day of the shootings, maybe she was really only identifying the guy who was arrested for the crime. That kind of thing can happen."

George has a point. If Brenner had not been able to pick out Carr's photo on May 20th, wasn't that something that Keefer should have confirmed through disclosure? If the prosecution was going to use the June 16th lineup as evidence of Carr's guilt, shouldn't it be obliged to turn over any other evidence it had that tended to undermine the validity of that evidence? Isn't that exculpatory evidence that the prosecution was obliged to disclose?

Gochenour adds that it was during July 1988 that he and William Costopoulos had found out where the sand was that had been taken from Susan Reinart's toes at her autopsy and tended to show both that she had been killed at a beach and that Jay Smith had not participated in her murder (see Chapter 4). The sand had been in the state police's possession throughout Smith's first trial in 1986, but its existence had never been disclosed to the defense. Gochenour suspected that Trooper John Holtz might have been involved in keeping the existence of the sand secret. So, when Keefer turned over the discovery package in the Carr case, Gochenour's first thought was that maybe Holtz was up to his old tricks.

"Let me tell you a story about what the police did in the Carr case that made us think that they were hiding evidence," says Gochenour. "I went to the state police barracks down there in Gettysburg to inspect all the physical evidence that they had accumulated in the case. After I had looked at a few things, like the gun and the tent fly, and other things, I told them, 'Now bring out the toys. I want to see the toys.'

"Well, they looked at each other, looked at me, then looked back at each other, and then told me that they didn't know what I was talking about.

"I said, 'You know, the toys, the sex toys that were at the scene of the murder.'

"They said they didn't know anything about that. Later I heard through the grapevine that [Corporal Matthew] O'Brien and the others were furious. They wanted to know who was leaking information to George and me. They thought that someone was leaking info because there *had* been sex toys at the scene—vibrators and such—but the police had returned them to Brenner and the Wight family. Of course, they returned them because they didn't want us to find out about them through discovery. In effect, they sidestepped the discovery process by giving the evidence back to the families.

"But now that they knew that we knew, they wanted to know how we found out about it. They thought that one of their own—a cop—had to have talked. They came up with their number one suspect and I was told that things went so far that they read him his rights. The joke is that there had been no leak. I found the sex toys in the periphery of the pictures of the crime scene by using a special magnifying lens. I do this all the time with police photos. I look at the photo generally, then I go over the entire photo under magnification, spot by spot, outside to inside. I found the sex toys using this method. It's a way of catching the police doing what they shouldn't be doing. In this case, what they shouldn't have done was return that evidence to Brenner. We should have gotten those sex toys."

Even if the Pennsylvania State Police did return to Brenner and the Wight family personal effects that included what Gochenour called "sex toys," it's unclear why the defense would be entitled to such evidence on the ground that it was exculpatory. The sand taken from Reinart's toes may have substantiated the conclusion that she was killed at a beach and that Smith therefore was innocent of her murder, and Brenner's inability to identify Carr on May 20th might to some degree undermine the credibility of her successful identifications of him on June 16th, but it's unclear how or why the presence of vibrators would have had any bearing on Carr's culpability. At the trial, the defense might argue that the women had somehow provoked Carr through their sexual activity, but it's difficult to think that this issue should legitimately revolve around whether the women were using vibrators. Neither is it conceivable that the presence of vibrators would have had a bearing on whether Carr was entitled to a diminished-capacity defense. What is far more likely is that if the prosecution had kept the "sex toys" and disclosed their existence to the defense, George and Gochenour would have used them to play on the conservative values of the Adams County jury. The name Gochenour used to refer to these items suggests as much.

After reviewing Keefer's answer to his request for discovery, George incorporated a motion to compel discovery into an "omnibus pretrial motion" that asked Judge Spicer to suppress Carr's confessions, gun, and hair samples. Refusing to explain why he thought the evidence was unlawfully obtained, George wrote only that the first confession was illegal because Carr "did not knowingly and voluntarily waive his constitutionally protected [Fifth Amendment] right to remain silent." The second confession, gun, and hair samples, obtained on the basis of this earlier unlawful act, were, to use the familiar legal metaphor, the "fruit of the poisonous tree," and therefore they too should not be admitted as evidence at Carr's trial, George maintained.

IX

The September 19th suppression hearing was held in Courtroom 1 on the fourth floor of the modern Adams County Courthouse. Approximately thirty people were present in the plain room, most of whom were sitting on the wooden pewlike benches reserved for the press and spectators. The jury box was on the left side of the bench with the seal of Pennsylvania above it. The flags of Pennsylvania and of the United States stood behind the bench, one on either side. Judge Spicer entered the room and sat down. In a sidebar conference with Spicer and Keefer, George asked that the witnesses be sequestered. He didn't want any of the police officers to know how the others testified.

"I had to be careful," George explains. "I didn't want to lose my constitutional objection to Carr's interrogation by my own sloppiness. I knew well enough that some policemen, being human beings just like the rest of us, might shade the facts about what happened during an interrogation. That's especially true if the shading was going to help put a murderer behind bars. Of course, that goal doesn't justify police perjury. Police officers are supposed to tell the truth, and most of them do exactly that. But there are some who will do whatever they think is necessary, including lying on the stand, if they think it will put a criminal away. And a few will do it just for their reputations, just so that they can be known as the guy who put so-and-so in prison."

Keefer said he had no major objection to the sequestration of the witnesses, but he didn't like the idea of Carr sitting at the defense table if the only officer in the courtroom was the one sitting on the witness stand. George solved this problem by letting Trooper Donald Blevins remain in the courtroom throughout the proceeding. Holtz and O'Brien, the two who conducted the crucial first interview of Carr, were the key witnesses. If the first confession was admissible, the legality of the second would be more or less beside the point.

Keefer's reaction to George's concession hinted that his earlier perception of a security problem was a smokescreen. "I am going to make a motion for Mr. George to state his reasons as to the request for the suppressions. There are no reasons given whatsoever in the motion. . . . I believe the policemen are entitled to know what they are going to testify to here, what the basis of sequestration is prior to their being sequestered."

George answered, "I am prepared to tell the court my exact issue; however, I don't see the need for the officers to know. Their testimony," he added somewhat disingenuously, "is going to be the same regardless if they know or not. How would it be prejudicial to the commonwealth?"

Keefer replied that he thought "any witness has a right to know what he's testifying about before he's called to the stand to testify"—a comment that seemed to lend indirect and unintended support to the defense's contention that a murder suspect ought to know beforehand what exactly he's going to be questioned about.

Judge Spicer sided with George, concluding, "If you're willing to sequester, then they should be sequestered while they are still untainted, so to speak."

George then revealed to Spicer and Keefer at the sidebar the nature of his constitutional objection to Carr's confession: "The issue is going to be whether or not my client was arrested on the charges on which he was being questioned. He was arrested on a fugitive-from-justice warrant. He was not told he was being arrested for murder until 3:10 that afternoon, although the questioning was specifically directed at the incident on May 13th, the alleged murder."

All that Holtz would have to do to make this constitutional objection to Carr's confession disappear was to testify that he had told Carr that he wanted to question him about the shootings on South Mountain. Would a police officer lie about something like that? A different question is whether a police officer *should* lie in such a situation. Carr had murdered one human being and seriously wounded another, which was far more culpable, both from a moral and a legal point of view, than an act of police perjury. What then should a police officer do when his testimony could have a decisive impact on a Fifth Amendment objection to a confession in a murder case like Carr's, where the prosecution's case would be seriously compromised if the confession was ruled unlawful?

Judge Spicer's reaction to George's argument suggested that he was on a wild goose chase.

| Judge Spicer: | So that everybody knows what the state of the law is on this: there are some cases which say that the defendant must have some general understanding of the seriousness of the charges against him, but it is not necessary to tell the defendant precisely what those charges are. . . . There's one case [where] a woman was arrested for failure to make restitution and during the course of that arrest was questioned about I think a homicide. |
| George: | The murder of a baby. |

The case Spicer and George were referring to was *Commonwealth v. Dixon*, 475 Pa. 27, 379 A.2d 553 (1977). Linda Dixon, who had earlier been convicted of malicious destruction of property and ordered to pay $500 restitution in $50 monthly installments, was arrested for failure to make the required payments. After she waived her *Miranda* rights, the police showed her a small black-and-white photograph of her missing child, Christopher, taken when he was ten months old. One of the police officers then asked Dixon, "Where is Chrissy?" The suspect wept for ten minutes before she said, "I did it."

The commonwealth claimed that Dixon's confession itself was a valid waiver of her Fifth Amendment rights, because she knew at the time she said "I did it" that the police suspected her of murdering her son. The Pennsylvania Supreme Court rejected this argument, denying that incriminating statements alone constituted a valid waiver of the right to remain silent. On the contrary, the court said, such incriminating statements revealed that the "compulsive force of the unintelligent waiver has already had its effect." Before Dixon's waiver would have been valid, the court maintained, the police would have had to take additional steps beyond indirectly informing her that they suspected her of her son's murder. They would have had to do something like readminister Dixon her *Miranda* rights.

After Judge Spicer reemphasized *Dixon*'s unique status and repeated that in Pennsylvania a defendant could make a voluntary statement if he had a general understanding of the seriousness of the charges against him, the sidebar ended. Keefer then called Holtz to the stand and asked him whether Carr had ever been advised of his rights. Holtz said yes, both at the Weaver farm, where he'd been arrested, and at the Carlisle State Police Barracks. In the later instance, Holtz said, O'Brien had read Carr his rights from the standard Rights Waiver Form and then had reread the form, stopping after each right and asking Carr whether he understood it. Each time, Carr said he did, and he signed the waiver form before the substantive interview began. After a couple preliminary questions about Carr's education and his use of alcohol and drugs, Holtz asked Carr "to account" for his time since he left Florida. Holtz then read from his official police report summarizing what Carr had said:

> On 05/24/88, this officer and Corporal Matt O'BRIEN interviewed Stephen Roy CARR, WN/M/27, at the Pennsylvania State Police, Carlisle Station. CARR was advised of his rights at 1204 hours by Corporal Matt O'BRIEN. CARR said he understood his rights and he had no questions. Corporal O'BRIEN again went over his rights, stopping after each right and asking CARR if he understood, or had any questions. After Corporal O'BRIEN advised CARR for the second time that "you have an absolute right to remain silent," he (O'BRIEN) asked CARR what that meant to him and CARR replied, "I can keep my mouth shut." Corporal O'BRIEN then told CARR for a second time that anything you say can and will be used against you in a court of law. Corporal O'BRIEN asked CARR if he understood and he said, "Yes." Corporal O'BRIEN then told CARR a second time that you have a right to talk to an attorney before and have an attorney present with you during questioning. Corporal O'BRIEN asked CARR if he understood and he (CARR) said, "Yes." Corporal O'BRIEN then told CARR for a second time that if you cannot afford to hire an attorney, one will be appointed to represent you without charge before any questioning if you so desire. Corporal O'BRIEN asked CARR if he understood and he (CARR) said, "Yes." Corporal O'BRIEN then told CARR, "If you decide to answer any questions, you may stop any time you wish." Corporal O'BRIEN asked CARR if he understood and CARR nodded his head yes. At 1208 hours, CARR signed the Rights Waiver Form. Refer to attached Rights Waiver Form.
>
> CARR was asked if he could read and write and he (CARR) said

yes, but he had trouble spelling some large words. CARR was asked how far he went in school and he (CARR) said the ninth (9th) grade. CARR was asked if he was under the influence of any drugs or alcohol and he (CARR) said no. CARR said he does not drink because of stomach problems he has with alcohol and the last time he used drugs was about two (2) months ago and that was some weed (marijuana).

CARR was asked to account for his time from when he left Florida until now. CARR said he left Florida in December of 1986. He went to the mountains in Tennessee, then hitchhiked to Pennsylvania, arriving in Shippensburg in January of 1987. CARR said he would stay with his uncle, Gordon LUCE, RD2, Box 683, Shippensburg, Pa. off and on but he stayed mainly in the woods. CARR said he built a cabin from logs. The logs were placed so they ran up and down and the roof was made of plastic. CARR said he had a stove in this cabin and on real cold days, he would stay in a sleeping bag. CARR said he remained in the mountains until last Tuesday (05/17/88). CARR said he then floated downriver in a tub, arriving at the WEAVER farm on Wednesday (05/18/88). CARR said he remained at the WEAVER farm until today.

CARR was asked how he survived while he was in the woods and he (CARR) said he would set traps, fish and hunt. CARR said he had a single shot .22 caliber rifle. CARR then said his rifle was stolen last Friday while he was napping along the Appalachian Trail. CARR was then reminded that he said he was at the WEAVER farm last Friday. CARR then said it was the Friday before that (05/13/88). CARR said he was napping along the Appalachian Trail in the afternoon. He was in his sleeping bag. When he woke up, his rifle, knife, sunglasses, blue knit hat and about one and one-half (1½) boxes of loose .22 caliber ammunition was missing. CARR was asked to describe the items he claimed that were stolen. CARR said the rifle was a single shot, bolt action .22 caliber rifle, that he bought at a flea market for thirty (30) dollars. The knife was a folding pocket knife with a black wooden handle. The sunglasses were all tinted and he got them from his aunt and uncle (LUCE). CARR said he used the blue knit cap to carry his loose ammo in. CARR said he got two (2) boxes of .22 caliber long rifle ammunition from his uncle (Gordon LUCE) and he took the ammo from the boxes and placed it in his blue knit cap. CARR said he left the empty .22 caliber ammunition boxes at his uncle's house. CARR was asked while he was on the Appalachian Trail did he see anyone and he (CARR) said, "Yes, two girls." CARR said he arrived at a shelter along the Trail around 0200 hours on Friday, 05/13/88. CARR said when he got up the next morning he saw two girls kissing. One of the girls went to the outhouse. She walked past his shelter, she was buck-naked. CARR said she asked him when he got there and he told her last night. She then went back to the other girl and they got dressed and left. CARR said he waited thirty (30) minutes and then he left. CARR said he never saw the two girls again. CARR said he took a nap in the afternoon along the Appalachian Trail and when he awoke, his rifle and other items were missing. He then went to his aunt and uncle's house (LUCE). CARR was asked what he was wearing and he said a maroon shirt and gray sweatpants and the sweatpants had a blue stripe.

At this time CARR was advised that his knife, sunglasses and blue knit hat were found at the scene of a murder, near the Appalachian Trail. CARR began crying and said, "Why does this happen to me?" CARR then said, I'd left the Trail. I went to my aunt's. I slept all day. My gun was stolen. I left the Trail and went to my aunt's. CARR was then told that he was seen by the GOLDEN family on Saturday morning (05/14/88) and there was talk about the shooting of two (2) girls on the Appalachian Trail. CARR denied this and said he first heard of the shooting on the news, on TV, at 1800 on Saturday evening (05/14/88). CARR was then told that one (1) of the girls lived. She said that she saw him a second time on the Appalachian Trail. She said that her and the other girl were looking at a map and he walked up to them and asked them if they were lost. That he had a rifle and was holding it across his shoulder. At this point, CARR began to cry again. CARR then said, "If I tell you what really happened, you'll put me away for a long time." CARR then said, "I should have run." CARR was then asked if the shooting was an accident? CARR was crying. After a minute or two, CARR said it was an accident. He was shooting at a deer. He saw movement. He shot four (4), five (5) times, maybe more. He heard the girls screaming.

He then got scared and ran to his camp. He had a camp along the creek. He packed his stuff and left.

CARR was asked where the rifle was and he said he buried it in the ground, along the power line. CARR was asked when did he know he was not shooting at a deer and he said, "When they screamed." CARR said he wanted a deer because he was hungry and he shot and shot and shot.

CARR was asked if he ever killed a deer with a .22 caliber rifle before and he said, no.

CARR was asked if he would take us to the rifle and he said, "Yes."

At the end of his testimony, Holtz added that Carr's requests for cigarettes and water had been honored throughout the interview, and at no point had Carr asked for an attorney or for an end to the questioning.

George's questioning of Holtz was tense. Holtz knew that George was attempting to substantiate some kind of constitutional objection to Carr's confession, but he didn't know exactly what it was. George first tried to get Holtz to admit that Carr was a murder "suspect" prior to his arrest. The following cat-and-mouse exchange took place:

George: When was the first time my client became a suspect in this crime?

Holtz: The Friday before he was arrested, I believe; he became of great interest to the Pennsylvania State Police on that Friday [May 20th]. . . .

George: He became of great interest; is that because he was a suspect in the crime?

Holtz: I don't know how you're defining the word "suspect." This is why I am having problems with it.

George: As of May 20, 1988, who was the main suspect in the shooting of these two people, in your opinion?

Holtz: Stephen Roy Carr's photograph that was telexed from Florida certainly bore a great resemblance to the composite sketch given by the surviving victim. We were very interested in speaking to Mr. Carr.

George:	Sir, that's a nice stance, but my question to you is, Who was a major suspect on May 20, 1988?
Holtz:	I think it was building, and I think he becomes a major suspect, if you're correct, when the shell casings match on the 23rd.
George:	Prior to the 23rd, between the 20th and the 23rd you suspected my client was involved in the shootings; is that correct?
Holtz:	Suspected, yes.

The next step was to get Holtz to say on record that his main purpose in interrogating Carr on May 24th was to get him to confess to shooting the two women. George wanted Carr's arrest on the fugitive-from-justice warrant to look like a pretext manipulated by the police to question Carr about the murder.

George:	Let's save everybody a lot of time, officer. Isn't it true you wanted to know where Steve Carr was on May 13, 1988? . . .
Holtz:	Certainly I did, yes.
George:	And you directed your questioning in that regard?
Holtz:	The questioning was leading to that area, yes.
George:	Officer, isn't it true that Stephen Carr was arrested on a fugitive-from-justice warrant so you can also charge him with murder charges?
Holtz:	No. I can't agree with that.
George:	Isn't it true, officer, that probably the only reason you were involved in the arrest on the fugitive-from-justice charges was because you thought he was also involved in a murder?
Holtz:	We knew that the police department in Florida was looking for him. They requested we arrest him, and we certainly weren't going to turn our back on that request. We certainly were interested in speaking to him about the murder of Rebecca Wight.

George:	Would you have been involved in his arrest if he was solely being arrested on a fugitive-from-justice warrant.
Holtz:	I couldn't answer that.
George:	You don't know?
Holtz:	No, I don't.
George:	Isn't it true you were specifically called down [from Troop H Headquarters in Harrisburg] to assist in a murder investigation of Rebecca Wight?
Holtz:	Yes.

With this cross-examination, George established that at the time of the interrogation, Holtz was working on the Wight murder investigation; that if Carr had not been a major suspect in the murder investigation, Holtz would probably not have been involved with Carr's arrest; and that Holtz's interrogation of Carr was "directed" or "leading to" the events of May 13.

George's cross-examination of O'Brien was less confrontational than his questioning of Holtz, perhaps because O'Brien was a local cop whom George knew and respected or perhaps because O'Brien answered George's questions in a straightforward manner. For example, George asked O'Brien, "Is it true, officer, at the time my client was arrested he was a major suspect in the murder of Rebecca Wight?"

In contrast to Holtz, O'Brien simply responded, "Yes." At bottom, O'Brien had no qualms about admitting the facts that George thought were crucial to his constitutional objection to Carr's first confession.

The next trooper to testify was Blevins, whose potential testimony presented George with a problem, because Carr's second confession seemed to be free of the constitutional objection George was leveling against the first one. To salvage the situation, George somehow had to link the potentially unlawful first confession to the second one, thereby making it as unconstitutional as the first one. To this end, he asked Blevins what Holtz had told him before he (Blevins) had interviewed Carr on the afternoon the the 24th.

| George: | At this point you met up with Trooper Holtz again; is that correct? Back at the barracks? |

Blevins: Yes, sir.

George: At that point were you aware that Stephen Carr had given a statement to Trooper Holtz.

Blevins: I was more aware of what he had said during the statement, yes. I knew he had given a statement before, but I wasn't sure what all he had said in it.

George: Trooper Holtz told you pretty much what he said?

Blevins: He briefed me, yes.

Perhaps without realizing it, Blevins gave George much of what he was looking for. The second confession was arguably unlawful because, before it had taken place, Blevins had been "briefed" about information that had been unlawfully obtained.

After Blevins's testimony, it was the defense's turn to call witnesses. The only possible witness was Carr himself. He could testify that, as he had earlier told George and Gochenour, he had asked O'Brien and Holtz for an attorney and for the questioning to be stopped. If Carr testified accordingly and Judge Spicer believed him, all the evidence that the police had obtained after he'd made these alleged requests would have to be excluded. Putting Carr on the stand was dangerous, however. He would have to face cross-examination by Keefer, and George feared a disaster, perhaps another confession.

George therefore decided to keep Carr off the stand, give up the objection that Carr had in fact requested a lawyer, and base his entire constitutional objection to the confession on the ground that Holtz and O'Brien had arrested Carr as a fugitive but interrogated him as a murder suspect. After all, the testimonies of the three police officers had not really disputed the defense's claim that Carr was arrested for one thing and questioned about another. It was a stretch, of course, to claim that Carr's later admissions and statements were all tainted by the original unlawful confession, but George thought it better to rely on that argument than to put Carr on the stand. The odd result was that if Carr was telling the truth when he said that he had asked the troopers for an attorney and for an end to the questioning, Judge Spicer never heard him say so.

Having decided not to call Carr to the stand, George told Judge

Spicer that he would like to write a legal brief in favor of his position that all the evidence should be excluded. Spicer's reaction cut off any hope that the defense would win their motion to suppress evidence.

"What purpose is there to brief?" Judge Spicer asked. "In my opinion the commonwealth has shown that your client was aware, A, that the police were looking for him in respect to the murder case, B, that he understood that it was a very serious matter and C, that knowing that it was serious, decided to talk. You may disagree with that."

"That's exactly why I'd like the opportunity to brief upon reviewing the transcript," replied George. "I don't think there is anywhere on the record [of today's hearing] that he had knowledge he was being sought for a murder charge."

Judge Spicer queried, "How else can you interpret, 'I knew on the 17th that you were looking for me'?"

"Which is the same day that Trooper Blevins began looking for him as a fugitive from justice," George reminded the judge.

"It doesn't matter what the police knew or what the police were going to do," responded Judge Spicer. "It's what your client thought or understood about what was happening. So on the 17th he says the police were looking for him."

"And," George repeated, "they weren't looking for him until the 20th.

"That doesn't have anything to do with his subjective understanding," explained the judge. "And he says 'I know that if I tell the truth I am going to go away a long time.' "

George countered that Carr made that statement halfway through the interview, well after his rights had been violated. To use statements that should be suppressed to justify a waiver was, in George's opinion, "a bootstrap argument," an argument that assumed what had to be proven.

Unimpressed, Judge Spicer observed that what Carr knew at the time he confessed had to be determined from all the circumstances of the confession. "It's an unambiguous situation. We say we're arresting you on fugitive from justice, but we want to talk to you about what's happened since you left Florida."

"No," George disagreed. " 'To account for your time between the time you left Florida and [the] present.' That's what the trooper told Carr."

Judge Spicer retorted, "But the scope [of the questioning] is definitely after the fugitive transaction [Carr's flight from Florida] is passed."

"We're dealing with the constitutional issue here. This isn't something to be taken lightly," George pleaded. "We can presume this, we can presume that, but that's not the standard of proof," suggesting once again that Judge Spicer was presuming what the prosecution had to prove.

Judge Spicer's tone took on a fatalistic and final quality. "All we have," he said, "is the statements that he made and the reasonable interpretation that flows from these statements. I think, Mr. George, that he was aware that he was being questioned with respect to a murder charge."

Mr. George resigned himself to the inevitable. "Well, I understand what the court's position is going to be. I would still like the opportunity to file a brief upon review of the transcript [of today's hearing]. I don't know if that's possible?" George asked.

"I am not going to delay trial while you brief it," Judge Spicer warned.

"I understand that," George acknowledged.

Judge Spicer then formally delayed his ruling on all suppression issues until after George filed his brief, but he made it clear that he was going to rule against the defense.

The murder case against Carr had just turned a corner. Without the confessions, the gun, and the hair samples, Keefer still would have prosecuted Carr, but he might have been acquitted. By the end of the suppression hearing, that possibility had disappeared. The confessions and the gun were going into evidence, and that meant a conviction. Carr might not be sentenced to death or even convicted of first-degree murder, but after Spicer's reaction to the defense's offer to brief the suppression issue, it was clear that Carr was going to be convicted of some form of homicide.

Judge Spicer's decision was ultimately based on his understanding of Stephen Carr's consciousness, in particular on the fact that Carr thought the police were looking for him on May 17th. It wasn't clear whether Carr thought the police were looking for him in regard to the shootings on South Mountain, his fugitive status, or some other criminal activity, but the irony was that the police were not looking specifically for Carr until the 20th. The judge's determination that Carr's confession had been voluntary was derived from Carr's mistaken belief. The truth—that

Carr's confession was voluntary—was derived from what was untrue—that the police were looking for Carr on the 17th. Spicer's reasoning reveals that the law's route to the truth is not always straightforward. At times, it's so full of twists and turns that the truth itself loses much of its clarity and distinctness. It seems as shadowy and uncertain as the fallible means by which it is ascertained.

The Pretrial Conference

seven

I

Immediately after the suppression hearing, Judge Oscar Spicer issued his rulings on all the motions included in Defense Attorney Michael George's omnibus pretrial motion except the suppression issue, which he had reluctantly given George permission to brief. His rulings rejecting outright two of the defense's discovery requests were potentially critical. Spicer ruled that the prosecution did not have to disclose any statement, information, or evidence that related to Defendant Steve Carr's mental state on May 13th or any "objects, statements, documents, photographs, or other tangible evidence which relates to any sexual or physical interaction" between Claudia Brenner and Rebecca Wight during the weekend of May 13, 1988. The defense had been hoping to find through discovery evidence that Carr was in a severe emotional state at the time of the shootings or that the women had in some way provoked him, either of which might have reduced Carr's culpability from first-degree murder to either third-degree murder or voluntary manslaughter.

On September 20th, Judge Spicer ordered the jury commissioners to draw 220 persons for jury service for the term beginning October 31st: a 150-person panel from which 12 jurors would be selected to decide the fate of Carr and a 70-person panel for all the other trials scheduled for the upcoming court session. The numbers suggest that Spicer thought that selecting a jury for Carr's trial was going to be a complicated, time-consuming affair, probably in part because of the victims' sexual orientation. Any prospective juror who could not fairly decide the facts of the case because of some underlying prejudice against lesbians or homosexuals would have to be excused. Evidently, Spicer thought that a pool of 150 was big enough so that 12 unprejudiced persons could be found.

Jury selection, called *voir dire*, is a tactical battleground, because the defense and the prosecution each want a jury predisposed to its side. To shape the jury, each side can "challenge" and thereby dismiss undesirable jurors. Challenges are of two types: a "for cause" challenge, which needs a reason, and a "preemptory" challenge, which does not. Whereas the judge decides whether "for cause" challenges are justified, preemptory challenges are largely arbitrary. In the Carr case, each side had twenty preemptory challenges.

In small communities like Gettysburg, a cheap and sometimes effective method for deciding how to use preemptory challenges is to run the list of prospective jurors by lawyers and staff of the office or law firm, asking for comment and input. In the Carr case, George received feedback of this type. Beside one name was this handwritten description: "May have file on him. He is a real character—similar to Carr." Another read, "Very old liberal; college prof.; probably would have no objection to lesbians—not a good defense juror." Other comments were as follows: "Used to live on 3rd floor. She would sympathize with women." "I think he is insurance man—numerous kids—probably not chauvinistic enough to condone shooting lesbians." "Would not be a good juror for D." During jury selection, George would rely on such "gossip" only because he didn't have the time and resources to gather information concerning prospective jurors by more reliable means.

During *voir dire*, both sides also base their decisions on hunches derived from their years of experience working with local juries. "Interestingly enough," Prosecutor Roy Keefer admits, "in the Carr case my feeling was that I didn't think women were the jurors we wanted. I would have avoided women because they may have been more inclined to judge Rebecca and Claudia more harshly than men might have been. If it would have been two males shot, I would have thought the exact opposite. I think I would have gone with women, instead of men, because the men would have been more likely to judge the behavior of the victims and feel personally threatened by it than perhaps women would be."

To help them make up their minds about which potential jurors fit their hunches and which did not, both George and Keefer would ask prospective jurors questions; however, neither side wanted to invite a preemptory challenge by asking questions that would identify a juror as biased in some way against the opposing side. To accomplish this difficult task, lawyers with the necessary financial resources rely on social scientists, psychological experts, and jury consultants. Lawyers without such resources, such as those in the Carr trial, rely on gossip and hunches. Needless to say, jury selection in such circumstances is not an exact science. It is an art that combines judgment, intuition, and luck.

II

Starting in September, the staff of Criminal Defense Investigator Skip Gochenour began interviewing people who had known Carr, so that Gochenour and George could plan their strategy for the trial and the penalty phase that would follow if Carr were convicted of first-degree murder. They had to have a pretty good idea of what a witness would say before they could put him or her on the stand. From these interviews and Carr's prison records from Florida, the defense learned a great deal about Carr's past life.

The second of four children, Carr was born on December 14, 1959, in Bath, New York, a small city south of the Finger Lakes region, about forty miles west of Ithaca. Richard, his father, and Irma, his mother, had married in 1954. According to Richard, Irma was very religious for the first ten years of their marriage. She made the children go to church twice on Sunday and sometimes on Wednesday evenings. Richard described himself as a workaholic. When he was not at the local Westinghouse plant where he worked, he was in his shop making things for his wife and kids. He thought giving his family material things was the right thing to do. He gave Irma all the charge cards he could, which produced some money problems, but even that didn't make her happy. Irma often complained that he didn't love her or the kids enough.

Both Richard and Irma confirmed that when Steve was young he had fallen out of a tree. The resulting injury to his head gave him severe headaches, his father recalled, which might have been the reason why he had an inferiority complex and had always been a slow learner. Irma also remembered that Steve, when he was about nine years of age, ran a fever between 104 and 105 degrees for a week. Afterward, she said, he turned into a monster. He developed a terrible temper and began to think that everyone was against him. During this same time period, when Carr was about eleven years old, a twenty-two-year-old man sexually assaulted him, an experience that probably exacerbated his aggressive tendencies.

Though Richard was convinced that Irma never really loved him, their marriage survived for twenty years. He noted that when he was dating Irma in 1954, he had heard rumors that she was a lesbian. When Irma's best friend Boots left her husband and moved in with another woman, Irma had asked him if he would still love her if anything "came out" during the divorce proceedings. Richard assumed that Irma was referring to her own lesbianism. Soon thereafter, someone told Richard he saw Irma kissing Boots at a restaurant. Richard didn't know whether the story was true. In her interview with Gochenour's staff, Irma insisted that the rumors were false. She and Boots were just good friends.

The marriage collapsed after Steve, who was then about twelve years of age, introduced Irma to Curt Watkins, who was, according to Richard, a very feminine boy a few years older than Steve. To Richard's surprise, his wife and Curt took all the furniture and moved into the second floor of the Carr residence, putting locks on the doors so that Richard couldn't gain access to the upstairs. All the children except Steve lived with their mother. Steve lived downstairs with his father while, strangely enough, one of his friends lived upstairs with his mother.

In 1974, Irma moved to Shippensburg, Pennsylvania, to be near her sister Lucille Luce. She took her other three children with her, but she left Steve with Richard. Irma claimed that Steve stayed with his father because he felt sorry for him, but she admitted that she and Steve could not get along. Richard and Irma soon divorced.

Richard said that Steve did not do well after his mother left. Steve liked to hunt and fish, but his friends were of the wrong type and he never had any girlfriends. Irma claimed Richard spent all his free time in singles clubs, while Steve was on his own, running around with other boys and getting into trouble. James Klempner, a fifty-one-year-old friend of Steve's who lived on Sand Bank Road, said he suspected that Steve's father had sexually abused him. Because Steve took over the household chores after his mother left, maybe his father expected him to take over the sexual responsibilities of a wife. Klempner said Steve had talked vaguely about what had happened but had never said anything definite.

After a year or so, Richard sent Steve to live with his mother in Shippensburg. From then on, according to Richard, Steve never had a fit place to live in. It was Richard's understanding that Irma and the kids had lived for a time in an old school bus and that they didn't want Steve to be there.

Irma confirmed that Steve remained a troubled youth after he joined her in Shippensburg. Always picked on by other kids, he got into a lot of fights at school. Kenneth Morgan, the guidance counselor at Shippensburg Junior High School, partially confirmed Irma's account. He remembered Steve as a tall individual with stringy blond hair, always dirty and unkempt. Perhaps because of his appearance, the other kids shunned and ridiculed him. According to Morgan, Steve didn't have one friend in the whole school. He would come into Morgan's office, crying and complaining that the other kids were picking on him, calling him "stinky," "fish lips," or "nigger lips." But Morgan couldn't remember that Steve had caused any trouble in school or that he had been in any fights.

Morgan assumed that Steve's home life was considerably less than ideal. School officials bought soap and shampoo for Steve and let him take his showers at the school, but they couldn't do much for his dirty clothes. Steve himself reported that his brother stabbed him once and he retaliated by stabbing him with a big fork. His mother finally threw him out of the house in 1974, when he was fifteen. At about the same time, Morgan reported, Steve dropped out of school.

When Irma moved her family to Florida in 1977, Steve went along. They lived in a three-bedroom mobile home in a trailer park in Zephyrhills, near Tampa. Curt Watkins lived in another trailer nearby. On January 15, 1979, after drinking some beer, Steve and a friend named Bobby Halls stole some mail out of the Sleepy Hollow Travel Park. They didn't find any money and no one would cash the checks they did find. Frightened that he might be caught carrying the checks, Carr flushed them down the toilet at the Sambo's restaurant in Zephyrhills. On January

24th a dectective from the Zephyrhills Police Department arrested Carr on a charge of grand theft. Carr confessed and was locked up in the Pasco County Jail for three days before being released on a $2,500 bond. On May 24th, based on an understanding with the prosecutor that he would not be sentenced to more than a year and a day, Carr entered a plea of *nolo contendere*, meaning that he wasn't going to contest the charge. The judge found him guilty and ordered a presentence investigation.

With his sentencing on the grand theft charge in front of him, Carr had every incentive to stay on the right side of the law, but at a restaurant in Daytona Beach, he ordered and ate a meal knowing he couldn't pay for it. He was arrested for obtaining food with intent to defraud, pleaded guilty, and spent ten days in the county jail. The real price for his misdemeanor in Daytona Beach came at his sentencing for grand theft in Pasco County. The parole and probation department formally recommended probation with strict supervision, but the written evaluation of Carr contained a lot of negative language. There "appears to be a lack of family unity and cohesion in the subject's family structure." In regard to Carr himself, the report said that he was immature and lacked remorse. His "arrest for the instant offense would appear to have no effect on the subject or deter his delinquent activities"—a clear reference to the incident in Daytona Beach. On September 13th, Judge Ray Ulmer gave Carr the maximum under the plea bargain: a year and a day in a state correctional facility, not in the county jail. Carr was going to do some hard time.

At first, Carr did not do well in Florida's prison system. On September 17th, while he was undergoing initiation and testing at the system's Reception and Medical Center (RMC), Carr was placed in administrative confinement because he failed to report to the Records Department for fingerprinting and a photograph. Then, just three days later, he was again confined for engaging in homosexual acts. According to the shift supervisor's report, "Inmate Carr stated that he sucked a black inmate's dick for 5 dollars—and then didn't get paid—and he felt like he should get paid." A psychologist who interviewed him on October 1st recorded that Carr denied any previous homosexual activity and said he did it "for the money." In part because Carr did "not indicate any remorse for his behavior," the psychologist's evaluation was sharply negative. Above average in intelligence, but poorly motivated, with no goals or skills to speak of, Carr was described as a "largely insecure and inadequate individual."

On the basis of the tests he took at the RMC, Florida prison admin-istrators assigned Carr to Baker Correctional Institution (B.C.I.) on Oc-tober 11, 1979. At B.C.I., Carr was written up a few times—for disobey-ing a verbal order, not making his bed correctly, and not being dressed properly—and in February his work supervisor called Carr "a constant problem" and asked that he be removed from the landscaping squad. B.C.I officials nonetheless approved Carr for a work release program on April 7th and transferred him to Tarpon Springs, a community correc-tional center. He got out on June 2, 1980. He had served less than nine months of his sentence.

Once again a free man, Carr left Florida, returning to the Ship-pensburg area of Pennsylvania. He worked at Musselmans Canning Fac-tory and lived with his friend James Klempner. Klempner said Steve had told him about what life in prison was like, saying that "to be famous one either had to have blood on his knife or shit on his dick." Despite Carr's legal troubles in Florida, Klempner said Steve was a nice guy. He would help people lost in the woods and would, for a pack of cigarettes, do odd jobs for people living in the neighborhood. Carr would take food from local gardens, but no one minded. Everyone in the area would plant a little extra so that he would have some food. And Steve was nonviolent, Klempner insisted, save for one peculiar incident. He and Steve were watching an Oprah Winfrey show that was discussing homosexuals and all of a sudden Steve said, "They ought to shoot the whole damn bunch of them." Klempner was surprised at this comment because it came out of the blue.

Carr one day put too much wood in the stove in Klempner's house, overheating it and burning down the house. It was a damn shame, Klempner said, but he was sure it was an accident. Carr then moved in with his aunt and uncle, Lucy and Gordon Luce, but that arrangement didn't work out well. Because he was also having trouble keeping a job, Carr moved back to Florida to live with his mother in 1982.

It didn't take long before Carr was involved in a number of burglar-ies. On March 31, 1983, at about 3:30 A.M., Carr cut out a screen panel on a sliding door and entered the patio area of a residence in Zephyrhills, Florida. He then forced a jalousie window and cut through the inside screen to gain entry into the house. After he cut the telephone line in the kitchen, Steve rummaged through the kitchen drawers and also the drawers of a desk in the living room, scattering several photos onto the living room floor and couch. The owner of the house, Greta Gullifer, a seventy-five-year-old white woman, was asleep in her bedroom. She later told a police officer that she woke up and saw a white man standing by her bed. She screamed and the man fled. Only later did Gullifer discover that she was bleeding from her side.

Gary Pierce, the Zephyrhills Police Department detective who investigated the incident, believed that Carr had something else on his mind besides burglary when he entered Gullifer's bedroom. Pierce said that the woman had told him that Carr's face was only six inches from hers and that she had seen his right hand reaching out toward her when she screamed. Pierce explained that he had always thought that Carr was a "peeping Tom" because he had observed him numerous times sneaking around neighborhoods late at night. Another detective who worked for the Pasco County Sheriff's Department described Carr in the same way: a "peeping Tom" who was certainly capable of rape.

Before Carr was arrested for this assault and burglary, he and his friends engaged in a number of robberies, mostly of churches. On December 4, 1983, they got away with $450 worth of different items from the Faith Baptist Church; on December 15th, Carr, his cousins Mark and Tom Ricks, Gerald Foley, and Steve Fogarty stole a $2,000 stereo system from the New Hope Baptist Mission Church. Fogarty took the stolen property and gave the other four $150 worth of marijuana to split up. In both cases, Carr and his associates gained entry to the churches through a broken window. On January 3, 1984, Carr removed a window from the First Presbyterian Church and stole $42.50; on January 6th, he took a public-address system worth $558 and a violin of unknown value from the Wesleyan Church; on January 13th, Carr broke into a motor home on Zephyr Avenue and took a car stereo, a couple of speakers, and two eight-packs of Coke; on January 15th, he broke into Sergio's Restaurant on Highway 54, picked up a cake, and threw it on the ground outside near a water pump shed; on January 17, he broke into a travel trailer and a parked car located at 4 Manor Drive; and on January 23rd, he stole a rifle from a utility shed at 13 Beltram Drive. He fled the scene, but Detective Pierce picked him up with the gun still in his possession. Soon thereafter, Carr confessed to all the crimes he had committed since March 1983.

The charges against Carr were nine counts of burglary, two counts of grand theft, and one count of aggravated assault—the stabbing of Gullifer. On March 30, 1984, Judge Wayne Cobb sentenced Carr to three years for each of the twelve counts, but the sentences were to be served concurrently, not consecutively. In other words, Carr got only three years for twelve felonies, and he was given credit for the sixty-nine days he had already served. Records indicate that Detective Pierce, upset about the light sentence, said in open court that Carr "deserved a hell of a lot more than three years" for having committed multiple offenses against old ladies and churches. In his view, Carr had no morals or scruples.

On his second time through the system, RMC classified Carr as a medium-custody inmate and shipped him to the O unit, which Florida prison officials describe as a work camp. Carr arrived at the unit on May 11, 1984 and left it on August 2, 1985. Sentenced to three years, Carr served only about a year-and-a-half behind bars.

Three weeks after Carr got out, he and his cousin Tom Ricks stole a 1975 Jeep Wagoneer. Carr's story to the police was that he didn't know the jeep was stolen. Ricks had told him that the jeep belonged to a friend. The police discovered the wrecked, partially stripped, and abandoned jeep in an orange grove on the outskirts of Zephyrhills on December 6, 1985. The police arrested Carr for grand theft auto and he spent a week in jail before his mother bailed him out. His trial was scheduled for mid-1986, but he ran. Carr first went to Bath, New York, but his father drove him back down to Florida. Late in 1986, after his trial had been delayed, he ran again. For a couple of weeks, he stayed with a friend from prison who lived in Tennessee. He arrived back in Pennsylvania in January of 1987.

On his return to the South Mountain area, Carr was befriended by the Golden family. They had known the Carrs before they moved to Florida and had socialized with Steve when he lived in the Shippensburg area from 1980–1982. Alice Golden said that Carr had always been good to her family, especially the kids. He'd take a meal with the family and he'd help out around the house, doing the dishes, hanging the wash, or splitting some wood. He never stole anything and he never took food or coffee without first asking for it. Around women, Carr was extremely quiet. Alice had never heard him say anything vulgar or "off-the-wall" to a female. He did have a rifle that he always had with him when he was up on South Mountain.

Alice's husband, Larry, added that Carr's rifle was in bad shape. Larry had tried to shoot-the-weapon-in by adjusting the sights, but he said he couldn't get a pattern smaller than a square foot. And the ejector on the gun was not working. Carr had to pry out the empty shell casings with a pocket knife. According to Larry, Carr was a loner who lived on the mountain because he did not like to be around people. He was extremely quiet and kept to himself, but he never hurt anyone. Golden trusted Steve and considered him his friend.

John Golden, the seventeen-year-old son who had talked to Carr the morning after the shootings, said he got up around 8:00 A.M. that day and found Steve sitting in the kitchen, smoking a cigarette. Carr did say that he had done something awful, but John said he didn't seem upset. He added that during prior visits Carr had made similar statements, usually related to shooting a deer out of season or something like that.

Carr's criminal record and the defense interviews of Carr's friends and relatives were a mixed bag for the defense. They showed that except for the stabbing incident, Carr did not have a history of violent crimes. On the other hand, the overall pattern of criminal activity might suggest that Carr, as Detective Pierce had said, didn't have a conscience. If Carr took the stand, Keefer could use his criminal record to make him look un-redeemable. There was also the homosexual incident in prison. Would Keefer notice it, and what would he do with it if Carr testified? He could try to get Carr to say that because of his homosexual experiences in prison, he hated all homosexuals. After all, Klempner had heard Carr say that he thought all homosexuals should be shot. The defense hoped that Keefer would not find out about Carr's comment to Klempner. It would give Carr a clear and definite motive for the shootings.

III

In early October, George and Gochenour were also considering the best way to attack Brenner's credibility. At the preliminary hearing, George had asked Brenner whether she had told the police what she "could remember" each time she had spoken to them. Brenner had answered, "I always told them whatever I could. First to help them catch the guy who shot us and whatever help they wanted to work on the case, yes." But through discovery George and Gochenour had obtained police reports indicating that Brenner hadn't told the police about her sexual orientation until four or five days after the shootings, which left an impression that she hadn't told the whole truth at the preliminary hearing.

"So," George explains, "my first line of questioning at the trial would have been to address this issue: 'If you didn't tell the whole truth to the police when you were in the hospital because you were afraid, and if you didn't tell the whole truth at the preliminary hearing, why should we believe that you're telling the whole truth now? If being afraid once made you not tell the whole truth, why wouldn't it make you not tell the whole truth again?' That would have been the strategy. If, at that point, she admitted to doing things that teased Carr, great; if not, then our hope was that the jury would think she was lying. That's playing hardball, but that's what I would have had to do if the Carr case went to trial."

Brenner's medical records, which the defense obtained by subpoena, gave George additional ammunition. One medical report indicated that Brenner had told a doctor that she and Wight had exchanged "sharp words" with Carr, but in her testimony at the preliminary hearing, all that Brenner had said was that Carr had asked the women if they were lost, and Brenner had replied, "No, are you?"

"Brenner would have had to explain," says George, "why she told that doctor that there had been sharp words when she didn't describe them that way at the preliminary hearing."

Another statement that caught the defense's attention was one Brenner made to a medical technician on the helicopter that took her to Hershey Medical Center on the night of the shootings. She told him that she and Wight were camping in the woods "when a man shot at them with a shotgun approximately 30 feet away." The reference could be interpreted to mean that Brenner saw the gunman, which also conflicted with her testimony at the preliminary hearing.

"Lying," Gochenour observes, "is an intellectual process. If Brenner were like most people, she would have been so traumatized that she would have told the whole truth because she wouldn't have been able to muster the energy, the wherewithal, to calculate that she had to tell the story this way. To say this, but not that. But it looks like Brenner immediately went into a defense mode. She was going to take control of this. That can tell you a lot about her. She even gave Hershey Medical Center a wrong home address. She did the same thing with Chambersburg Hospital and the Shippensburg Ambulance Service. Now maybe she would say that she didn't tell the truth because she was terrified, but that's just my point. We had this evidence that suggested that when she's afraid, she perhaps has a tendency to lie or, which is the same thing, not to tell the whole truth. So maybe, just maybe, she was afraid to admit the truth about whether the women teased Carr."

Gochenour's explanation of the apparent discrepancies in the medical, police, and court records perhaps reveals more about him than it does about Brenner. Gochenour's years as a criminal defense investigator have shaped his outlook at the most fundamental level. Having seen so much violence, he's constantly on the lookout for it. Sensible people carry firearms and know how to use them, he believes; they stay alert, ready for the unexpected; they are careful and don't take foolish risks. That's the way Gochenour has lived his life. He's careful and prudent, but ready and able to defend himself. He therefore often perceives victims of homicidal violence as weak, foolish risk takers who are partly to blame for what happened to them. It was with this perspective that Gochenour dipped Brenner's story into the acid of his professional and personal distrust and cynicism.

The defense's planned attack on Brenner's credibility was meant to level the playing field. Brenner's sexual orientation combined with the idea that she was not telling the whole truth about what happened on South Mountain might be enough to convince a conservative Adams County jury to bring back a verdict of voluntary manslaughter or third-degree murder. Moreover, person after person living in the South Mountain area described Carr as a quiet, pleasant person, one who would never have shot the women for no reason at all. If Carr took the stand to testify at his trial, these potential defense witnesses might be able to lend him some credibility with the jury.

IV

While the defense was evaluating the relative credibility of Brenner and Carr, Dr. John Hume conducted his psychological examination of Carr. After meeting with Carr for four-and-a-half hours, Hume informed

George and Gochenour on October 10th that he couldn't testify that Carr was insane or had a mental abnormality of the type Pennsylvania required for diminished capacity. According to Hume, Carr was mentally ill, but his psychological disorders did not affect his understanding of what he was doing at any particular time. He was an angry, frustrated person, but he could plan ahead, consider different options, and reflect on the consequences of his actions. He could, in other words, perform all the mental operations necessary for a person to deliberately and intentionally kill another human being.

If Pennsylvania followed the Model Penal Code (MPC) of the American Law Institute, a code that serves as a model for states to consider when they revise their criminal laws, it would have been much easier for George to introduce evidence of Carr's mental condition at his trial. First, the M'Naghten definition of insanity used by Pennsylvania limits the defense to defendants who do not know what they are doing at the time of the crime, or, if they do know what they are doing, they don't know it is wrong. In contrast, the MPC says that a person is insane, and therefore innocent of a crime, if at the time of the offense "as a result of mental disease or defect he lacks substantial capacity either to appreciate the criminality of his conduct *or to conform his conduct to the requirements of law*" (Section 4.01) (emphasis added). Also, the MPC reduces murder to manslaughter when the homicide is "committed under the influence of extreme mental or emotional disturbance for which there is reasonable explanation or excuse" (Section 210.3(1) (b)). This provision adds that the "reasonableness of such explanation or excuse shall be determined *from the viewpoint of a person in the actor's situation under the circumstances as he believes them to be*" (emphasis added). If either of these provisions had been operative in Pennsylvania in 1988, Hume would probably have been able to testify that Carr's mental illness eroded his capacity to conform his conduct to the law or affected his understanding of his situation, perhaps giving him a reasonable explanation or excuse for what he had done. Pennsylvania's definition of insanity and diminished capacity precluded Hume's testimony, however, and Carr had to go on trial for his life without the benefit of favorable expert psychiatric testimony, increasing his risk of receiving a death sentence. Because states have the authority to define relevant defenses differently, capitol homicide defendants across the country have different odds of

activity that had taken place between the two women. And later, they made a big deal of the fact that the police had returned some irrelevant evidence to the relatives of the victims. They interpreted that as a way of avoiding discovery, but the way I looked at it, it was just common sense. The police don't have to keep everything they pick up at a crime scene. If some object has no value as evidence, then of course it can be returned to the victims' relatives."

In Paragraphs 7 through 9 of the formal motion he filed with the court, Keefer indicated what evidence he wanted to exclude from Carr's trial.

7. It is the position of the commonwealth that the relationship or life-style of the victims is totally irrelevant to the prosecution at bar.

8. It is also the position of the commonwealth that the intimate activity of the victims immediately prior to and at the time of the shootings is irrelevant in that such testimony does not rise to the level of serious provocation or serve as a basis for diminished capacity under the laws of this commonwealth.

9. The interjection of such testimony into the trial would be highly prejudicial.

In his accompanying brief, Keefer explained that the law had to assume that the average person would not "lose control" at the sight of lesbian lovemaking, because homosexuality was legally protected by the Pennsylvania Constitution. In *Commonwealth v. Bonadio*, 490 Pa. 91 (1980), the Pennsylvania Supreme Court had ruled that the state constitution barred imposing criminal penalties on homosexual types of sexual activity. Moreover, courts of other states had ruled that "homosexual advances" could not legally meet the requirements of provocation. If Homosexual A invites Heterosexual B to engage in sodomy, B can't kill A and then claim that A's invitation provoked him. In Keefers's opinion, if enduring an unwelcomed homosexual advance couldn't constitute provocation, then *a fortiori* watching lesbians make love couldn't, either. The evidence of lesbian sexual activity prior to the shootings was therefore irrelevant and "highly prejudicial."

"After all," says Keefer, "think of who would be on the jury. Since each and every one of the jurors would be local residents of Adams County, not only was it very likely that none of them would be lesbians, but it was also probable that no one on the panel could count a lesbian among their friends, relatives, or even acquaintances. Indifference, if not outright hostility, to Rebecca Wight and Claudia Brenner might tempt the jury to find provocation, even though legally there weren't any grounds for such a conclusion. And once the evidence concerning lesbian relationships and sexual activity was introduced at the trial, no one, not even Judge Spicer, could stop a determined jury from bringing in a verdict of voluntary manslaughter if that is what it wanted to do. The only way to prevent the possibility of this result, or at least reduce its likelihood dramatically, was to keep the prejudicial evidence entirely out of the case. Judge Spicer had the power to do just that."

When George got a copy of Keefer's motion *in limine*, he knew that the case had come to another turning point. At the upcoming pretrial conference that Judge Spicer had scheduled to hear argument on the issue, George had to convince the judge that the evidence Keefer wanted out had to go in. In preparation for the conference, George filed two of his own motions *in limine*.

VI

The pretrial conference took place on the afternoon of October 24th in a half-empty Courtroom 1. It began with a surprise. As soon as Judge Spicer took his seat on the bench, Keefer introduced him to Abbe Smith, an attorney representing Brenner. Smith, a graduate of New York University School of Law, was a feminist criminal trial attorney affiliated with the Defender Association of Philadelphia, the National Lawyers Guild, and the American Civil Liberties Union. On the record, Spicer did not formally greet Abbe Smith or ask Keefer what she was doing at the table reserved for the prosecution. Wasting no time on pleasantries, he immediately got down to business, referring to Paragraph 7 of Keefer's motion. "I really don't think that the relationship [between the two victims] has any relevance to this case." However, "the intimate activity of the victims immediately prior to and at the time of the shootings" was something else. The activity might be "irrelevant from the standpoint of serious provocation," but Spicer said he didn't "know how in the world you could keep it out" of the trial. He explained, "It's just like extra judicial declarations to explain conduct. Explaining conduct has no legal relevance . . ., but if it makes more meaningful the description of the incident, it's always admissible as an exception to the hearsay rule."

In other words, the evidence of sexual activity prior to the shootings wasn't relevant to provocation, but it was relevant to understanding what happened on South Mountain. Accordingly, Judge Spicer was inclined to admit the evidence at Carr's trial unless its prejudicial character outweighed its evidentiary value. Keefer insisted that it did.

> Keefer: If . . . the court is going to rule as a matter of law and so instruct the jury that it's not something that can be considered in terms of provocation, . . . then I think there's no question, Your Honor, that the possible prejudice regarding the sexual orientation of these two people would vastly outweigh any evidentiary value of this particular piece of information. As a matter of fact, it would have no evidentiary value. The only way it would come in is [as] a footnote, if you will, on the testimony regarding the case.

> Judge Spicer: But practically every detail is a footnote.

Keefer had not convinced Spicer. The sexual activity of the women might be a detail, but Keefer had not established that letting it into the trial would unjustifiably hurt the prosecution.

George spoke up, insisting that the defense was going to present, contrary to what Judge Spicer and Keefer were assuming, a provocation defense. The skeptical judge asked what evidence in the case could the defense possibly use to substantiate a defense of provocation. Prior to the conference, George and Gochenour had worked out a tactic "to duck" this question.

> George: I am going to object to this court making a pretrial determination as such, simply because it's forcing me into a position of making an offer of proof prior to the trial even beginning. If I am forced to make an offer of proof, I am implicitly forced to admit that my client may have been at the scene and I don't

think I am in a position to do that at this point. I don't think the commonwealth has proved it at this point. I don't think I should be forced by the Court to do so.

Judge Spicer: Your're saying this should be something not deter-mined *in limine.*

George: It should be reserved for issue and depending on the evidence at trial.

As a step in the defense's plan to get the evidence of sexual activity in front of an Adams County jury, George was insisting that his client should not be forced to incriminate himself before trial. Keefer stepped back into the fray, broaching for the first time the issue of how the evidence would affect jury selection and the jury at the trial itself.

Keefer: This is a matter that has to be determined *in limine.* Due to the prejudicial nature, it would have a great bearing in terms of voir dire of the jury whether or not this evi-dence, number one, is going to be admissible, and, num-ber two, [for] what purpose is that evidence admissible. I don't see how we can possibly individually voir dire 150 jurors to make sure they can reach a satisfactory and unbiased verdict in this case without knowing whether that testimony and to what extent that testimony would be acceptable.

Spicer faced a dilemma: should he force a defendant to incriminate himself or risk a biased jury? He turned to George.

Judge Spicer: Speak in [the] hypothetical how in the world this evidence [can] be possibly relevant . . . to prov-ocation?

George: . . . I am not expecting the court to hold this as an offer of proof as far as what the defense is going to establish. I don't think I should be in that position prior to trial if we're speaking purely hypothetically.

Judge Spicer: Hypothetically.

Spicer seemed to be giving the defense a blank slate to write on, but George knew better than to stray too far from what he understood to be the facts of the case. Though he had used the word "hypothetically," Spicer in fact wanted to know what the defense intended to prove at trial if he let them make a claim of provocation. The word "hypothetically" was for the record. Its purpose was to show that Spicer was not doing what in fact he was doing—forcing the defense to concede implicitly that Carr had shot the two women.

George replied, "If the defense is able to present [evidence of] a life which has been dominated by sexual assaults by homosexuals, sexually assaulted in prison by homosexuals, evidence potentially . . . that the defendant's mother may have been involved in lesbian relationships, evidence that from the time this person was in society to any extent, he has been looked upon as a, quote, 'freak.' He has been rejected by every advance he ever made towards women and on the date of the incident in question, hypothetically speaking, he was again rejected by these women after being presented to whatever activity they may have been engaged in. . . . He was rejected thereafter to the point that it pushed him over the edge."

"If you're talking about provocation," Judge Spicer answered, "flatly, unequivocally, this would not amount to provocation. So if you want that in the form of a ruling, I will make it. You're talking about diminished capacity. That's something else, because diminished capacity obviously refers to [the] subjective state of mind [of the defendant] and I have no idea what the subjective state of mind was or what kind of testimony you would have with respect to subjective state of mind. . . . [E]xcept you have to give some notice of intention to claim the defense of diminished capacity."

"I understand that," George replied.

"Have you given it?" Spicer asked, not knowing that Dr. Hume had taken away the option of pursuing a diminished-capacity defense.

"No, I understand that is not going to be an issue at this trial," George replied.

"Then I will rule that it's not relevant," Spicer concluded.

Judge Spicer was not going to let George argue to the jury that Carr's life of deprivation, rejection, and sexual abuse had a bearing on whether he was legally provoked. Spicer then turned to the other side of his dilemma, asking, "How are we going to approach voir dire at this point?"

George:	I am entitled during voir dire to elicit prejudice. . . . If favoritism or disdain for homosexuals is a prejudice, I am entitled to know that from the jury or from a potential juror member.
Keefer:	Only if there's evidence of that in the case.
Judge Spicer:	You're only entitled if it is going to come into the evidence. . . . Are you still proceeding on the death penalty?
Keefer:	Yes, sir. The evidence that Mr. George talks about may be admissible in terms of penalty phase.
Judge Spicer:	If it is admissible in the penalty phase, and I think it would on the hypothetical, then it's a proper area for voir dire.

An ironic twist. The fact that the commonwealth was seeking the death penalty in the case came to the defense's advantage. If a jury convicted Carr of first-degree murder, that same jury in a separate proceeding would consider whether he should be executed. Since Carr's background included incidents of homosexuality, Keefer and George would be granted wide latitude to examine potential jurors' attitudes toward sexual orientation. Surprisingly, the ruling in favor of a wide-open voir dire was based on Carr's sexual history, not the victims' sexual activities at the time of the shootings. Carr's sexual history was not relevant to provocation, but it was relevant to whether a jury should sentence him to death.

All that Judge Spicer had decided so far was that Keefer's voir dire problem did not require a pretrial ruling that excluded evidence of the victims' sexual activity from the trial. He had not yet made up his mind whether he would, per George's request, delay until trial his ruling on whether the defense could raise a provocation defense. At this point in the conference, the only specific rulings Spicer had made were that Carr's sexual history was irrelevant to provocation and that the victims' sexual activities were relevant to what had happened on South Mountain. He had not yet decided whether this latter evidence, despite its relevance, was so prejudicial to the commonwealth's case that it should be excluded, anyway.

The only issue George wanted to delay until trial was the question of whether the defense could explicitly raise the defense of provocation. He was prepared to argue immediately that the evidence of sexual activity had to go into the trial because the commonwealth was going to introduce Trooper John Holtz's report of Carr's confession, which included a reference to what Carr had seen the women doing. He then added,

> George: Additionally, there's evidence that a third party may have been involved in this shooting, a third party who has made threats to homosexuals, a third party who was in the area at the time the incident took place. We're entitled to introduce evidence that a third party may be responsible for the shooting. I can go through a whole list but I don't think I want to bore the court with that at this point.

George was referring to the police report that indicated that Paul Drixell had suggested that homosexuals should be used for target practice. The defense was entitled to introduce evidence that Drixell, not Carr, shot the two women. If the defense did introduce such evidence, it would obviously have the right to present evidence that Brenner and Wight were engaged in lesbian sexual activity at the time of the shootings.

Judge Spicer noted a problem with George's line of reasoning. There was no evidence that Drixell had seen the women at all, much less at the time of the shootings.

> George: I don't believe that the defense is forced with the proposition [of] proving the third party is involved or responsible. I think the defense is entitled to present evidence that the third party may be involved. The burden is not on me to prove this third party guilty.
>
> Judge Spicer: That's true.
>
> Keefer: But they can't just talk about third party without any evidentiary material being in the case, either.

Judge Spicer: It would seem to me that the description of what
occurred is going to be admissible. It would also
seem to me that the jury is going to be told that that
cannot be used as serious provocation.

George had won a victory. The evidence of the victims' sexual activity
was going into the trial so that the defense could, if it decided to do so,
implicate an innocent person by publicly exposing his homophobic prejudices. Even if Judge Spicer eventually ruled at the trial that the defense
could not raise a provocation defense, at least some evidence of lesbian
sexual activity would be placed in front of the Adams County jury.

Since Judge Spicer had reserved his ruling on whether the defense
could explicitly raise the issue of provocation with the jury, Keefer asked
whether Smith, Brenner's attorney, could file an amicus brief in opposi-
tion to the defense's plan to raise a provocation defense at trial. Keefer's
request was somewhat unusual, but not necessarily illegitimate. Statements by victims at sentencing hearings have become a regular feature of
the American justice system, so why shouldn't victims have a right to
influence the trial process itself?

Judge Spicer, however, at first reacted negatively to the request, telling Keefer that he and he alone was responsible for prosecuting Carr.
Smith then addressed the court for the first time.

Smith: I am certainly not employed by the commonwealth;
nor do I intend to represent them in any way. I am,
however, retained by Miss Brenner who is, unusually
is, a surviving complainant in a homicide prosecution. I say "unusually." Usually, complaining witnesses—they're dead. The case is of particular im-
portance to her. I think the court knows there are a
number of issues that are rather intimate and private. She, like any other citizen, has a right to privacy. My interest in the case, Your Honor, is clearly
on her behalf and also [as] a friend of the court. If
the court or defense counsel wants, I could file as
amicus formally.

Judge Spicer: If you enter special appearance on behalf of a witness
to protect her right of privacy, that's something

else. At least you're representing someone's interest. You're not just coming in as a proponent of the concept of justice which is an *amicus curiae* position. It's entirely a different matter how you are viewed in this particular case. You say that she has certain rights of privacy. I agree with you. I think that's very relevant, but that's something different than being a friend of the court.

Sensing that Judge Spicer was about to allow Smith to file her brief, not as an amicus curiae, but as a private attorney protecting Brenner's right to privacy, George objected to her entry in the case. Spicer emphasized the limited character of Smith's appearance, noting that she would not participate in the trial itself.

George: Your Honor, it's gone beyond that respect when she's starting to file briefs and argue legal issues. There's legal issues before this court. They're being argued by the victim, the commonwealth. They're making an issue out of the very issue they don't want to make an issue out of.

Judge Spicer: I didn't understand she wanted to argue. She just wanted to file a brief.

Keefer: That's right.

George: Isn't that another way of arguing?

Judge Spicer: I suppose. We'll allow her to file a brief on behalf of the witness.

After conceding that Smith's brief was a form of argument, Spicer let her file it anyway.

George thought that Judge Spicer was making a mistake. He acknowledged that Brenner had a right to retain an attorney, whether to protect her right to privacy or for some other reason, but Smith's brief focused on provocation, not on Brenner's rights of privacy. A victim, a probable witness, was attempting to influence how Spicer resolved the legal issue that was at the heart of Carr's death penalty case. Now George would have to respond to the arguments of both the prosecutor and the surviving victim's lawyer, thereby upsetting the level playing field of the adversarial system.

After Judge Spicer granted Smith permission to file her brief, the conference moved to the defense's motions *in limine*. One concerned a quotation carved into the stock of Carr's gun: "I will give up my gun when they pry my cold dead fingers from around it." George believed that this inscription was irrelevant to Carr's guilt and should be excluded from the trial on that basis. Keefer disagreed.

> Keefer: [In regard to] that statement carved into the stock of that rifle with its, if you will, sentiment towards that gun and the right to carry that gun, we can certainly contrast that statement with the defendant's actions of disassembling the gun, packing it in plastic and hiding it in the woods under a rotted tree stump to show the obvious guilt that he felt after the time of the shooting and can argue to the jury that [it] is evidence of guilt that they can consider in terms of finding the defendant guilty or not guilty of homicide of the first degree or any other crime.

Seeing the gun, touching it, handling it, and, yes, reading the inscription and feeling the carved lettering—that was an experience that Keefer wanted to give to the jury at Carr's trial.

George responded that before the prosecution could use the inscription against Carr, Keefer had to prove that it was he who carved it into the gun stock. Realizing that he had no such evidence, Keefer gave up. The gun would be allowed into evidence, but Keefer would not be allowed to show the inscription to the jury.

"What else?" Judge Spicer asked.

George explained that the defense would stipulate that the victim was in fact Rebecca Wight, therefore making it unnecessary for Mr. Wight to identify his dead daughter on the stand. Citing two Pennsylvania Supreme Court opinions in support of his position, Keefer argued that there could be no such stipulation unless the commonwealth agreed. Judge Spicer ruled, "That's obviously correct and that [defense] request is refused." George's rather transparent attempt to keep Mr. Wight off the stand had failed. Even if Mr. Wight's testimony was designed to elicit sympathy from the jury, the prosecution could still put him on the stand.

Before adjourning the conference, Judge Spicer summed up what had been accomplished: Mr. Wight could testify; the inscription on Carr's gun was inadmissible; the defense would not be allowed to introduce evidence concerning the past relationship of Brenner and Wight; Smith could submit her brief on provocation; and the issues of how much evidence of the victims' sexual activities would be admitted and whether the defense would be permitted to argue provocation to the jury were reserved for trial.

The Decision

eightchapter
eight

I

After the pretrial conference, the defense had little time. Jury selection would begin the following Monday, October 31st, and all that Defense Attorney Michael George could argue was that Steve Carr should be convicted of nothing more than voluntary manslaughter, because the women had legally provoked him. To succeed, George would have to convince first Judge Oscar Spicer and then the jury that Carr had been in a rage at the time of the shootings (the subjective requirement of provocation) and that the women had done things to him that would have provoked a rational person to violence (the objective requirement). At the time, George's only idea was to hook some of the sorry aspects of Carr's life on the subjective requirement. He'd try to prove that Carr was in a rage the whole day by showing the jury how Carr's life had turned him into a bitter and frustrated young man, full of hate.

"In other words," George explains, "all this testimony that Judge Spicer thought was relevant only to diminished capacity, that Carr was rejected and sexually assaulted—I would try to get it in through the back door. I wouldn't use it to prove that Carr acted as a rational man would have acted, but rather to prove that at the time of the shootings Carr was in a very emotional and irrational state. The beauty of it was that individ-

174 ·

ual jurors might start to sympathize with Carr because of what he had been through, connecting what happened on May 13th with all the bad things that had happened to him. It would then be difficult for them to answer the question of how a rational man would have reacted in an objective fashion. Hopefully, mercy would creep into the picture."

But who would testify that the women had done things to Carr that would have provoked a rational person? Obviously, Brenner was not going to admit to any such conduct, and, according to Criminal Defense Investigator Skip Gochenour, it was no accident that Troopers John Holtz and Donald Blevins and Corporal Matthew O'Brien would not testify that Carr had told them that the women had teased him.

"What you've got to understand," says Gochenour, "is that today's police officer usually is not interested in the truth, or should I say, the whole truth. What he wants are those parts of the truth that enable him to get a conviction on the most serious charge possible. For example, Holtz's question to Carr: 'Did you really see those girls kissing?' That was a well thought-out question to get Carr to incriminate himself. But did Holtz follow up? Did he ask Carr why he shot the two women while they were engaged in sex? No, he did not. Why? Because the last thing Holtz wanted in his possession was information that might help the defense. Police officers are trained to interrogate a suspect in this way. They want admissions of key facts, not full confessions."

George could put Carr himself on the stand, but here too there were obstacles. First, there was Carr's appearance: tall, thin, gaunt, hollow-faced, missing most of his front teeth, deep-set eyes. "We feared that some of the jurors would find him menacing even in the courtroom," says George. Second, if Carr took the stand, Prosecutor Roy Keefer would ask him whether he pulled the trigger. "The whole idea of trying to get Carr's confession thrown out on appeal would, more or less, have just gone up in smoke," George insists. "The appellate court would find out through the grapevine that at trial Carr had admitted to the shootings. So, putting Carr on the stand had the effect of putting all his eggs in one basket, the provocation basket. I didn't think that was wise at the time, and I still don't. We had a good Fifth Amendment argument. Why throw it away for something that was probably not going to work, anyway?"

Also, George doubted that Carr could have answered Keefer's questions without inadvertently undermining his claim that the women had legally provoked him. Carr just didn't have the intellectual training or capacities to stand up to a hostile cross-examination. The impoverished background that perhaps disabled Carr from having adequate control over his violent inclinations also disabled him from taking the stand in his own defense.

Lastly, there was the character of the shootings. The murder weapon, a single-shot .22 caliber rifle, had to be reloaded manually after each shot, which required some dexterity. In addition, because the ejector that spits out the spent shells from the chamber wasn't working, Carr had to be able to dig them out. The knife found at the crime scene was probably used for this purpose.

"Then look at the shooter's success," Gochenour points out. "There was indisputable evidence that from a distance of eighty-two feet the shooter hit his target with seven of eight bullets. Five of the shots hit Claudia Brenner within a seven- or eight-inch circle of her head, indicating that a skilled and calm marksman was trying to kill the two women. You take an inexperienced hunter out in the woods, and I don't care how well he can shoot at a target, if a deer jumps out of the woods fifty feet away, nine times out of ten the inexperienced hunter won't hit a thing. He has buck fever. His body dumps adrenaline into his system. The result: he loses a lot of his fine motor skills and coordination. Look at how a basketball player can't even make a free throw because he gets too nervous in a big game. You see, Adams County is a big hunting area. The hunters on the jury would have known that whoever shot those women was not in some kind of rage. They would have known that the shooter wasn't out of control, but in control, completely in control of the situation. I didn't know if Keefer would focus on these facts, but I didn't think he had to. I think the hunters on the jury would have figured it out all by themselves."

Though Keefer had always thought that an Adams County jury posed a problem for him, George and Gochenour thought that the social reality was the exact opposite. The men of Adams County would never have bought the idea that Carr satisfied the subjective requirement of provocation. Of course, George and Gochenour did their utmost to make Keefer think that he had a jury problem by spreading publicly the impression that the murder was a vicious hate crime. But they spread this impression to give Keefer some incentive to make a deal, not because they believed it.

"If Carr shot those women," Gochenour insists, "he didn't do it because they were lesbians. Hell, why would he follow them around all day if he wanted to kill them because they were homosexuals. He knew what they were in the morning. He had his gun, no one was around. And you got to remember that Carr had a homosexual incident in prison. He filed a complaint against the other guy, but that was only because he didn't get paid. Now is that the type of guy who's going to shoot someone because he or she's a homosexual? Does that make any sense at all? So, the idea that this was some sort of hate crime was a distortion that the defense fed into, but it really was a case of letting Keefer, the police, the victims, and the media think what they wanted to think anyway."

"This kind of mess," Gochenour continues, "arises when politics gets mixed up with the criminal justice system, when political perceptions and fears start to influence what the decision makers in the criminal justice system are doing. The facts of the case receive less attention than some politically inspired guess about the motive of the killer. Other facts can't get into evidence, because the police are trained to be ignorant of them because, politically, they want the public accolades that go along with big convictions. I think all of this, or maybe I should say most of it, is politics: the politicalization of the American criminal justice system, a system that once was the best in the world. Maybe it still is, but it is not as good as it used to be."

Despite Gochenour's suggestion that the American criminal justice system once operated more in accordance with "the facts" than it does today, it would be incorrect to think that there ever was a golden age when American criminal courts assessed culpability in a manner divorced from the surrounding political and social context. Many legal doctrines and principles cannot be applied without making subtle value judgments that are inescapably political in character. It is possible, however, that today's criminal justice system is more self-consciously political than yesterday's. Contemporary Americans are perhaps more sensitive than previous generations to the underlying political commitments involved in defining criminal law categories. These categories therefore become contested, mirroring broader social and political disagreements.

Issues of insanity, diminished capacity, provocation, the right to remain silent, hate crime, date rape, crack cocaine use, child abuse, battered woman syndrome, and recovered memory all have a political profile. Today's American criminal justice system perhaps functions more than it once did in a political spotlight. If so, not all the effects of this spotlight are necessarily beneficial. For example, despite Gochenour's lament for a bygone era of American criminal justice, he and George were apparently willing to use the political aspects of the Carr case to gain for their client a perhaps undeserved leniency.

According to George and Gochenour, Carr shot Wight and Brenner because they didn't treat him with respect. Carr, an outcast of society, rejected by family and society, went off to live in the woods. Here he had some control. He knew how to survive and people left him alone. Then Carr ran into these two women at the campsite, two middle-class college students who were succeeding in the world in which Carr had failed. Whatever happened between the women and Carr, he got pissed off, George and Gochenour believe. Maybe he had to take this kind of abuse in town—the giggles, the finger pointing, the stares—but he was not going to put up with it on his own turf. The woods were his home.

"You see," Gochenour explains, "middle-class people construct an artificial world around them and then they believe that that's the way the real world is. They believe that discussion will solve everything, that if you have good intellectual tools, you can out-argue anybody and out-intellectualize the next guy. And that's how you will prevail. But Steve Carr didn't resolve disputes in the middle-class way. He wasn't going to try to out-argue or out-intellectualize anyone. He had his own way of winning arguments.

"Carr may have hated the women," Gochenour concludes, "but he hated them because they were from a culture that despised him, loathed him as a creepy subhuman animal. There was a clash of cultures up there on South Mountain. I remember Mike described it once that way. But it wasn't the clash of heterosexual culture against homosexual culture. It was a clash of the culture of the underworld—the culture of the failed, the rejected and the despised—against the culture of progressive middle-class America. If one of the women had been a male, or, for that matter, if both had been heterosexual males, the same thing would probably have happened.

Though the defense fully intended to put witnesses on the stand who would testify that Carr was a peaceful, shy, somewhat reclusive individual, Gochenour in fact perceived him as a violent social outcast. He was not a hometown boy; he had a long criminal record; and he had a scary, wild look about him—the mountain man look. He was the kind of person who's often executed in this country. One of the freaks. The ones who have been rejected their entire lives get one last big rejection.

For all these reasons, the defense was ecstatic when they heard that Keefer was willing to cut a deal. It gave Carr a way out. George immediately called Keefer and told him that Carr might consider a deal if he could avoid the death penalty. The two lawyers talked about what each wanted. George didn't want to give up the right to appeal the *Miranda* issue. That complicated the situation, because a convicted defendant can appeal, but not one who pleads guilty. To get around this problem, George and Keefer worked out the arrangement of a non-jury bench trial. Keefer would drop the death penalty and all the charges except one count of first-degree murder. In return, the defense accepted a stipulated set of facts that made it a virtual certainty that Judge Spicer would convict Carr of first-degree murder and, as Pennsylvania law required, sentence him to life imprisonment. If the defense later won its case on appeal and got a new trial, Carr's confessions, gun, and hair samples would be excluded from it, but the commonwealth could then resurrect the death penalty and all the other charges.

"After Keefer and I worked out this deal," George recounts, "we both went back to talk to our respective parties. I laid it out for Steve. I told him he had two doors in front of him: one door was marked TRIAL, the other DEAL. I told him that we couldn't be sure, at least not entirely, of what was behind each door. We knew some of what was behind each door, but not all. If he chose the door marked TRIAL, then he would have a jury trial. He could be convicted of first-degree murder and get the death penalty or life imprisonment, or, if he got lucky, he could be convicted of either third-degree murder or voluntary manslaughter. No one knew what was going to happen, but I told him that in my judgment a voluntary manslaughter conviction was not likely. If he took the door marked DEAL, we knew he wouldn't be executed. He probably would be convicted of first-degree murder and sentenced to life imprisonment, but we could still appeal the *Miranda* issue. On the other hand, we did not know if the appeal would go anywhere. It might lead to a new trial, a trial where Steve would be in a much stronger evidentiary position, but then again it might not. And if we lost the appeal, we didn't know how many years Steve would be in prison. He might spend the rest of his life behind bars, or he might at some point get a pardon. It was his choice. Which door did he want? I didn't envy his decision. I think if I had to make a decision like that, I would choose the door marked TRIAL because I'm something of a natural gambler. But who knows how one would choose in such a situation? It's a terrible spot to be in."

II

"Why did I decide to go the route of a deal?" says Keefer. "Well, in the end, I think it had to do with the type of case it was. There was a surviving victim, Claudia Brenner, who would have had to testify if the case went to trial, and her testimony would have had to deal with some very intimate activities. It might have been a very painful experience, both for her and for the family of Rebecca Wight. So, I decided to leave it up to Claudia and Mr. Wight. If they wanted a trial and a chance for the death penalty, I would go for it. If, on the other hand, the victims were satisfied with a sentence of life imprisonment and wanted to avoid a trial, then I would go forward with the arrangement that George and I had worked out."

Keefer met with Brenner and Mr. Wight in his office in the Adams County Courthouse on Wednesday, October 26th, two days after the pre-trial conference. Three of the police officers who had worked on the case—Blevins, Holtz and O'Brien—were also there, along with Brenner's attorney, Abbe Smith, and Mr. Wight's daughter Judy. They sat in a circle so that they could talk directly to one another. Keefer quickly explained the specifics of the deal that he and George had talked about. Both Brenner and Mr. Wight indicated that they were not inclined to take the deal if there was a strong likelihood that Carr would win on appeal. They didn't want to come back in three years and testify at Carr's new trial. Keefer assured them that Carr's Fifth Amendment appeal wasn't going anywhere.

"I tend to think it was one of those CYA [Cover Your Ass] motions that defense lawyers have to file to protect themselves. Even if Carr won the appeal and the confessions and the gun were thrown out, it would have been a big mistake for Carr to come back and argue to the jury that he didn't pull the trigger. No jury would buy that. In fact, the quickest way for Carr to have gotten the death penalty, at least in my opinion, was for him to come in and say, 'Wasn't me.' His best option was to admit that he did it, but argue that 'Yeah, I was enraged because I had such an unhappy life.' That way, you're hoping not to get murder one, but even if you get it, you're laying your foundation for the penalty phase. But Carr already had that option in the first trial. So, if he wanted something better than a sentence of life imprisonment, he had to risk the death penalty. That was the real choice facing Mr. Carr. I had him pretty well cornered."

Keefer also explained to Brenner, Mr. Wight, and the others what life imprisonment meant in Pennsylvania. Under former Governor Milton Shapp, people sentenced to life imprisonment usually got a pardon after seventeen or eighteen years in prison, but Governor Richard Thornburgh had not pardoned anyone who wasn't on his deathbed. Keefer refused to make any predictions about the future. The case against Carr, of course, was airtight. At the preliminary hearing, Brenner had proved that she could talk about her sex life on the witness stand without losing her composure, and Keefer knew of no real inconsistencies or discrepancies in her testimony. The only question mark in Keefer's mind was how the jury would react to the victims.

"What you want," Keefer explains, "is to have the jury sit in the box and think, 'There but for the grace of God go I. That could have been me that was shot.' I don't think we would have had that kind of identification in this case, not with Claudia and Rebecca. The jurors would not have sat there and said, 'That could have been me.' In fact, I feared that some of them might be rather disgusted by what Claudia and Rebecca had been doing up there on South Mountain. I even told them, which was true, that I personally had run into people I knew, respected people here in Gettysburg, who made comments like, 'I can see why he did it.' As I recall, Don Blevins had also heard some similar things from some people on the street. We told Claudia and Mr. Wight about these comments, not to scare them, but to let them know that there were people in the community that had that sort of attitude."

According to Keefer, Brenner approached the issue of the death penalty from a more intellectual, less emotional perspective than Mr. Wight did. She wanted to know the likelihood of all the outcomes of the various options. Smith helped her frame questions and assess the possibilities. Keefer sensed that Brenner was more willing to deal than Mr. Wight because she realized the risks of a trial. A conviction of third-degree murder would result in a ten- to twenty-year sentence for Carr, with a chance of parole in seven years. Voluntary manslaughter, which was a possibility if the case went to trial, amounted to only five to ten. And, even if Carr were sentenced to death, no one had been executed in the commonwealth in twenty-five years. So why gamble?

Keefer emphasized that if Mr. Wight and Brenner decided to go for the death penalty, he would give them 100 percent. On the other hand, if Brenner opted for the deal, Keefer made it clear that he was not going to run the risk of a trial if his major witness was not on board with that decision. Mr. Wight understood what Keefer was saying. The meeting then broke up. Mr. Wight and Brenner were to inform Keefer of their decisions the following morning.

III

Leon Wight's reaction to his daughter's murder stemmed from his own personality and the nature of his relationship to her. Mr. Wight set high standards for himself and for those around him, especially his children, in whom he tried to instill the values of hard work, independence, and self-reliance. In part because Rebecca embodied these values, Mr. Wight always introduced his eldest daughter as "Rebecca, my daughter, of whom I am exceedingly proud." Mr. Wight was also, however, a man who sometimes drank too much, which made him impatient and irritable. He would therefore occasionally find fault with his daughters and say things he would later regret.

Such a situation arose in May 1988. Mr. Wight's second wife worked for an international organization that would occasionally give home leave to its employees and their dependents. In the case of the Wight family, that meant the organization would provide free transportation to the Philippines for her and all her dependents, including any adopted children. Rebecca and her sister Evelyn wanted to take advantage of this opportunity to travel, but they hadn't supplied the organization with the required itineraries. On Monday, May 9th, Mr. Wight got a letter from Rebecca that only vaguely described her travel plans. He had been drinking, and the letter made him angry. He called Rebecca up and chewed her out on the phone. He told her point-blank that her explanation for her irresponsibility was "inadequate."

On Wednesday, Rebecca wrote her father a letter explaining why the itineraries were late. "I see this itinerary," she wrote, "as one of many situations where we just didn't understand each other very well." Their inability to communicate had two sources, she wrote: Mr. Wight's feeling unappreciated and his alcoholism.

> I am trying to understand exactly where the distress is rooted, and I think it comes from your feeling unappreciated. I want you to feel appreciated, and I think no matter how much you are appreciated you have to feel that way inside about yourself. I don't think it is something I can provide.
>
> When you yelled at me about my inadequacy over and over I felt as if you must have been told that yourself sometime (maybe you tell yourself that over and over in your head) but it simply is not true. We are both fine people who have a hard time understanding each other. . . .
>
> And no matter how much we understand that you have a disease and that I am dealing with the symptoms of a disease and not the real and wonderful you, I do react irrationally out of my own emotional distress about the ongoing poor communication that is inevitable. . . . But you know, it is not my job to keep straight in my heart and mind the real YOU and the alcoholic not-YOU.

Rebecca closed her letter with an expression of her love for her father and an apology for the sometimes complicated character of their relationship.

Rebecca's response further irritated her father. He immediately sat down and wrote his reply, expressing his bewilderment as to why his two daughters could not give him the information he needed, information that was for their, not his, benefit. He could only conclude that Rebecca "must have terrible problems" with her priorities and values. In its closing paragraphs, Mr. Wight's letter took on an angry tone as it highlighted Rebecca's ingratitude and irresponsibility.

> You cannot imagine how I now feel about my daughters. Your lack of care, interest and efforts, and your selfishness and stupidity have hurt me tremendously. I have always respected you for your intel-

ligence, your independence, and your ambition, but this recent incident and recent visits have damaged my confidence in you. I feel estranged from you. . . .

Mr. Wight, a frustrated parent whose pride in his children led him to write things he didn't mean, wrote the above letter on the evening of May 13th and it was there on his desk the next day when he found out that Rebecca had been murdered.

The pain Mr. Wight felt rereading the letter was excruciating. He'd lost a daughter to a violent death. That was bad enough, so bad that Mr. Wight had trouble accepting the reality of it. But the realization that he had lost Rebecca when they were estranged and that they never would have the opportunity to patch things up doubled his pain, hurting him in an almost physical sense. The existence of the letter intensified his grief. Of course, Rebecca hadn't seen the letter, but there was no getting around the fact that he had written the sharp words at approximately the same time that his daughter, alone in the woods in Pennsylvania, was dying. This unnerving image preoccupied and depressed Mr. Wight during the months after the murder, perhaps explaining in part why he wanted Carr executed.

"At the meeting, Keefer told me to call him the next day, to tell him what I thought he should do, even though it was pretty clear to me that Claudia Brenner was ultimately going to be the one who made the decision," says Mr. Wight. "That hurt me. That hurt me very much. The more I thought about this deal, the more it sickened me. And the more I realized that I couldn't do anything about it, the angrier I got. I called him that morning. That was on the morning of the 27th. I know, because I wrote down on a piece of paper what I intended to say and I still have that piece of paper. I kept it. Go ahead, read it."

10/27/88
Telecon to Roy Keefer, D.A., Gettysburg, PA

- Plea bargain = a quick, easy, cheap success for the prosecutor. He gets credit for a conviction without the labors of a trial. It's a cop-out.
- Why the rush? Why do you need a decision from me on such an important issue in less than 24 hours? Is it because you're afraid

that Carr's lawyer may withdraw the offer to plea-bargain? Why do you have this fear? I conceived Becky, my first child, and raised her for 18 years until she went away to college. Why must I make a decision in as many hours re the disposition of her murderer? For your convenience? For the court's convenience? Fuck you! I don't care about your inconveniences. How many technical errors will result from the rush?

- What about the charges related to the attempted murder of Claudia? Have you bargained them away? Is this justice? It's like Carr never committed these crimes. You have given away too much.

- Are there any other elements you have overlooked—technical or otherwise—that the defense may use to reduce the assurance that Carr WILL spend the rest of his life in a maximum security prison with no possibility of parole?

- You have personally called Claudia and/or her lawyer many times to keep them informed re developments. You have never called me. Why not? You personally called Claudia to request her presence at yesterday's meeting. You did not call me. Why not?

- I have been provided/informed of *no* information since the initial hearing.

- I agree to the plea bargain for the following reasons:
  a. Carr would never be executed even if he were convicted and received the death penalty[,] based on the fact that there have been no executions in Pennsylvania in 25 years and there are now about 200 convicted felons on death row.
  b. I have little confidence that you could/would prosecute this case with sufficient aggressiveness to succeed. You're a nice guy and you are an ambitious politician in Gettysburg. Do I need to elaborate on that subject?
  c. Based on your description of the process of two trials—one for conviction and another for penalty—I have strong doubts—I fear that Carr could end up with a lesser penalty than life imprisonment without parole.
  d. I have little respect for the system of so-called justice in this country based on what I have experienced.

    e. Carr will be vulnerable to rape and murder as an ordinary con-
      vict; he will not enjoy the protections he would on death row.

- "Life imprisonment without parole." What does it really mean?
  How many are free today? How are they freed? Does it really
  mean what it says?

Mr. Wight can't recall whether he addressed every one of these points
when he talked to Keefer that morning, but he's sure he touched on most
of them. Whether he did or not, they are an accurate representation of
what he was thinking and feeling on the day Keefer and George cut their
deal in the Carr case.

IV

Brenner returned to Keefer's office the next morning, Thursday, October
27th. She had stayed overnight in a motel and hashed things out with her
lawyer. She told Keefer she preferred the deal.

"The trial was just too big of a gamble," Keefer observes. "It meant
turning over the decision of what happened to Carr to twelve people who
were complete strangers to her. She just didn't want to do that. Maybe it
was because she has seen so much prejudice against gays and lesbians, but
I also think Claudia wanted to be in control of the situation. I had made it
clear to her that I was going to abide by her decision. That kind of influence can be psychologically comforting to a victim, especially one who's a
member of a discriminated-against group. On the other hand, even if
Carr would never in fact be executed, I think it would have been enor-
mously gratifying for Claudia to have twelve jurors sentence Carr to
death, to have them say that Carr no longer deserved to be alive. A symbolic death sentence might have satisfied Claudia. It might have given her
some real assurance that the criminal justice system did not discriminate
against homosexuals. That homosexuals were people, too. But in the end,
Claudia wasn't all that confident that she would get the desired result. She
gave up the opportunity to test the system for the sure thing—a sentence
of life imprisonment. Her fears ultimately won out over her hopes."

V

Before the meeting on the 26th, Don Blevins had run into Keefer in the
hall and asked him what was going on. Keefer told him about the possi-

ble deal in the Carr case. Blevins recalls, "My attitude was, 'Whatever you think is best.' If Keefer thought the right thing to do was to cut a deal for life imprisonment, it was his call. As a state trooper, my view was that he knew more about it than I did. But I did wonder, why make a deal? A confession is the ultimate. Why deal a case when you had the guy cold? That was my question, but I didn't push it."

Blevins says he can't recall Keefer's ever having a meeting like the one he had in the Carr case. Usually, Keefer would just call the victim on the phone, give him or her a sales pitch, and the person would buy the deal that he had arranged. Sometimes he'd call the arresting cop and let him or her know what was happening, but other times the cop would find out by reading the newspaper. Blevins says he can't help thinking that the meeting was to put extra pressure on Brenner to take the deal. The cops were there to cheer the deal along, but they didn't have a vote. Keefer didn't care what they thought.

Blevins doesn't remember having a lot of input at the meeting. He might have said some things to Brenner about how juries were unpredictable, but at that point he was following Keefer's lead. At first, Blevins didn't think Brenner was going to buy the deal. She was really upset when she was told that all the charges involving her would be dropped if the deal went through. Says Blevins, "Claudia was thinking, 'But what about what Carr did to me?' That concerned her, but eventually she started looking at the whole picture. After all, how many times can you serve a life sentence? I think her lawyer, Abbe Smith, who if I remember correctly was personally opposed to the death penalty, probably had a lot of influence. She helped turn Claudia around."

In contrast to Brenner, Mr. Wight could not be reasoned with, Blevins recalls. Of course, he adds, many Americans wouldn't have bought that deal if their child had been the one murdered. Mr. Wight's opinion didn't matter much, anyway, because he didn't have a veto on the deal. This wasn't stated explicitly, but it was implied; at least that was Blevins's impression. Brenner was a victim; Mr. Wight was only a relative of a victim.

"I know I felt sorry for Leon Wight," Blevins recalls. "I knew he felt betrayed by the system. His daughter had been killed, and he had no real influence on what was going to happen to the murderer. It bothered Keefer, too. He wanted Wight's approval of the deal, but he never really got it. I remember after the meeting, Keefer said something in the hall-way like, 'I sure wish it could be different.' Maybe it bothered Keefer so much because he froze Wight out of the decision for the very reason that he knew that Wight would never come down on the side that Keefer wanted him to come down on: the side of the deal. And maybe Keefer left the decision in Claudia's hands for that reason, too. He guessed that she'd eventually take the deal, so he let her make the decision. I don't know if that's what happened, but that's possible, very possible."

VI

The role that victims should play in plea bargaining is a matter of dispute. In the past, their influence has been limited, because crime was perceived as a violation of the public's peace and the state took full responsibility for prosecuting and punishing criminals. Today, there is a developing appreciation that the traditional outlook is perhaps insensitive to victims' feelings. The role that Brenner and Mr. Wight played in the Carr case shows both the problems and the benefits of expanding the role that victims play in plea bargaining. For example, Keefer gave Brenner the power to veto the deal. Was that justifiable? As the district attorney, should he have made the decision alone? Alternatively, if it was okay to give Brenner veto power, should he also have given it to Mr. Wight? After all, why should Brenner have a veto if the deal meant that the only charge against Carr was the murder of Mr. Wight's daughter? On the other hand, would it have been improper to give Mr. Wight veto power because of the kinds of emotions he was experiencing? Lastly, if Blevins is correct and Keefer gave Brenner a veto because he was pretty sure that he could manipulate her decision, is this unethical conduct on Keefer's part or a shrewd way of handling professional responsibilities?

Keefer is a person who presumably would not be allowed to serve on a jury in a capital punishment case, because his religious beliefs prevent him from sentencing anyone to death. Nevertheless, he believed that his personal reservations concerning the death penalty had no effect on Brenner's decision to opt for the deal and that he would have been an "aggressive advocate" in favor of sending Carr to his death if Brenner opted for a trial. Keefer may be right on both counts. The human mind is complicated, capable of much that appears contradictory, whether the issue is why a victim opted for a deal, why a prosecutor sought the death penalty in a particular case, or why a murderer killed someone. After all, St. Augustine long ago argued that a true Christian could execute a condemned criminal as long as it was done in the spirit of love. If a true Christian can manage such a psychological feat, it's certainly possible that a district attorney could be an "aggressive advocate" in favor of inflicting a sanction that he or she personally abhors. In today's world, perhaps professional responsibilities enable human beings to do what once required religious inspiration.

chapter nine

The Trial

I

The bench trial of Stephen Roy Carr, in which Judge Oscar Spicer would decide whether Carr, in killing Rebecca Wight, was guilty of first-degree murder or of a lower form of homicide, began about 3:25 P.M. on the day Claudia Brenner accepted the deal that Defense Attorney Michael George and Prosecutor Roy Keefer had worked out. The same people who had attended the preliminary hearing, the suppression hearing, and the pretrial conference were once again gathered in Courtroom 1 on the fourth floor of the Adams County Courthouse. The four state troopers who had played pivotal roles in Carr's capture—Corporal Matthew O'Brien and Troopers Donald Blevins, Denny Beaver, and John Holtz—were present, as were the handful of reporters who had been covering the case for the local newspapers and TV channels. Leon Wight, his wife, and his two daughters, Evelyn and Judy, sat together with Claudia Brenner, Abbe Smith, and approximately eight other women behind the table occupied by Keefer and his assistant. George, Criminal Defense Investigator Skip Gochenour, and Carr sat at the defense table on the left side of the room. Because no one from Carr's family was present, the benches immediately behind the defense table were empty. The proceedings began immediately after Spicer entered the sparsely filled room and took his place on the bench.

After Keefer summarized the terms of the agreement for Judge Spicer's benefit, George announced that he would not proceed until Spicer made his formal ruling on whether he (George) could raise the defense of provocation at Carr's trial. Timing was crucial, because Carr could appeal only judicial rulings made before the agreement. George then made "an offer of proof" that recounted Carr's history of sexual abuse and social rejection and noted that "the women were engaged in a lesbian act at the time the incident occurred." Though Spicer observed that such evidence might be relevant to diminished capacity, he ruled that it did not constitute legal provocation.

The ruling reveals the all-or-nothing character of categories of criminal culpability. Perhaps Carr could have presented evidence that would have satisfied some but not all of the requirements of diminished capacity. Perhaps he also could have presented evidence that would have satisfied some but not all of the requirements of provocation. But since he could not satisfy all the requirements of either, Carr had no excuse whatsoever. He was not permitted to add whatever he could present with regard to diminished capacity to what he could present with regard to provocation so that a jury would have a full picture of him and of what he had done. The law's commitment to "the whole truth" must be understood accordingly. The law often ignores relevant facts that are not enough to turn the color of a legal litmus paper, and it doesn't matter how many pieces of litmus paper there are in a case. Just because Carr had a plausible argument that the police violated his Fifth Amendment rights did not mean that the law would extend to him a wide conception of either diminished capacity or provocation.

After making his final ruling on provocation, Judge Spicer turned to Carr and told him that a jury might return a verdict of voluntary manslaughter, but that he, as a judge, would be "less inclined to dispense mercy without [a] rational basis." So, the judge continued, "if you elect to proceed to a trial by the Court alone, . . . you're basically giving up your right to a voluntary manslaughter verdict. Do you understand that?"

"Yes, Your Honor," Carr replied. His fear of the death penalty outweighed his hope that a jury would treat him leniently. His fear and hope were the reverse of Brenner's.

With the provocation issue out of the way, Judge Spicer entered into a long dialogue with Carr, directing at him questions that were, in the main, the standard ones that judges across the country ask when they are taking a defendant's guilty plea. One purpose of this somewhat ritualized conversation (called "the colloquy") was to insulate the deal George and Keefer had struck from later appellate attack. This was accomplished by creating a record indicating that Carr knew what he was doing and that he was doing it voluntarily.

Judge Spicer began with a series of questions concerning Carr's emotional and psychological health and then turned to Carr's relationship to George. Carr's answers to these questions, which were part of the price of the deal, would make it more difficult for him ever to argue on appeal that he was incompetent or that Pennsylvania had supplied him with ineffective counsel.

After asking Carr whether he could make an "intelligent decision about how you are proceeding today" and getting an affirmative reply, Judge Spicer remarked, "Just tell me what you think we're doing in your own words. What's happening today?"

Unable to respond, Carr said, "I am not Michael George. I understand but, you know, it's putting it into words."

Judge Spicer described for Carr the constitutional rights that he would be waiving if he took the deal: his right against double jeopardy (the right not to be prosecuted twice for the same crime) and all the rights associated with a jury trial, including the right to confront witnesses. To save himself from a death sentence, Carr "freely" gave away these rights. Perhaps he knew what he was doing, perhaps he didn't. Certainly it was a lot of ground to cover for someone with only nine years of education.

Keefer suggested that Judge Spicer tell Carr that because of the deal, "he may be giving up some [non-specified] due process rights."

Spicer responded, "That really won't mean anything. If you have some in mind I'd be glad to talk to him about it. But I am sure he won't understand what a due process right is." This doubt was in contrast to Spicer's confidence that Carr understood the more specific constitutional rights he had just discussed with him.

Was Judge Spicer's confidence misplaced? Was it possible or likely that, throughout the colloquy, Carr was claiming that he understood things that he in fact did not understand or understood only superficially?

At the end of the colloquy, Judge Spicer asked Carr whether anyone had "pressured" him into accepting the deal. Carr replied, "No, sir," implying that Keefer's decision to seek the death penalty had not pressured him into a plea bargain. In this fashion, the criminal justice system used the death penalty both to pressure Carr into waiving his right to a jury trial and then to pressure him into saying that no pressure had been applied.

At this point, the stipulation of facts prepared by Keefer and agreed to by both sides as a condition of the deal was introduced into the formal record of the case. It contained a devastating amount of evidence of Carr's guilt. The defense conceded that "numerous people" had identified Carr as the person depicted in Brenner's sketch, that the shell casings recovered from the Golden residence came from Carr's gun, that ballistics tests confirmed that the eight spent shell casings found at the scene came from the same gun, and that the women began screaming after the first shot. In short, Keefer designed the stipulation of facts not only to ensure Carr's conviction of first-degree murder, but also to provide a foundation for Carr's reconviction if he got lucky on appeal. It was all a part of the price of the deal.

Keefer called first Holtz and then Blevins to the stand. Their testimonies were not part of the agreed-upon stipulation of facts, because the defense intended to appeal its Fifth Amendment objection to Carr's confessions. Both troopers repeated what they had said at the preliminary and suppression hearings. George had no questions. Keefer rested his case.

Judge Spicer turned to George. "Anything that you want to present?"

George replied, "Your Honor, again, pursuant to our understanding, we have no evidence."

All that remained were the defense's and prosecution's closing arguments. Mike George went first. Because Judge Spicer had the power to bring in a verdict of less than first-degree murder, George made a pitch for mercy.

> . . . I guess what I ask the court to consider at this point is that Steve Carr has lived in the mountains of Adams County since 1986. Com-

mon sense is certainly something to take into consideration. Over that period of a year and a half to two years it makes sense that he has come across other people. He has come across a variety of people, yet not until May 13, 1988, has Stephen Carr been charged with murder for any incidents occurring up in those mountains. . . . [I]f the court determines that Steve Carr is in fact the person who fired that weapon, what caused him to do that on May 13th that didn't cause him to do it on any other occasion prior to May 13th?

I guess the critical issue before this court is going to be the issue of premeditation. . . . If Stephen Carr had intended, had premeditated to kill those women, why didn't he just walk up and shoot them in the head? There is nothing, there is no explanation why he just didn't shoot the both of them and drag them off into the woods and have nobody ever find them again. If he premeditated murder, he was certainly capable of carrying that off. He knew the mountains. Those women were by themselves up there in isolation and he easily could have walked up to them and shot them in the head, but that didn't happen. It's more likely that there was something up there that happened that triggered him to the point where he shot, if again we assume he is the person who shot. During the course of that shooting, he heard a scream, he panicked and ran. No premeditation. . . .

Steve Carr submits himself to this proceeding today, this proceeding where we have all stipulated to the facts, we have stipulated to the admission of a confession, and he submits himself to this proceeding knowing what this court has determined pretrial and it's for that sole reason we are here today and we are proceeding in this manner.

The court has ruled that the confession of Steve Carr is admissible and has ruled that it is a valid confession. The defense submits that the confession was a result of an illegal interrogation and as such it shouldn't have been admitted. The court has admitted it. We maintain that Stephen Carr, well, we maintain that an illegal interrogation has resulted in many improper convictions and we ask the court to consider that.

Without uttering a word, Spicer turned to Keefer.

. . . It is an important fact in this case, Your Honor, that at least the first five shots which were fired with this weapon . . . struck Claudia Brenner. This rifle, because of the way it is built, necessitates that after each shot is fired a shell casing must be ejected, and another projectile must be put into the weapon. It must be cocked and fired again. This took place at least five times prior to the final two shots which killed Rebecca Wight. Your Honor, premeditation does not mean sitting down and writing out a plan, as I know the court knows. Premeditation means that prior to pulling the trigger on those final two shots, those two shots which killed Rebecca Wight, the defendant had a fully formed intent to do just what he did, and that is to shoot her and to kill her. . . .

In addition to that, Your Honor, there is the testimony that Mr. Carr had lived in these woods for approximately two years prior to the time that the shooting took place. The trail in which these women chose to walk that day as stipulated was a loop. They went around one side of the loop and found a place to stay. As they went down that loop, interestingly enough, Stephen Roy Carr was at the head of the trail, the only trail which intersects with Rocky Knob Trail, the loop which the women had chosen to walk on that day.

Your Honor, the Commonwealth does not think it was mere circumstance or happenstance that Stephen Roy Carr walked upon these people later in the afternoon. It would be submitted, Your Honor, and the evidence is there based upon the stipulation that this court could find if it so chooses, that Stephen Roy Carr in fact stalked and hunted these two people as a hunter would hunt game in these woods and that after stalking and hunting them, based upon the evidence, this court, essentially, has no other verdict except that this case is an intentional, premeditated shooting, that it caused the death of Rebecca Wight and therefore rises to murder of the first degree.

Spicer thanked Keefer for his closing argument.

The courtroom then became very quiet. The attorneys and their assistants, Brenner and her friends, members of the Wight family, newspaper reporters, the state troopers, and the two deputy sheriffs in charge of transporting Carr to and from the Adams County Prison waited for the verdict. The trial had been a strange one. Though the defense refused to concede that Carr was Wight's killer, it had accepted a stipulated set of facts that seemed to indicate beyond a reasonable doubt that Carr had indeed pulled the trigger. As the minutes ticked away, the anxiety mounted. Judge Spicer, sitting on the raised bench in the front of the courtroom, a Pennsylvania flag and an American flag standing on either side of him, was deep in reflection. Was he going to convict Carr of first- or third-degree murder? Keefer was becoming increasingly concerned and George, increasingly hopeful.

Finally, after about ten minutes, Judge Spicer announced, "The verdict of the court is that the defendant is guilty of murder in the first degree." It was 5:12 P.M. The trial of Stephen Roy Carr had taken less than two hours.

II

As a necessary step in the process of appealing to the Pennsylvania Superior Court (an appellate court that usually sits in three-judge panels), George filed on November 7, 1988, a postverdict motion, along with an accompanying brief, that asked Judge Spicer to overturn Carr's first-degree murder conviction and grant him a new trial. On April 4, 1989, Spicer handed down an opinion that once again rejected George's Fifth Amendment objection to Carr's confession, restating his belief that Carr knew from the beginning of his interrogation that the police wanted to talk to him about a murder.

That left only provocation. In his brief, George for the first time had focused on Wight's and Brenner's activities, rather than on Carr's history of sexual abuse. "[T]he victims," he wrote, "put on what the Defendant perceived to be a show: they walked in front of him while they were naked; one woman excreted in front of him; and they hugged and kissed each other in front of him. Later in the afternoon, the women partook in oral sex with each other before his very eyes. Not only was he forced to isolate himself from society because of constant rejection, but also, society was following him, in his isolation, and once again throwing rejection in his face." Based on these "facts," George claimed that it was "quite possible" that a reasonable man in such circumstances would have become impassioned to the point of losing his capacity for cool reflection. At the very least, George insisted, whether Brenner and Wight had provoked Carr should have been decided by the jury, not by Judge Spicer.

George's "new" offer of proof angered Keefer. In his answering brief, he called it "nothing more than a ruse in order to slander the victims" and perhaps hinted that George's own homophobia was the underlying motive for the attack. "There is little question," Keefer wrote, "but that no such argument would have been advanced if a heterosexual couple would have been shot under similar circumstances." Brenner had lost her lover and nearly her life because of a homophobic killer, Keefer thought, and now she was perhaps in danger of losing her reputation because of the homophobia of the man who was defending the murderer. "There can be no doubt," Keefer concluded, "but that the court acted properly in rejecting the defendant's ploy in this matter."

In his opinion rejecting the defense's contention that the issue of provocation should have gone to the jury, Judge Spicer began by noting that George's new offer of proof went "somewhat beyond the offer [at trial] and the record." What he meant was that there had been no evidence at the preliminary hearing or in the stipulation of facts at the trial that the women had done what the defense was now claiming they'd done. The record indicated that the women had been naked and that they had engaged in sexual activity, but that was all. There was no evidence in the record that either woman had defecated in front of Carr or rejected his sexual advances. In a postverdict proceeding, Spicer was not about to reopen the case. In his view, the crucial facts contained in the record were that the sexual conduct in question had "stimulated" Carr's preexisting "murderous impulses." The question was whether, given these facts, the law should recognize Carr's reaction as a potentially "reasonable" one, such that a jury should have decided whether it constituted provocation.

Judge Spicer conceded that in *Commonwealth v. McCusker*, 448 Pa. 382, 292 A. 2d 286 (1972), the Pennsylvania Supreme Court had ruled that a husband who killed his adulterous wife did have the right to bring in expert psychiatric testimony explaining why he reacted "reasonably." In *Commonwealth v. Stonehouse*, 521 Pa. 41, 555 A. 2d 772 (1989), the same court had decided that expert testimony was also admissible to determine whether a battered woman acted "reasonably" in self-defense when she killed her husband. If the husband and the battered woman had the right to present such expert testimony to a jury, the question was why Carr shouldn't be allowed to have a psychiatrist testify that a history of sexual abuse had affected his mental state at the time of the shootings.

Ultimately, Judge Spicer argued, the reason Carr should be treated differently from the *McCusker* and *Stonehouse* defendants was based on policy, not logic. To substantiate his position, Spicer quoted from *Commonwealth v. Weinstein*, 499 Pa. 106, 117, 451 A. 2d 1344, 1349 (1982), a Pennsylvania Supreme Court case on "irresistible impulse."

> The law, in its effort to shape a rational social policy, . . . cannot admit that acts an individual carefully plans and carries out to advance his own desire . . . will not be punished simply because of the intensity or strangeness of that desire. Such an admission proceeds imperceptibly to the absurd result that the more strange and brutal the act the more likely the actor is to be relieved of its criminal consequences. Along the psychoanalytic continuum the outrageous proves the innocence. In an oddly circular fashion the act establishes its cause as mental illness and the mental illness determines the act. Such analysis may be medically useful. It is not legally useful.

A mentally ill person who intentionally killed another, even if he or she was motivated by an "intense," "irresistible," and "strange" desire, was not entitled, on that ground alone, to introduce expert psychiatric testimony as to the nature of the impulse. "Likewise," Spicer continued, "a person who intentionally kills a stranger should not be able to expect a lessened punishment because of revulsion or disapproval of the victim's conduct." There had been no relationship between Carr and his victims, and the women's sexual activities had not harmed any of his legal interests. Therefore, even if Carr's sexual history could explain why he fell into a murderous rage when he saw lesbian lovemaking, it made no sense for the law, in its "effort to shape a rational social policy," to let such evidence into a trial. Maybe what the women were doing had provoked Carr, Spicer concluded, but it had not legally provoked him.

Judge Spicer's opinion contained a valuable insight. Criminal law categories are often perceived as black or white. Depending on whether a defendant has crossed a precisely drawn line or not, he or she is guilty of first-degree murder, third-degree murder, or voluntary manslaughter. What Spicer's opinion suggests, however, is that the lines of the criminal law are sometimes too fuzzy to decide the defendant's level of culpability. When judges find themselves in such a situation, they have no choice but to make a policy decision. In doing so, they make one or more of the fuzzy lines a little more distinct, but that does not mean that the law is achieving some kind of overall clarity. As one line of criminal liability becomes more clear and precise, others become less so as society's social and political attitudes evolve. For this reason, the criminal justice system can never be completely separated from the culture that gives it life and substance, and the assessment of criminal culpability can never take place in a political vacuum. As the professionals and jurors in the criminal justice system decide which homicides are worse than others, they are not only sifting and sorting the guilty. They are also at times helping to create the kind of world they want to live in. They are playing a political policy-making role.

III

On May 17, 1989, the final act of the Carr case—the formal sentencing hearing—took place in a nearly empty Courtroom 1. Before imposing on Carr the sentence of life imprisonment without parole, Judge Spicer permitted both Brenner and Mr. Wight to read victim-impact statements. Brenner read her statement in a clear and loud voice that revealed her emotions.

> I wish I did not have to make this statement. I wish that my experiences in Adams County, Pennsylvania, had ended, as planned, on May 15, 1988. I wish that Rebecca and I were making plans for where we wanted to hike and backpack this summer. I wish that the inconceivable pain and horror I experienced were fears with no basis in reality, that the sound of shots, that shattering reality in my mind, was a bad dream from which I could awaken. . . .
>
> I wish that Mr. Michael George had found a way of defending his client that did not attempt to blame the victims, that did not add sensationalism for the media to exploit, that did not augment the pain I had already endured through the vicious and murderous actions of his client.
>
> At one level, I am furious. I am outraged that Stephen Roy Carr, for whatever savage personal reasons, violently imposed his will on my life. I am angry that our victimization could be portrayed by the defense attorney in inflammatory and distorted terms, and that he would attempt to exploit the fact that we had a lesbian relationship. . . .

Mr. Wight then read his statement, his voice echoing his bitter frustration.

> The defendant, Stephen Carr, murdered my 28 year old daughter, Rebecca Wight, a year and 5 days ago. He murdered her suddenly, brutally, and senselessly. He also tried to murder her companion, Claudia Brenner, by shooting her in the head four times.
>
> There are many other victims of Stephen Carr's horrible crime of murdering my daughter. Her parents, grandparents, sisters, brothers, many other relatives, and many, many friends are also all victims. The defendant's murderous actions have, in effect, placed a lifetime sentence on all of us—a lifetime sentence of mourning the loss of Rebecca forever.
>
> It is difficult to measure the value of a life. . . . [Rebecca] was a lovely, bright, intelligent, and valuable human being. She was a vital, caring person who helped many people. She no longer exists because this "thing" murdered her.
>
> Stephen Carr has been found by this court guilty of murder in the first degree of my daughter. He has made many legal appeals, but the court has denied each and every one of his appeals. He has received the full consideration and benefits of our legal system.
>
> It is my understanding that, according to the law of Pennsylvania, the penalty for his horrible crime is mandatory life imprisonment without possibility of parole. There is no other choice or possibility. His past criminal history and bizarre personal behavior indicate that he is a dangerous subhuman misfit, and he will always be a serious, dangerous threat to society. Any consideration of possible rehabilitation of Stephen Carr would be absurd.
>
> I want the defendant sentenced to death. His life is worthless, useless, dangerous, and he killed my daughter. But, through plea bargaining, and other elements in our system of justice, he was able to avoid this fate, with the understanding, I was told, that he would spend the rest of his unnatural life in prison. While in prison, he will be fed, clothed, and sheltered. Although life in prison can be difficult, he will be able to taste food, read books, write, make friends (if he is able), probably watch TV and movies, listen to music, see the sky—live and breathe. My daughter cannot because she is no longer alive—she is dead. He killed her.

After Mr. Wight's harsh words died away in the courtroom, Judge Spicer sentenced Carr to life imprisonment. Unless he received a pardon or won his appeal, Carr would spend the rest of his life behind bars.

The next day, the *Gettysburg Times* published an account of Carr's sentencing that included Brenner's victim-impact statement. In response to the article, Clayton R. Wilcox, a prominent Gettysburg attorney, wrote a letter to the editor that touched on several of the important social issues that surfaced in the murder trial of Stephen Carr: the death penalty and its seemingly random imposition; the rights of individuals, no matter what their sexual orientation, to life and personal happiness; the devastating effects of murder; and the deranged character of the defendant. The central point of Wilcox's letter, however, was to take exception to Brenner's negative portrayal of Mike George.

> . . . The sexual preference of the two victims did not lessen their right to life and personal happiness. Nevertheless, the violation of that right by Mr. Carr does not lessen the duty of his defense counsel to commit himself to his defense with all the vigor permitted by law.
>
> Few attorneys in any community are willing to represent persons accused of serious crimes. The reasons given are varied. However, it is suggested that one significant reason is the perception that the community will see them as one of the obstacles to the pursuit of wrongdoers. . . . The thought of being perceived in that manner is not comforting in today's social and political environment.
>
> There is irony in the comments directed toward Mr. George. He did not seek the role he played in this unfortunate real life drama. He was requested to act in the capacity of defense counsel by the court. The fees generated based on court established hourly rates do not come close to traditional billing rates for this area. He accepted a case which an experienced defense counsel would perceive as "a loser."
>
> These comments . . . are made to bring into focus the role of defense counsel in our society and to recognize the difficult, yet vital, role carried out by Attorney George.

In his letter, Wilcox suggests that George had a professional obligation to "inquire" into the "sexual relationship between the two victims and the irrational effect [it had] on the defendant." In carrying out such an inquiry, George might appear to be an "obstacle to the pursuit of wrong-doers," but he is in fact "an essential aid to the preservation of basic rights guaranteed to all citizens."

Wilcox's depiction of the defense attorney's role is a traditional one, but it doesn't necessarily justify everything that George did in the Carr case. For example, the defense never thought that Carr was in a rage at the time of the shootings, even though they used the provocation defense to bluff the prosecution into a deal. Thus was Keefer right that George's brief supporting his postverdict motion was "nothing more than a ruse" to slander the victims? Should defense attorneys be permitted to seek unwarranted defenses for their clients in this way? Are such tactics really essential to the preservation of individual rights? What specific rights do such tactics preserve?

Conversely, in fulfilling their professional obligations, defense attorneys may be called on to expand legal defenses in ways they do not themselves politically support. If, for example, George did believe that Carr was in a rage at the time of the shootings, perhaps he would have had a duty to argue that Carr should be allowed to plead provocation to an Adams County jury. It's a close call, because asserting what kind of conduct would provoke a rational person to violence is a value judgment that a defense lawyer should only rarely make unilaterally. It's an issue for the judge or the jury. Accordingly, a defense attorney might have an obligation to make such an argument even if, by doing so, he is working to create a society he or she would personally abhor. This is one of the psychological strains that an adversarial system of criminal justice imposes on defense attorneys. For the benefit of their clients, who are often individuals they despise, they have to try to reshape the law in ways that undermine their own political values.

Wilcox's letter was in some ways the last word on the Carr case. By the time it was published in the *Gettysburg Times*, more than a year after Rebecca Wight's murder and six months after the plea bargain and Carr's conviction, the local community had tired of the case. In one place, Wilcox's letter echoed the popular feeling: "The Stephen Carr homicide prosecution is complete. He is rightly tucked away in a penitentiary for life without parole. Good riddance, Mr. Carr, and the entire community justifiably shares a sense of relief that the prosecution has been successfully completed." Whereas bitterly contested, high-profile murder trials, such as the O. J. Simpson trial, can maintain a high degree of public interest for a considerable length of time, murder cases that are plea-bargained—as the majority of homicide cases in the United States are—cannot do so. The deal is a fait accompli that punctures and deflates the public's curiosity. Accordingly, murder cases usually come into the American criminal justice system with a bang and leave with a whimper.

The Aftermath

I

In her book *Eight Bullets: One Woman's Story of Surviving Anti-Gay Violence*, Claudia Brenner describes the four stages of recovery she went through after her violent encounter with Carr on South Mountain.[1] The first step was to feel safe again, to have a sense of security, to be free from fear and paranoia. The second was to grieve: to remember and mourn the loss of Rebecca Wight. The third was to put the shootings into an intellectual context. Having grown up in a safe, white, middle-class world, Brenner had to come to terms with the possibility that lethal violence could erupt unexpectedly and that she, as a lesbian, a Jew, and a woman, was vulnerable.

Brenner's fourth stage of recovery transformed her into a political activist. Just a few weeks after Carr was sentenced to life imprisonment, she stood next to Kevin Berrill, the director of the National Gay and Lesbian Task Force (NGLTF) Anti-Violence Project, at a press conference in Washington, D.C. The NGLTF was about to issue its annual report on

---

[1]Claudia Brenner and Hannah Ashley, *Eight Bullets: One Woman's Story of Surviving Anti-Gay Violence* (Ithaca, N.Y.: Firebrand Books, 1995), p. 154.

anti-gay violence in the United States. After Berrill summarized the report, Brenner stepped up to the microphones and into the limelight.

Over the next few years, Brenner spoke at demonstrations and rallies, appeared on talk shows and news programs, and gave interviews to the press. Since she was not a theoretician or statistician, her role was to tell her story, giving "the human dimension" and revealing "the truth of the personal."[2] In 1990, with the help of a new partner, she crafted a speech entitled "Eight Bullets" that she delivered to a demonstration in front of the state capital building in Albany, New York. Recounting what happened to her and Wight on Rocky Knob Trail, Brenner highlighted the personal tragedies implicit in the impersonal numbers of anti-gay crime statistics. She had once thought she was safe because she played by the rules, but she had been viciously assaulted and Wight had been brutally murdered. The rules hadn't kept them safe and they wouldn't save other homosexuals from violence. Feeling the scar tissue on the side of her tongue caused by the bullet that had struck her in the face—the fourth bullet—Brenner asked the members of her audience to commit themselves to "action, education, and change."[3]

The speech was a turning point for her, Brenner says in her book. She felt she had made a real contribution in the fight against anti-gay violence simply by being herself. Her personal life was therefore no longer separate from the social and political world around her. She once again felt connected to other people. Though most victims of violent trauma do not become political activists, the knowledge that she was making a difference in the fight for gay-rights and the recognition she received for her efforts were for Brenner the "fuel" for her "survival."[4]

II

Over the years, Leon Wight has not talked much about his daughter Rebecca's death, though he's thought about it a great deal, wondering why he lost his eldest child at such a young age, so cruelly and unnecessarily. He says he doubts whether people ever think much about the harm mur-

---

[2]Ibid., pp. 190, 193.
[3]Ibid., pp. 194–97.
[4]Ibid., p. 204.

derers do to the living, especially to those who have lost forever the opportunity to say, "I'm sorry," to the person who's gone. That's a pain that's very real for Mr. Wight, and, as long as he is alive, it will never disappear.

Though at the trial Mr. Wight wanted Carr executed, he doesn't care much about it anymore, he says, as long as Carr in fact spends the rest of his life in prison. Mr. Wight, however, is still ambivalent about the way Carr escaped the death penalty. The deal was for the convenience of the prosecution and the court, he believes. No one cared about what he thought, even though he in fact had lost the most. A part of himself died with his daughter. Ever since the murder, there's been a dead spot in his life, but the system didn't give a damn about his grief or his feelings, he says.

Mr. Wight has a similar, though less extreme, reaction to Claudia Brenner's decision to promote her career as a gay activist by going public with her story of the shootings. The problem was "Grandma," Mr. Wight's ninety-four-year-old mother, who knew that Rebecca had been killed but not the circumstances of her death. Brenner's outspokenness meant that his mother might learn of her granddaughter's sexual orientation, but so far the Wight family has been lucky. Grandma hasn't yet found out the whole truth about how her granddaughter died.

Mr. Wight himself hadn't known about Rebecca's sexual orientation at the time of the murder. Not until weeks later did his daughter Evelyn tell him that Brenner was going to testify that she had been Rebecca's lover. Mr. Wight remembers how the news stunned him. Though he'd never been hostile to gays or lesbians, he couldn't understand homosexuality. Eventually Mr. Wight talked about his dead daughter's sexual orientation with a counselor, who advised him that he should be thankful that Rebecca was a person who could love and be loved. It took time for this advice to sink in, but it finally reached him, he says. Now he is convinced that Rebecca's sexual orientation was just a small part of who she was and the fact the Rebecca could love another human being tells much more about who she was than does the sex of the person she loved. Whatever he thought at first, that's the way Mr. Wight looks at it today.

III

Both Roy Keefer and Michael George are still practicing law in Gettysburg, but their roles have reversed. George defeated Keefer in the 1995

Republican primary election for the district attorney's office of Adams County and ran unopposed in the general election. He took office on January 1, 1996, and, within a few weeks, confronted his first death penalty case. James Brooks, Warren Bibbs, and Donald Copenhaver were accused of severely beating a man in his seventies, John Aiken, and then shooting him in the head execution-style. Despite his general doubts about the value of capital punishment, George sought the death penalty. The alleged aggravating circumstance was that the three men murdered Aiken while in the perpetration of another felony—robbery. Keefer took on the perhaps unpleasant task of representing James Brooks. Judge Oscar F. Spicer, still president judge of Adams County, would have presided over the trial had there been one, but all three defendants avoided the death penalty through plea bargaining. In exchange for their guilty pleas, Brooks and Bibbs, the two who went into the house and robbed and shot Aiken, received life sentences; Copenhaver, the driver who stayed in the car, got a twenty- to forty-year sentence. Perhaps the executions by lethal injection of Keith Zettlemoyer on May 2, 1995, and Leon Moser on August 16, 1995, Pennsylvania's first executions since Elmo Smith went to the electric chair in 1964, had something to do with Brooks's and Bibbs's decisions to take the deal George offered them.

Judge Spicer says he has no regrets about his ruling that Carr's psychosexual history was inadmissible, even though it imposed a difficult choice on Carr: take the deal offered to you or run a significant risk of a death sentence at a trial. In a letter, he explains why.

> . . . I watched William Kuntsler in a T.V. interview say that the American criminal justice system should be destroyed. He was, at the time, attempting to represent the man who calmly walked through a train and methodically killed people whose only sin (at the moment) was being able to afford a train ticket. He spoke of raising black rage as a defense, which brings to mind a suggestion that recognition of such defenses as emotional distress, or battered person syndrome, really requires that each and every person charged with taking another person's life has the right to parade a history of grievances before a jury in hopes of either creating sympathy or confusion. . . .

Although I think the criminal justice system has its failings, it obviously works. . . . However, one of the reasons it does not work as well as it should is its total lack of predictability. Scholars can debate the finer points of intent as long as they wish, but the public can smell a decision gone haywire quite easily. A successful twinkie defense [see Chapter Eleven] erodes public confidence and trust in the law. Shooting wealthy parents in the back and claiming abuse made you do it fares no better.

Should we blame the first [Erik and Lyle] Menendez jury for going off the deep end? Before we say yes, we should understand that any juror may be bewildered by a mass of complex and confusing information in an unfamiliar surrounding. If a judge tells a juror that he or she should consider all that has transpired in a defendant's life in determining sanity, or gradations of an offense, it stands to reason that the more gruesome the crime the greater the likelihood of a defense-oriented verdict. Sometimes judicial thinking is somewhat akin to hypnosis, which involves the suspension of reality in cognitive functioning.

There are, I think, many trial judges across the United States who would agree with Spicer. Their names may not often get into the national newspapers, because the homicide cases that come before them usually end up in plea bargains, which only rarely capture the media's attention.

IV

All the police officers who played a major role in the investigation of the Carr case have retired from the Pennsylvania State Police. Matthew O'Brien retired in 1991 and became the head of security at the Adams County Courthouse. John Holtz retired under a dark cloud after Jay Smith's conviction and death sentence were overturned on the ground of prosecutorial misconduct. Skip Gochenour, who is still a defense homicide detective operating out of Harrisburg, played an important role in the reversal of Smith's conviction and perhaps indirectly in Holtz's retirement.

After his retirement in 1991, Denny Beaver joined the Loss Prevention Department of the Pennsylvania State Employees Credit Union. He never thought about the Carr case until Claudia Brenner sent him a copy of *Eight Bullets*. In general, he thought the book was an accurate and perceptive account of the case. Brenner's memory played only one trick on her, says Beaver. When she was in the hospital, she couldn't identify a photograph of Carr that Beaver showed her. In her book, Brenner claimed she couldn't identify Carr because the photograph was a ten-year-old picture of Carr wearing a costume at a party.[5]

"That's just not true," Beaver asserts. "I don't think Claudia is lying, or anything like that, but she is definitely not remembering the way it was. It happens all the time in criminal cases. People get confused; things get turned around. The photo I showed her in the hospital was a telex of a mug shot taken of Carr down in Florida. About that, I am absolutely certain."

Donald Blevins retired in 1992 and opened a shop that specialized in buying, restoring, and selling classic cars. Like Beaver, he was reminded of the Carr case when he received a copy of *Eight Bullets* in the mail. Blevins says he doesn't like all the foul language in the book, but he found it generally accurate. She doesn't have all the facts right about the investigation, but that's to be expected, he says. After all, she was a patient in a hospital. There are bound to be some discrepancies.

"There's only one other thing about Claudia's book that I can't figure out," Blevins adds. "She says that Rebecca Wight was fully clothed, except for her sneakers, at the time of the shootings, but that can't be right. On the night of the shootings, I turned Wight's body over and saw all these twigs and leaves and dirt stuffed inside the back of her jeans and her underwear was lying on the ground five feet away from the body. At first I was puzzled. 'How in the world did that stuff get into this woman's jeans.' But then it came to me. I already suspected that the two women were lesbians, so the answer was that they were naked when they got shot. Wight was hurt too badly to pull her pants on while standing up, so she pulled them on while sitting on the ground. Maybe Claudia helped her. That's how she got all those twigs, leaves, and dirt into the backside of her jeans."

If Blevins is right, if that's the way it happened, why would Brenner lie about it, both at the preliminary hearing and, years later, in her book? Blevins admits that he doesn't have an answer to that question, but he's confident it doesn't mean anything. Just a "loose end," he calls it.

---

[5]Ibid., p. 98.

V

"Yes, if a person had need, I'd still let him stay in my house," declared Chester Weaver, now in his fifties, but with the same round, friendly face. "I wouldn't hesitate. Christian charity is first."

I had telephoned Chester and Esther Weaver a few days before to see if they and their sons, Nevin and Curtis, would talk to me about Steve Carr. Chester had told me to come by on Thursday after supper. I arrived about 6:30. Chester and Nevin, still in their work clothes, and I chatted as Esther and Nevin's wife, dressed in long, plain dresses and wearing lace head coverings, cleaned up the dishes. Curtis and his wife, who still lived on the farm next door, arrived, and soon we were all sitting around the kitchen table. Two children played on the floor nearby.

"If somebody had need," Chester continued, "it would be cruel to say, 'No, I don't trust you. You keep hoofing down the road.' And the Bible says that sometimes you can entertain angels unawares if you just take care of somebody in need."

"Our opinions are based upon the Bible," Nevin asserted. "We try to read the Bible literally and do what it says."

"What does the Bible say about punishment and forgiveness?" I asked. "And how would you apply those doctrines to someone like Steve Carr?"

"Well," Chester replied, "the Bible says if you do me harm and I don't forgive you, then I can't be forgiven. We are forgiven as we forgive."

"So you think Mr. Wight should forgive Carr?"

"He should try, else he'll never find peace," Curtis said softly.

"Did he ever talk to Steve?" Chester ventured.

"No."

"Maybe it would be a good thing if they did talk, but both would have to change their attitudes," Esther commented quietly, rubbing her hands anxiously in her lap.

"What Steve has to do," Chester continued, "is to sincerely repent for what he has done—feel sorry for what he did—and ask God's forgiveness. And anybody he has hurt, he should do whatever he can to right that, but that doesn't mean that society doesn't have the right to take his life. The Bible says that if a person sheds blood, his blood shall be shed. An eye for an eye, a tooth for a tooth, and I don't want to speak against the way God says things should be done."

It was somewhat odd to hear this old biblical adage of retribution coming from the mouth of such a peaceful person, but I had no doubt that the smiling man beside me was quite serious.

"The state's responsibility," Nevin chimed in, "is law and justice. They're ordained by God for that purpose."

"But if you or I had been kicked out of our homes at the age of fourteen or fifteen, like Steve Carr was," Esther said pointedly, "what would we have been like?"

I glanced at the two children playing happily nearby.

"It all goes back to one thing," Curtis insisted. "Steve had no morals, no teaching. He was at a loss. What is right, what is wrong, I mean—"

"I'd like to ask you a question," Esther interjected, turning toward me in her quiet, forceful way. "How do you feel about parents punishing their children? I mean spanking them when they do something bad, because that's where it all begins."

"The Bible," Nevin announced, "says that if parents ignore their child, then they're responsible for that child—to pay the price."

"So," I said, trying to sum up where the conversation had taken us, "you're saying that even if we punish Steve's parents, and even if Steve is sincerely sorry for what he did, you would still say that Steve should be executed?"

"Well," said Chester, somewhat apologetically, "I'm not going to say he should have his life taken, but he should be punished. The state sets the price and Steve has to pay the price, whatever it is. But the most important thing for Steve now is to face his sin. He must acknowledge it before God and do what he can to reconcile with the people he's hurt."

"I heard say," Curtis remarked, "that if a man's truly sorry, he'll no longer beg to get out of prison."

"I heard that too," added Esther approvingly.

"God is at the center of what Steve must do," Nevin insisted, "just as He is at the center of what our society should do. If we continue to ignore God, take Him out of our schools and don't respect His commandments, we can't expect God's honor upon us. As we move away from those principles, it's going to get worse and worse. After all, if you take religion out of life, then what is life? Without religion, where does man end up?"

"Ends up with Steve Carr, that's what," Chester declared.

VI

In July 1989, Steve Carr entered the walls of Graterford Correctional Institute as number AT 1414. The million-square-foot facility, located northwest of Philadelphia, is staffed by 700 guards and houses approximately 3,500 inmates, including many of Pennsylvania's first-degree murderers, in 2,756 cells. At first optimistic about his future, Carr instructed Defense Attorney Michael George to pursue his appeal to the Pennsylvania Superior Court in Harrisburg. "I understand and I think you should go for it. All I can do is hope and pray that things work out and they don't raise the death penalty." He also asked George for a transcript of his trial and studied the publications *Federal Rules of Evidence* and *Pennsylvania Mental Health Defense*. However, he also communicated to George that certain aspects of his confinement were troubling. His "celly" was stealing his things, he had dropped out of school, and his health was suffering. "I was told that I might have a heart disease."

On September 24, 1990, the superior court handed down its decision rejecting Carr's Fifth Amendment objection to his confession and upholding Judge Oscar Spicer's ruling that his psychosexual history was inadmissible. The court pointedly concluded, "An accused cannot, by recalling some past injury or insult, establish a foundation for a manslaughter verdict."

Disappointed but still determined to keep fighting, Carr begged George to file an appeal to the Pennsylvania Supreme Court, writing, "Go all the way. I not just going to rot my life away!" Several months later, however, George informed Carr that the state supreme court had refused to hear his appeal. Carr had only one option left: to file a habeas corpus petition in federal court on the ground that his confession violated the U.S. Constitution. Over the next few years, Carr pestered George to file the necessary papers, but George refused, perhaps because even if Carr won in federal court on the Fifth Amendment question, the Pennsylvania ruling in regard to his psychosexual history would still stand. If Carr won a new trial, he would face the death penalty and he would not be able to introduce at trial the kind of evidence that might induce a jury to treat him leniently.

In February 1995, Carr wrote George, "What going on? Did you send in to the 3 cir[cuit]? Let me know. I don't want to give up. I want out!" He then sent George a list of questions, asking in a cover letter, "Are you going to investigate this for me?" A month or so later, George, Criminal Defense Investigator Skip Gochenour, and I visited Carr in Graterford. The four of us entered a small lawyer-inmate conference room with a table, three chairs, and a barred window. Gochenour leaned against the window ledge, and the rest of us sat down, Carr and George taking the two chairs at the table.

Carr spoke first—loudly and angrily. "Why don't you answer my letters? You my lawyer ain't you? Why don't you tell me what's going on? I writes a letter to you, six months, no answer. What the fuck is that? I's getting fucked over here. I can't stand it no longer. You is my lawyer. You is supposed to be helping me and you ain't doing shit for me. I's just rotting away in here." He looked sick and desperate. The deal that he had accepted seven years earlier had saved his life by reducing it to something that had no value.

George responded by telling Carr that he could no longer be his lawyer. The news visibly stunned and dejected Carr. George added that if Carr wanted to file a federal petition, he might be able to convince someone from the Federal Public Defenders Office to pick up his case.

Reacting to the hopelessness of his predicament, Carr commanded, "Write the address down." He couldn't stop George from withdrawing as his attorney, but he could for the last time jerk his chain by ordering him to do something.

George hesitated for a second, but then pulled out his pen. He gave Carr the address but advised him not to file a petition because it would destroy any chance for a pardon. The smart move was for Carr to do his time and hope for the best.

"That's why I think you should talk to Professor Pohlman here. He wants to write a book about your case, give you an opportunity to tell your side of the story. Skip and I came down here with him to see what you wanted to do about it. We think you should go ahead. It might help you get a pardon if your side of the story came out. Maybe you would get a little more sympathy if people knew what you've been through."

The room fell silent. Frowning, Carr stared into space. Should he give up fighting? Should he resign himself to spending the rest of his life in prison?

"By the way, Steve," Gochenour asked, breaking the silence, "how many visitors do you get here? Do many people come by to see you?"

Carr slowly looked up at Gochenour's face. He knew what Gochenour was getting at. His face grim, he finally answered, "One visitor. I's been here over five years and one person—Chester Weaver—came to see me."

"Then maybe you'd like it," Gochenour added gently, "if the professor here would start coming by to see you. Give you something to look forward to."

Carr turned toward me. Vacant eyes set in a hollow, expressionless face stared at me. I waited without saying anything, trying not to squirm or in any other way reveal my discomfort. I wondered what it would be like to be a convict with no one on the outside, not one human being in the world caring whether you were dead or alive.

Finally, his voice weary with loneliness and frustration, Carr said, "Yeah, he can come back if he wants."

Conclusion
chapter eleven

I started this book at the onset of the O. J. Simpson trial and am finishing it after one jury sentenced Timothy McVeigh to death for the bombing of the government building in Oklahoma City and another jury deadlocked on the fate of his partner Terry Nichols. There is, of course, nothing wrong with Americans learning something about their law and their courts from high-profile murder trials such as these. A problem arises only if viewers and readers do not realize that they are unrepresentative of what normally goes on in the criminal justice system. Given the time and resources invested in them, perhaps high-profile trials do a fair job of uncovering the facts that are relevant to an assessment of a murderer's culpability, but that doesn't mean that the American criminal justice system does an adequate job of uncovering the truth in the typical homicide case.

The Stephen Roy Carr case shows how difficult it is to ascertain all the relevant facts in a standard homicide prosecution. Not only do witnesses often disagree about what happened, but prospective jurors often have biases that predispose them in one direction or the other. Defense lawyers care less about the truth than about their clients' interests and rights, including their right to remain silent and their right to an attorney, while the overwhelming majority of prosecutors want big convictions. In such an adversarial context, the search for truth can quickly degenerate into a matter of strategy, tactics, spins, and bluffs. Ultimately it becomes something of a game, each side intent on victory rather than finding out what "really" happened and why. Perhaps such a system can uncover some of the truth, but rarely will it uncover the "whole truth." As each side highlights only "facts" that support the result it seeks, all too often elements of the truth fall through the cracks.

Presiding over such a contest, of course, is the judge, whose rulings on the admissibility of evidence can have a huge impact on how the system processes a particular case. For instance, though Carr's confession indicated beyond a reasonable doubt that he had shot Rebecca Wight and Claudia Brenner, there was a chance that it would be ruled inadmissible on the ground that it had been obtained in violation of Carr's right to remain silent. The police had tricked him into incriminating himself, perhaps in part by failing to inform him that he was a murder suspect at the beginning of his interrogation. Should the right to remain silent be understood to cover a confession taken in such circumstances?

The American criminal justice system prides itself on its commitment to the presumption of innocence and competitive fairness. The state bears the burden of proving the defendant guilty of the crime charged through an adversarial system of legal representation. Tricking defendants into confessing to a crime before they have a lawyer and then using the confession at the trial to convict them is arguably in tension with these underlying principles. These principles, of course, would not prevent repentant defendants from voluntarily confessing to their crime and pleading guilty before a judge, but Carr's confession was not voluntary in this sense. He inadvertently implicated himself. Perhaps if he'd been better educated or had had a lawyer present at his interrogation, he would have avoided the traps Trooper John Holtz and Corporal Matthew O'Brien set for him. But the more Carr talked to the police, the deeper into trouble he got. Does the use of such confessions to convict ignorant, mentally challenged defendants truly respect their right to remain silent, their right to an attorney, and the principles of our accusatorial model of criminal justice? This is a political question. It cannot be answered without considering our country's social and political aspirations.

The practice of plea bargaining exacerbates the adversarial system's fact-finding deficiencies. When a defendant takes a deal in a homicide case, there is no clash of "truth." The opposing sides' interpretations of the facts never join in battle before a jury or a judge. Instead, as in the Carr case, the defendant's culpability is brokered without either side's formally defending its version of what happened or probing the validity of the other side's interpretation. Defense Attorney Michael George and Prosecutor Roy Keefer didn't know how strong each other's arguments really were. They did not even know the strength of their own arguments, because they didn't know what the other side had to undermine them. In such circumstances, bluff and spin can have a large impact on the nature of the deal that is finally struck.

Of course, a formal trial in the Carr case would not have ensured that more of the truth would have come to light. In the criminal justice system, there are no surefire solutions, only probabilities. The Carr case nonetheless shows that plea bargaining sharply increases the risk that significant facts of homicide cases never see the light of day. After all, do we really know what happened up there on South Mountain on May 13, 1988? We know that Carr pulled the trigger, but what about the specific facts bearing on which degree of homicide Carr was guilty of? In particular, what was the nature of the interaction between Carr and the two women on the morning of May 13th?

The formal record of the case reflects only one side's version of these events, because Carr took the deal. If Carr wanted to testify that somehow the women provoked him, the law would have given him his chance, but only if he ran the risk of incurring the death penalty. Since Carr chose not to take this risk, the plea bargain buried his version of the truth. Though it is quite unlikely that the women did anything to Carr that would have constituted legal provocation, it is possible that an Adams County jury would have convicted him of a lower form of homicide if he had testified as to his version of the morning's events.

Carr's decision to take the deal has a bearing on the legitimacy of the death penalty. The death penalty is usually justified on the ground that it will deter future murderers, balance a cosmic scale of justice (an eye for an eye), or provide an outlet for society's feelings of vengeance. There are well-known objections to each of these rationales, but the traditional debate obscures the death penalty's most obvious purpose: it gives prosecutors enormous leverage to get homicide defendants to plead guilty.

Without the death penalty, defendants charged with first degree murder would risk only a life sentence by taking their case to trial. My guess is that many who would not risk their lives would risk life sentences. Accordingly, the question that must be asked is whether it is morally justifiable to execute several dozen murderers each year, or whatever number is necessary to maintain a credible threat, so that prosecutors can dispose of a great many homicide cases by plea bargains. I believe this is an important question. Trials cost time and money. Without the death penalty, the number of homicide trials would presumably go up sharply, overwhelming an already overtaxed criminal justice system.

When homicide defendants give up their right to a trial, they also give up their right to present to a jury mitigating evidence that might reduce their culpability. In some states, for example, Carr would have had a legitimate right to raise a defense of diminished capacity, but the death penalty might have dissuaded him from pursuing the defense, for fear that the jury would reject it and sentence him to death. The fact that the death penalty discourages defendants from raising borderline defenses at trial is a troubling aspect of the existing criminal justice system. The law governing defenses can never be crystal clear, but it's anomalous that some defendants pay with their lives if they guess wrong about the meaning of the law or misjudge a jury's reaction to the "facts" of their cases.

The public's opinion of the diminished-capacity defense is too often based on what has happened in high-profile trials. For example, in 1978 Dan White shot and killed George Moscone, the mayor of San Francisco, and Harvey Milk, a gay-rights activist and member of the city's Board of Supervisors. After hearing psychiatric testimony indicating that White had been depressed, the jury returned a verdict of manslaughter. White's depressed state was variously ascribed to the stress of his job, his childhood, and junk food ("the Twinkie defense"). In the end, despite strong evidence supporting a verdict that he had, with the utmost premeditation, intentionally killed two human beings, White was sentenced to seven years and eight months in prison and in fact served only a little more than four-and-a-half years.

The public outrage at White's verdict and sentence eventually led to the abolishment of the diminished-capacity defense in California. Because a homicide defendant unjustifiably benefited from the defense in a high-profile trial, it became impossible for a defendant like Carr to plead diminished capacity in California. This perhaps is an example of how reforms of the criminal justice system can go wrong when they are based on the exceptional case, rather than the typical one.

Is Pennsylvania's approach to diminished capacity, which confines this defense to cases of mental illness that erode the defendant's cognitive capacities, the right one? Or, as the Model Penal Code permits, should mentally ill homicide defendants such as Carr have a right to introduce evidence that they didn't have substantial control over themselves when they intentionally shot someone? Just because White should have been convicted of first-degree murder does not establish that our criminal justice system should not treat a homicide defendant who has a serious mental illness brought on by a lifetime of abuse more leniently than it treats the average killer. It is a political issue, largely dependent on the kind of society we want to live in. Do the victimized who lash out violently deserve from us less punitive vengeance and more therapeutic compassion?

Homicide defendants, of course, might want to raise at trial a defense to which they are clearly not entitled. This was presumably Carr's goal in regard to provocation. Accordingly, opponents of the death penalty who think that Carr's life sentence was the punishment he deserved should consider the fact that it was the conjunction of the death penalty and plea bargaining that delivered this result. If the death penalty hadn't been a part of the equation, there is a distinct possibility that an Adams County jury would have convicted Carr of third-degree murder or voluntary manslaughter and he might have been released from prison inside of ten years.

Plea bargaining in death penalty cases is an extremely efficient method of discouraging homicide defendants from pursuing undeserved or borderline defenses. Unfortunately, this method of resolving homicide cases rarely provides the sort of accurate assessment of culpability that the application of the death penalty would seem to require. Supreme Court decisions restrict capital punishment to cases of first-degree murder in which statutorily defined aggravating circumstances outweigh any mitigating factors. Applying the death penalty in this way is thought to be fair because all those executed have failed this test of culpability and are in that sense equally culpable. However, this argument ignores those guilty of aggravated murder who have escaped the death penalty through plea bargaining. Many of these murderers are as culpable as those who are executed, but they escape the ultimate punishment, which introduces a serious element of arbitrariness into the system of how the death penalty is applied. Any moral legitimacy that the death penalty has in terms of its contribution to institutional efficiency has to be balanced against the immorality of treating people unfairly and arbitrarily.

For example, the plea bargaining that took place in the Carr case precluded an authoritative finding of Carr's motive for the shootings, which conceivably had a bearing on his intent and the applicability of certain defenses. Keefer became convinced early on that Carr's motive was homophobic in character, and the defense did everything in its power to encourage this interpretation as a way to increase the likelihood of a deal. Once the deal was in place, the significance of certain evidence as to Carr's motive never came to light. The evidence I am referring to has a bearing on why Trooper Donald Blevins can't figure out why Brenner states in her book that Rebecca Wight was clothed during the shootings.

Blevins may be right. Perhaps Brenner hasn't been telling the truth and both women were at least partially naked at the time they were shot. After all, Wight's autopsy report confirms that broken leaves and seeds were on both buttock areas. On the other hand, Brenner could be telling the truth. If so, either Wight hiked the entire day in a tight pair of jeans without underwear but with the debris in her pants, or Carr removed Wight's pants and underwear after Brenner left the crime scene to get help. Though Wight's autopsy found no signs of sexual activity, Carr could nonetheless have undressed the body and then partially redressed it, getting the debris inside her jeans and leaving the underwear lying on the ground nearby.

Which of these scenarios is true has a direct bearing on the nature of Carr's crime and on how an Adams County jury would have evaluated it. If Carr's motive was homophobic in character, if the shootings constituted a classic hate crime, that fact would arguably elevate his culpability, perhaps to the point that the death penalty would have been an appropriate punishment. At a minimum, a motive of homophobia would all but have precluded any kind of provocation defense. But Keefer, fearing that a conservative Adams County jury would react to the perceived hate crime by extending a large amount of undeserved leniency to Carr, pushed for a deal that put Carr in prison for life. Imagine, then, how this same jury would have assessed Carr's culpability if Keefer had argued at trial that the murder of Wight and the wounding of Brenner, at their most fundamental levels, had been sex crimes. The physical evidence mentioned above is certainly compatible with such a conclusion, and there are other bits and pieces of evidence scattered along the trail of this case that support this interpretation of the incident.

My point is not that the shootings were a sex crime, but that the adversarial system of plea bargaining, which is at the center of how homicide cases are resolved in this country, did little to find out why Carr in fact pulled the trigger of his .22 caliber rifle eight times. Keefer quickly concluded it was a hate crime; George encouraged this spin but apparently viewed the incident as a class crime, the act of a violent social outcast who had been provoked—perhaps not reasonably or legally provoked, but provoked nonetheless. Yet in my conversation with him in prison (see Epilogue), Carr told me that George had instructed him never to talk about what he'd admitted to Dr. John Hume: the fact that he'd thought about raping the women but didn't. If Carr's recollection is true, perhaps George's depiction of Carr's crime as the violent reaction of a provoked outcast, like his characterization of it as a hate crime, was just another spin that he put on the facts to hide the underlying reality of Carr's crime. In either case, the adversarial system of plea bargaining failed to pin down crucial facts in the Carr case. Truth was sacrificed in favor of a quick and easy disposition of an adversarial contest.

Of course, the categories of hatred, class resentment, and lust are permeable and overlay each other. All three motives can be intertwined in one act of violence, and perhaps Carr's crime was one of this sort. It is still true, however, that the system never came close to figuring out Carr's motive for shooting the two women and that his crime takes on different degrees of blameworthiness depending on what his primary motivation was. Legitimately or not, it's likely that Adams County jurors would have assessed Carr's culpability quite differently depending on whether they concluded that his motive was primarily one of hatred, rejection, or lust.

We will never know the whole truth about what happened on South Mountain on May 13, 1988. The system, not the people involved, failed to find out all the facts relevant to Carr's culpability. Now it's too late. Perhaps Carr is serving the sentence that he deserves, perhaps not.

The adversarial system of plea bargaining lends itself more to disposing of cases quickly than to punishing criminals at the level of their culpability, and this tells us something about who we are as a people. American ideals of criminal justice are beautiful to behold, and perhaps they are approximated in some of the high-profile cases that capture the attention of the American public, but they can also be the source of our illusions. On display in the high-profile cases, they hide or mask the reality of plea bargaining. Perhaps, in the end, it's all to be expected. A society always on the go, adept at marketing, and fond of fast food and sports has found a way to feel morally good about itself as it quickly and cheaply disposes of homicide cases through an adversarial process of plea bargaining. The challenge confronting those who are morally uncomfortable with this system is to formulate reforms that take into account both our ideals and the practical realities, bending and adjusting each to the other.

A Conversation with Stephen Roy Carr

A month after Michael George, Skip Gochenour, and I had visited Steve Carr at Graterford Correctional Institute, I returned to Graterford alone to talk to Carr. We met in the same lawyer-inmate conference room where the four of us had talked earlier. This time, I was sitting at the small table, with the barred window to my right. Carr sat across the table from me with his back to the door. Through the door's window, I could see the officer in charge of the visiting room at his large desk and he could see me.

"So what's prison like? Do you want to talk a little bit about that first?" I asked Carr.

"Well, if that wall wasn't so high—," he said, a small grin playing upon his thin, hollow cheeks.

"You'd be out of here, huh?"

The grin disappeared from Carr's face. In a desperate tone, he replied, "Driving me crazy in here."

"Why don't you tell me what a day is like?"

The words tumbled out of Carr's mouth and soul. "Sitting in my room, talking to myself, dreaming about my family."

"Your family?"

"Yeah and dreaming about the future, getting out."

"Does dreaming help you get through your day?"

"I get to the point that I don't feel like doing nothing. Just sit there," Carr said.

"And prison does that to you. It makes you—"

"Lazy," he said. "You got to fight the boredom."

"Fight boredom, huh. With what? Do you have a TV in here?"

"Yeah, I got a TV," Carr said without enthusiasm. "I have to hold the fine tuning together with rubber bands, so I can get the picture in. But I don't watch TV that much anymore."

"Do you ever work on your case?"

"Nighttime, when it's quiet," Carr replied. An indifference in his tone suggested to me that he only rarely worked to make his dream come true.

"Anything else you can say about prison life?"

"Sleep, eat and walk away," Carr chanted in reply, a grin returning to his gaunt face.

"Sleep, eat and walk away," I repeated, puzzled.

"Walk away from fights."

"Oh, that's the way you keep out of—"

"I only got one misconduct in here for being lazy on my job."

"What is your job?"

"Polishing brass handles on the doors."

"And you've done that for seven years, or do they move you around?"

"Nah. Nah. I was going to school when I first got here, but I lost my attitude with it."

"Why? What happened?"

"My GED. One point missed it."

"That's a shame," I sympathized. "Are you going to try and get it yet or have you lost interest in that, too?"

"I just lost it. And more important, I mean, they could of just given me that one point," anger creeping into Carr's voice as he gestured with his large right hand. His forearm was long and lean. I could easily see that at one time Carr had been quite muscular, but his body had atrophied during his seven years of confinement.

"And now you don't have much interest in working at it?"

"Nah, I just went through so much bullshit down there that I just got tired of it. Got the fuck away from there. Now they say they got a mile-long list and I can't get back in."

"So prison has worn you down so that you've lost interest in things? In your GED degree? In your case? Is that what's happened?"

"Yeah. I lost the motivation to do anything. Started smoking marijuana. I run back to my house [cell] after doing it and it's like I have no motivation to do anything. It's like, I don't know, I'm running from society or running from this society in here, you know. Staying away from everybody, trying to keep my nose clean."

"The newspapers described you as a loner when you lived out on South Mountain. Are you telling me that you've become a loner here in prison, too?"

"Yeah," Carr replied cautiously.

"How do you understand that? In your own mind, why are you such a loner?"

Carr sat there across the table from me, his head down on his chest. We both knew there was little reason for me to be there unless Carr was willing to talk about himself. He moved his chair so that he could extend his long legs off to the side of the table. He sat there a while with his arms crossed on his chest, thinking about what he should do. Finally, without changing his position, staring out the window to my right, he spoke.

"Well, it started out because I brought this guy home. His name was Curt Watkins."

So began Carr's explanation of how he turned into a loner. I already knew most of the story, but it was fascinating to hear Carr retell it: his mother living upstairs with Watkins and the other three Carr children, while he lived downstairs with his father; his father beating him severely for stealing some coins; his brother introducing him to theft and drugs; his family and relatives conspiring against him and blaming him for anything that happened. For example, he said his mother arranged to have a neighborhood boy break a lamp so that she could blame it on Carr and thereby have a reason not to take him along with her when she moved to Pennsylvania. And after Carr joined his mother and siblings in Shippensburg, they purportedly instigated neighborhood kids to pick fights with him. Soon thereafter he got into a fight with Watkins.

"The next thing my mom's kicking me out the door. 'Here's twenty dollars Dad sent you,' she says, 'get the fuck out.'" Carr spoke bitterly.

"And this happened when you were only fifteen?"

"Yeah," Carr replied firmly. "It was 1974. I lived up in the mountains for three years."

"Where did you sleep?"

"Well, the neighborhood kids had built an A-frame up there. I lived in that A-frame."

"Did you go to school?"

"Nah, I was kicked out."

"Did you enjoy living up in the mountains all by yourself?"

"Damn straight I did," Carr exclaimed, sitting up in his chair. "It was peaceful. Everybody wasn't out to get me. People were leaving me the fuck alone," Carr said, biting off the last three words.

"Why don't you describe for me a perfect day on South Mountain?"

"Hunting all the time, fishing—ahh, a couple a people had their own bass ponds—and stuff like that."

"You'd just put your pole in their ponds?"

"Better than that," Carr chuckled at the recollection. "You take yourself one of those long skinny plastic pipes, you put a couple of empty milk gallons on one end of it so it will float above the water and you put the other end in your mouth. Then you tie rocks and stuff to your legs, and get yourself a bow and arrow. Then you just walk into the water and go spear-fishing."

"Let me get this straight," I asked, "you're under water, breathing through this plastic pipe, shooting bass with a bow and arrow?"

"Yeah, it's a helluva lot of fun," Carr said, smiling, his chin in his palm. "Being free. Not a care in the world."

"Tell me, how do you rate yourself as a person who can live off the land?"

He seemed embarrassed for me that I had asked such a question. Finally, he said, "I'd say I'm pretty good at living up there."

"Did you have any kind of income?"

"Aluminum cans, scrape aluminum. There's dumps all over those mountains. People partying and stuff. You can go to town and sell the aluminum cans and ah, buy your 22 shells and any other supplies that you might need."

"You say there were parties up on the Mountain?"

"Kids go up in those mountains and party all the time."

"Were you able to get drugs from these kids?"

"People plant dope all over those mountains."

"So, did you ever try growing marijuana up there?"

Carr paused and vaguely responded, "Uh huh."

"As I understand it, it's very easy to grow, right?"

Carr lost whatever inhibition had been bothering him. He bragged, "In the mountain laurel, along the creeks, I had twenty-five foot plants."

"What the hell did you do with all that pot?"

"Sold it."

"So that's how you made money up there, right?" I guessed.

"Uh huh," Carr replied, amused that I had discovered his secret. In an understated way, he added, "Keeps you living for a while."

"You made how much a pound?"

"Oh, back then it was about $260."

"When did you start growing marijuana?"

"All the way down through the line."

"You mean you were growing and selling pot when you were 15?"

"Uh huh," Carr said with a patronizing air.

"What else? Anything about your life on South Mountain that we haven't talked about yet?"

"Well," Carr remarked with a sly grin, "there was adventuring. Just going adventuring. Just doing what you want."

"What did this 'adventuring' involve?"

"Well, the first thing you got to understand is that all those cabins up on that Mountain are potential stores."

"Potential stores? You mean you'd take things from them?"

"Sometimes, you know, I might see something and pick it up and put it in my knapsack. Now I might just put it in someone else's cabin, just for the fun of it. I might take a TV out of here and put it in the cabin up the road."

"For the fun of it? Make people wonder what the hell is going on?"

"Yeah. Just for the helluvit," Carr said merrily. "Being free, you know?"

Carr looked at me for some indication that I knew what he was talking about. Smiling and nodding my head, I asked, "But you also took things from these cabins for your own personal use, right?"

"This is the way to think about burglary," Carr replied, as if he were giving me some professional advice. "When you go up to a cabin, and it's got like Cadillacs all over it and stuff, and if the windows be open, okay, you take the screen off gently. Nothing causes much damage. Or you take the whole window frame out. You crawl in. Take a shower. Cook a little food. Maybe you see something you like. You takes that with you. But when you done, when you leave, you put the screen or the window frame back where it belongs."

"So you take a little here, a little there, but you leave the place pretty much as you found it—that's how you operated?"

"Yeah, like the bandit of the mountain," Carr laughed.

"What kind of stuff did you get?"

"I got all kinds of stuff. I got old coins and different kinds of antiques I buried in some of the places that I got up in the mountains. I built, like, shelters underground. Put a generator in, with the creek bed and stuff, piped it in here, set up the heater system and timers and stuff, set up a little bed there, and a camp stove like in a motor home and stuff. I had my own house set right up."

Hiding my disbelief, I asked, "How could you have built that many underground shelters? Did you finance this with your marijuana sales?"

"No, I stole all of it. You take a little bit here, a little bit there. They ain't going to miss it."

"You're telling me that you stole a bunch of antiques from the cabins on South Mountain and that you hid this stuff in underground shelters that you built, and that it's all waiting for you when you get out of prison?"

"There's about fifteen–twenty of them."

"So, tell me, how much loot do you have stashed in these shelters?"

"About $230,000."

"$230,000!" I first thought Carr was making a joke, but the man across the table from me was serious. All I could say in reply was, "You're a rich man."

"It don't do me no good in here, but it'll be there when I get out," Carr stated confidently.

I hadn't anticipated this delusional side of Carr's personality. I knew that he'd had a rough childhood and had engaged in a lot of minor thefts, but talking with him now convinced me that he had a strange dark side. His mood could quickly shift from deep pessimism to wild optimism.

His contact with reality fluctuated in the same way. One minute he was a lethargic, burnt-out drug addict, and the next a rich man who would soon reap the benefits of all his treasures. Pervading this combination of contradictions was more than a hint of cold-blooded malice and pathological indifference. A complicated and puzzling piece of human machinery, Carr was, as George had once said, a man "you'd hesitate to get close to."

Perhaps it was inevitable that Carr would get in trouble with the law. Having little or no feeling of connectedness to his family or to other people, he had no respect for the community's rules. They were something alien to him. If there came a time when he felt he could get away with it, there was nothing stopping him from crossing the line. For Carr, the step from a troubled and vicious childhood to a life of crime was a small one.

"So eventually you moved to Florida?" I inquired.

"Yeah, that was in 1977."

"You were back living with your family. How did that work out?"

"In '78 I got arrested. Then I went to Daytona Beach and got arrested for dining-and-dashing. I was lucky there cause they just let me out, so I took off up to Pennsylvania. Got arrested up here and they brought me back and I got a year-and-a-day. Second time was for, ahh, ten counts of burglary and aggravated assault. I was in some lady's trailer and it was like, ahh, she woke up and grabbed the phone and hit me in the head. I jumped up, I had a knife in my hand, and took off running. Hell, I didn't even know I stabbed her. I never knew anything about it until, ahh, my cousin Markie got busted on a pound of dope and next thing I know I'm getting pulled in on that stabbing."

"A family member turned you in?"

"Hell yeah," Carr replied heatedly. "About fifteen of us were doing these burglaries, but I was the only one who got arrested for them." Loudly and angrily, he repeated, "I was the only one!" A guard outside the room looked at Carr through the door's window. I waited until Carr calmed down.

"Were you perhaps the oldest?"

"Nah. Nah. My family, my own family, and their friends snitched me out. Tommy was the one who drove the jeep, so that only made me an accessory to the crime, but he walks. They didn't want him cause he was

young, only sixteen years old, and I was already in prison onc
know. They first attacked this other guy, Steve. They arrested hin.
burglary charges and he's the one that snitched Tommy out and Tomn.
snitched me out. But now they're sitting back and saying I was the one
that snitched," Carr screeched, flabbergasted at the obvious unfairness of
it all.

The unsmiling face of the guard appeared on the other side of the
door's window. He tapped on the glass with his knuckle. Carr turned,
saw who it was, and immediately became submissive. The guard's face
disappeared.

"Your family says you snitched Tommy out to the police?"

"Yeah," Carr replied, his voice full of hurt. "That Tommy did all this
and did all that." After a pause, Carr said with quiet fury, "Damn right I
snitched the motherfucker out after he snitched me out. But they don't
want to hear that. Anybody in the family can steal something, but I get
the blame for everything."

Carr's life in Florida was a textbook case of the conjunction of a
dysfunctional family, drugs, and crime. Theft and getting high had become a way of life for Carr, one financing the other. His bonds to other
people, including members of his family, had continued to deteriorate
under the pressure of his self-destructive lifestyle. He'd had no way to
extricate himself from the downward spiral that had become his life
other than to flee from society and family. He took refuge in the wilds of
the South Mountain area.

"Did you know that you were heading for the South Mountain area
when you left Florida?" I asked.

"Oh yeah, I knew exactly—" Suddenly Carr's head jerked sideways
and he sat bolt upright in his chair, rubbing his eyes and shaking his
head.

Alarmed, I asked, "What's the matter?"

Carr calmly replied, "My mind just went dead."

"What's that? Did you say your mind just went dead?"

"Yeah," Carr answered with a sad grin on his face, enjoying the
attention he was getting.

"Does that happen often?"

"I been doing drugs since I was fifteen years old," he said, as if that
were all the information I needed.

"And you think drugs have screwed up your mind?"

"Yeah. Just goes black. And I got high blood pressure too. Sometimes I have to sit down and wait till it clears up a little bit so I can see."

"Headaches?"

"Yeah, I get migraine headaches."

Carr certainly didn't look healthy. His pale complexion, bony frame, hollow cheeks, dull eyes, and listless manner left the impression of a man with a slow degenerative disease.

"When you got back to South Mountain, did you go back to the same lifestyle that you had back in 1974–77, hunting, fishing, stealing stuff from the cabins, and growing marijuana?"

"I had marijuana growing all over my aunt's property. That's what I was doing when these shootings happened. My aunt told me that the police was showing my picture around and I was rushing round getting that marijuana off her property. I was planning on going to Virginia, so I was getting my shit together."

"But that's not what the police reports say," I observed. "They say that your aunt told you that the police were looking for you after the shootings, not before?"

"I told them cops right straight out," Carr retorted vehemently, "that my aunt told me that the police were showing my picture around before all this happened up on the trail. But the police didn't want to listen to that. They wanted to make up their own story."

"You're saying that in their reports the police moved events around in order—"

"Yeah, to suit themselves," he interrupted. "To make their stories stronger, you know, to make the confession legal and to make this into some big hate crime."

"Do you understand," I asked, "that Judge Spicer ruled that your confession was legal in part because the police officers testified that you told them your Aunt Lucille had told you the police were looking for you after the shootings? If she told you that at that time, then you would have known that you were a murder suspect?"

"Yeah, but that ain't what happened. My aunt told me that the police were looking for me before the shootings. I think it was on the 11th that she told me that. That's when I started chopping down my marijuana, selling it, and getting ready to hit the road. That's why I went up to the

Appalachian Trail that night, to get away from my aunt's place, cause I figured that's where the police would be looking for me."

I wondered whether it was possible. Could his Aunt Lucille have told Carr that the cops were looking for him as a way to get rid of him? Carr then would have had a reason for arriving at the Appalachian Trail shelter in the middle of the night. After all, why would Carr's aunt have told him that the police were looking for him after the shootings? It wasn't true, and his aunt had no reason to think he was a murder suspect during the first few days after the shootings, when Carr was staying at her house.

"You arrived at the shelter late Thursday or early Friday morning?" I asked.

"I don't know exactly when I got there. It was in the middle of the night."

"So," I asked lightly, wondering what Carr would say, "what happened that morning?"

He didn't hesitate. Gesturing first with one arm, then the other, he said, "They woke up. They were out there pissing in the woods. They were running round naked. They were going to the outhouse. If they knew I was there, why were they doing all this. I mean, like, they weren't trying to hide anything. It was right out in the open. I mean if these girls didn't want somebody to see them, then why are they running round naked. Indecent exposure and shit."

"You're saying the two women knew you were in the shelter?"

"They had to know," Carr insisted. "Their tent was only thirty, forty feet away from me. I had a campfire. I was cooking coffee. The smoke was going right down their way."

At my request, Carr drew a map on a sheet of paper. He then continued with his story, using the map to help me visualize what he was saying.

"Their tent was northwest of the shelter, about ten–fifteen feet off the Appalachian Trail. They had to smell the smoke. They had to see the fire. The girl who went outside to piss and shit—that had to be Claudia because Rebecca was the one that went to the outhouse and I saw she had, you know, the bald pussy. Anyways, Claudia had to walk right through the smoke cause I was burning green wood."

"You're claiming that in the early morning Brenner walked through the smoke of your campfire?" I asked.

"Yeah. She had to."

"Wasn't there another shelter in between the shelter you were at and the women? Could you see the campsite clearly from where your campfire was located?"

"Yeah. That other shelter was off to the side. I could see directly past it down there to where the women were. When Claudia went out into the woods, aahh, aahh," Carr stuttered, paused, and then added sheepishly, "I had to go up and around the backside of the shelter to see her."

"And where was the outhouse?"

"The outhouse was behind the shelters on the south side," Carr said, pointing to his map. "That's why Rebecca walked through the shelters, right by me, to get to the outhouse. We talked and then she went back down and told Claudia and they moved on out of there. So apparently they didn't know I was there the whole time."

The words had slipped out of Carr's mouth.

"I thought you said they had to have known you were there? Did they know or not?" I asked.

"I don't know," Carr said, looking genuinely undecided. He then shook his head and repeated, "They were completely naked."

Since the nudity clearly stood out in Carr's recollection of the events of that morning, I asked, "Were they naked after they knew you were there?"

"They were out running 'round naked for almost two or three hours that morning. I masturbated, I dunno, three or four times, you know. I wanted to get involved."

I had not expected Carr to admit to me in person that he had masturbated on the morning of the shootings. Sensing what Carr wanted to talk about, I asked, "You had never seen anything like this before?"

"I'd never seen it in real life. I've seen like porn movies and stuff, but not in real life. It was, you know," Carr searched for the right word, "intriguing, ahhhh, interesting, fascinating, to see this, you know."

He turned to me, seeking confirmation for what he had just said. His eyes were bright, suggesting to me that he could still visualize in his mind's eye what he had seen that morning.

"You thought that you had come across two free spirits out there in the woods, didn't you?"

"Yeah."

"Did you think these two women were looking for sex?"

Avoiding my question, he said, "I been doing without it so long, it doesn't even bother me no more." Then Carr paused, sighed, and admitted, "I wanted it. I wanted to know what it feels like."

"There's the suggestion that the two women teased you. If they did tease you, what did they do?"

"Rebecca stood right here in front of me," Carr said, stretching out his arm. "I could of reached out there and grabbed that puss, that's how close she was. She didn't have a thought or care in the world, you know."

"You mean, she wasn't embarrassed at all?"

"It was like she was in a nudist colony or something," Carr said, shaking his head in disbelief.

"Did you think, by being naked, she was trying to mock you, or irritate you, or make fun of you?"

"I dunno," Carr said quietly.

"Did they get dressed immediately when Wight went back to their tent?"

"No," Carr replied firmly.

"They stayed naked?"

"They took their tent down, they set there naked, they were packing up their stuff and they got—"

I interrupted him. "They were naked outside of their tent after they knew, for sure, that you were there?"

"Yeah. It wasn't that long, cause they took the tent down. They had all their clothes and everything, knapsacks and everything there. They were going through their stuff and getting their clothes together. But they took the tent down—"

"While they were naked?"

"Yeah, I was watching them."

"What was going through your mind as you watched these two naked women?"

"I told you, I wanted to get involved, but I never raped a girl in my life and I wasn't going to start there. As bad off as I was, hard up and stuff, I still wouldn't rape 'em. The thought crossed my mind, you know, but I never raped a girl. I even told that to the psychiatrist."

"Hume?"

"The one that Michael George got for me. I never raped a girl, but it had crossed my mind: that's basically the statement that they didn't show in court. That's what Michael George won't let me talk about," Carr added lamely.

"About what you told—"

"The psychiatrist."

"Why won't he let you talk about it?"

"I dunno." Carr paused and recrossed his legs. He was thinking. Finally, he said, "Maybe we shouldn't talk about it, either." A long pause followed before Carr added, "Maybe I shouldn't never have brought that up."

"Well, that's fine." I replied. "We don't have to go into it any further. But what you told Hume was that you thought about raping the women, but you didn't do it, right?"

"Yeah," he said. "The thought crossed my mind, going down there and getting a pussy. Just knocking them out and taking it, you know. But, ahhh, I've never done it and I wouldn't know how to go about it, really. Attack two girls and stuff, so ahh—"

"At any point, did you ever think that these two women might be receptive to what you were after?"

"Yeah."

"So, why didn't you ask them?"

Carr frowned, lowered his head and shook it sadly. He hesitated more than once before he finally said, "I only had sex with women three times in my life. I've never picked up a woman. It breaks down."

Carr's tone and manner convinced me that he had not made any sexual advances to Wight or Brenner. "Did you exchange any sharp words with the women at all that morning?"

"Nah, not then. It was later, when they were going down the Rocky Knob Trail. They were looking at a map and I was asking them if they were lost. Claudia said, "No are you," in a real pissy way. And I'm like, 'What the fuck did I do to you, cunt.'"

"So what did you do then?"

"When the girls went down the Rocky Knob, I went on down the Appalachian Trail. The rental cabin over there, I robbed that place," Carr calmly admitted. "I took a couple of sleeping bags, a camera, and a few other things from there."

"So what did you do next?"

"Then I came back over across the trail, cause I was going back down there to watch those girls. I thought by then they ought to be, ahh, settled back in, you know." I jumped a deer just on that side of the ridge. I chased it right over the ridge and down to the creek. Have you ever been out deer hunting?"

"No."

"You never shot a deer with a 22?" Carr asked in disbelief. "Not even when you were a kid?"

"There weren't many deer in the farm country where I grew up," I answered somewhat defensively.

"Well, you wouldn't even know what I'm talking about then," Carr observed derisively.

"Try me, tell me about it," I responded.

"Well," he began, "with a 22 you'd have to shoot a deer two, or about eight to ten times, fifteen times to drop it. If you drop a deer, chances are if you don't go over and slit that deer's throat, that deer's going to jump up and run away, cause all you did is stun him, you know. I've seen deer jump up when you shoot them with a shotgun. A slug right through the heart, and they still jump up and run three or four miles."

"So, what does that mean?"

"It means that I was shooting at a deer and nobody wanted to listen to what I had to say," Carr cried out.

"Oh, I see. You're explaining the eight shots?"

"Yeah. I shot more than eight times. I had a whole mouth full of fucking 22-shots. I started on the ridge and ended up by the creek."

"You mean you were shooting as you were moving?"

"Yeah."

"But the police found the eight empty shell casings at one spot," I reminded Carr.

"Yeah. Where the girls were sitting there along the creek, that was the point where I ended up shooting at, but I started way up there in the pines," he explained.

"So, you're sticking to the story that this was a hunting accident?" I asked, keeping my voice nonjudgmental.

"I knew I was shooting at deer," Carr cried desperately. "Cause I jumped him up in the pines."

"And the fact that the empty shells were found at a place where there was—what has been called—a window through the laurel, that fact doesn't affect your claim that you were shooting at a deer. Is that what you're telling me?" I asked gently.

"Yeah," Carr replied stubbornly.

"So, you were heading back to watch the girls, you see a deer, you shoot at it a number of times, and the deer just by chance runs to where the women were at by the creek. Is that it?"

Perhaps not realizing the point of my question, Carr replied, "When you're running a deer down, you don't look and see where you're going. You lose your sense of direction when you're chasing after a deer. You're mainly concentrating on that deer instead of where you're going."

I tried a different tack. "What were you expecting to see the women doing that afternoon? Did you expect to see them engaged in sex, as you had seen that morning?"

Without thinking, Carr answered, "I only saw them walking around naked that morning. I didn't see no sex. The sex didn't happen till next time."

"In the afternoon?"

"Yeah."

"But if you saw the sex in the afternoon, you're back to that problem of claiming that you were shooting at deer and, at the same time, watching the two women have sex? That's not really compatible, is it?" I asked softly.

Carr, clearly embarrassed and irritated with himself, could not figure out a way to reconcile what he had just said with his story of a hunting accident. Finally, he quietly said, "Yeah, that's a little full-of-it, cause . . ."

"What's that?" I interrupted, not quite sure of what Carr had said.

Changing his mind, Carr loudly insisted, "I was shooting a deer."

Not wanting to antagonize him, I changed the subject. "If it was really a hunting accident, why did you take the deal, knowing that you'd be convicted of first-degree murder?"

"Michael went after the passion defense," Carr explained. "And that's what hurt me."

"Hurt you? How so?"

"It was like, ahh, I went after these lesbians cause of what I seen them doing."

"You think now that it would have been better to stick to the hunting-accident story?"

"Yeah," Carr replied. After a pause, he continued, "They never even proved to me Rebecca was dead. I dunno if she's dead. I ain't never seen no body. All they showed me was a picture of her laying in the woods. She could've been unconscious. I mean, if you were shot in the head, and you were blacked out, and took you off to the hospital, and gave you a new name."

Carr's response stunned me. I didn't believe that he really thought that Rebecca Wight was still alive. He was only trying to weasel out of admitting that he had murdered her. Even so, what did it say about his mental state that he would make such a ridiculous suggestion? Earlier he was a rich man with $230,000 buried in underground shelters on South Mountain. Now the police had framed him for the murder of a woman who was still secretly alive. Carr was a social predator not fully in touch with reality.

"Do you think the plea bargain, looking back on it, was the right move?"

"No," Carr said forcefully.

"You now wish you would have taken your case to a jury?"

"Right. I wish I went all the way with it."

"So you're not happy with the job that George did for you?"

"Every time when I was in the hearings, like he'd stand up and say something, the judge would say, 'Sit down,' or, you know, 'Overruled,' or something. George never would argue the point with him. He would just sit right down and then that would be that. And then Keefer, he was just running off his mouth and shit. I mean if George is supposed to be my lawyer, why ain't he standing up for me?" Carr raged.

"So, you think you got the shaft?"

"I think my lawyer gave me the shaft."

"What about the judge?" I asked. "Do you remember Judge Spicer's questions. 'Do you understand what you're doing here Mr. Carr? Do you understand the rights you're giving away?' On the transcript it says that you always said, 'Yes sir.' Are you telling me that because of what you call your sixth grade education and because of your drug abuse, you really didn't understand what was going on around you?"

"I was given drugs at the prison for my nightmares—"

"You mean the prison in Adams County?" I asked.

"Two or three times, the paramedics would come in there. I'd be laying on the floor shaking, hyperventilating. I was on a bunk sleeping, and the next thing you know I'd be on the floor."

"What was causing these nightmares? Was it the fact that you were in a hunting accident or the fact that you knew you had intentionally shot those two women?"

"I dunno," Carr said sullenly, realizing that his story of a hunting accident made no more sense in 1995 than it had in 1988.

"You don't want to talk about that?"

"No," he answered angrily.

I backed off. "So, then, because of these drugs and your lack of an education, you didn't really understand what Judge Spicer was telling you. Is that what you're telling me?"

"Yeah," Carr said. "I just nodded my head and says, 'Yes sir.' That's all I could do."

"So, what now? The last time I was here you mentioned a federal habeas corpus petition. Are you working on that?"

Carr sat there silently, thinking. He was a beaten man.

He then said quietly, "No, not really. I don't do nothing but sit in my cell. I'm lost and I don't know what the fuck to do anymore."

"You feel completely alone?"

"I am alone. You're the only visitor I get."

He looked worn out. I asked him, "Do you want to quit for today? Do you want to head back to your cell?"

"Yeah," he answered in a dull, thick voice.

"Do you want me to come back? Does it do any good for you to talk about these things?"

In a pleading tone, he said, "Yeah. You can come back."

We left the lawyer-inmate conference room and shook hands, and then Carr turned toward the door that led to the cells. I watched the tall, gaunt man shuffle away, his shoulders hunched forward, his head hung down. The bargain he took in October 1988 had perhaps saved his life, but at the price of reducing it to a life of pain, frustration, and loneliness. I left Graterford Prison and haven't returned since. Carr of course is still there, alone.

Acknowledgments

During 1995 and 1996, a number of my friends in Carlisle, Pennsylvania, endured hours of seemingly endless conversation about the Steve Carr case and read bulky drafts of what later became this book. In compensation for their pains, I wish I could do more than express my gratitude to Lee Fritschler, Gene and Kathy Hickok, Jon and Nancy Tarrant, and John and Jane Ransom. Ash and Kim Nichols were especially helpful. At a time when I wasn't sure how I should proceed with this project, they helped me get my bearings. I also wish to promise the "Nicholettes" that I will never again discuss in their presence the contents of this book. As Molly would say, "Enough already."

Michael and Nancy Reed also deserve special mention. Michael, who is a lawyer, shared my fascination with the Carr case, and we tested Nancy's patience by talking about it for hours on end. Michael also carefully read the final draft of the manuscript, giving me the benefit of his good judgment on matters of both style and substance.

I would have missed an important piece of the story of the Carr case were it not for my dear friend Victoria Kuhn, who grew up in Adams County, Pennsylvania. Thank you Vickie!

A number of bright undergraduates read my manuscript and gave me useful hints on ways to improve it for a student audience. They were Sara Bryant, Andre Vanier, Ryan Green, Rachel DuFault, Jennifer Becker, Kim Demarchi, Valerie Hays, David Hollar, Mary Hale, Martha Pacold, Stephanie Kosta, Eric Gottesman, and Elizabeth Nahm. During 1997 and 1998, I had the pleasure of working with Jim Duff, Vanessa Yarnall, and Charlotte Suniega. Vanessa, who doesn't like to use one more word than is absolutely necessary, edited the manuscript more than once. Any felicity of style this book may occasionally have is largely because of her efforts.

It is always a pleasure to work with Clark Dougan, senior editor at the University of Massachusetts Press. It was Clark who guided my efforts to reduce what was an unwieldy manuscript to what is now, I hope, a readable book. My copyeditor, Deborah Klenotic, also did an excellent job. I am grateful to her for all her help.

Lastly, I wish to thank Patricia, Katrina, and Nathan. These three put up with a great deal of inconvenience for my sake when my survival depends on their patience and love.

Index

record in Florida, 152–57; raped in prison, 124–25; sexual experiences, 99; purportedly nonviolent, 154; police first learn of him, 52; police have probable cause for arrest, 59–60; interviewed by Matthew O'Brien and John Holtz, 69; police discovery of gun, 69; interviewed by Don Blevins, 70; incriminates himself, 71; gives Blevins samples of head and facial hair, 71; asks for attorney, 71–72, 115; role in the shootings, 99–100, 124–25, 235–37; testimony on morning events, 97–99, 232–35; thoughts about raping the women, 234–35; motive, 5, 80, 177–79, 220–22; homophobic remark to James Klempner, 154; mental condition (Dr. John Hume's report), 161–62; significance of mental condition, 102–3; mental condition the day after shootings, 57; at Weaver farm, 60–64; arrested at Weaver farm, 67; belief in God's will, 68; behavior at arraignment, 128; failure to testify at trial, 175–76; takes plea bargain, 179–81; colloquy with Judge Oscar Spicer, 192–93, 238–39; pursues appeal, 212–14

Cobb, Judge Wayne, 156
Commonwealth v. Bonadio, 163
Commonwealth v. Dixon, 137
Commonwealth v. McCusker, 197
Commonwealth v. Stonehouse, 197
Commonwealth v. Weinstein, 198
Competency to stand trial, 100, 102, 121–22, 127, 128
Copenhaver, Donald, 207
Costopoulos, William, 96, 133
Crotty, Don, 43

Dead Woman's Hollow Road, 16
Death penalty, arbitrary application of, 219–20; doubts of Roy Keefer, 76; doubts of Michael George, 84–85; doubts of Oscar Spicer, 90–91; and homophobia's effect on culpability, 80, 81; impact on Stephen Carr, 179–80, 192; George's thoughts on, 84; impact on borderline defenses, 218–19; Keefer's decision to seek for Carr, 74, 79–80, 81–82; and Pennsylvania's sentencing code, 77, 81; strategic advantages for prosecutor, 78, 217–18
Dillon, Larry, 37
Diminished capacity, 4, 127, 160, 191; Pennsylvania's definition of, 102–3, compared to Model Penal Code's provisions, 160, 219; public's view of, 218
Discovery, 131–33; and controversy about "sex toys," 133–34; Oscar Spicer's ruling on, 148
Dixon, Linda, 137
Donnelly, Trooper Frank, 65, 66, 67
Drixell, Paul (a suspect), 48–49, 54, 169

Eastern Pennsylvania Mennonite Church, 62

Fedok, Fred, 34
Fogarty, Steve, 155
Foley, Gerald, 155

George, Michael, 3, 4, 6, 128, 178; background, 83–84; bench trial, closing argument, 193; on Brenner's credibility, 157–59; on Stephen Carr's motive, 177–79; on right to remain silent, 135, 136, 143, 145–46; on